ADVANCED TOPICS IN UNIX

Processes, Files, and Systems

Ronald J. Leach

John Wiley & Sons, Inc.

New York • Chichester • Brisbane • Toronto • Singapore

Publisher: Katherine Schowalter
Senior Editor: Diane D. Cerra
Managing Editor: Maureen B. Drexel
Editorial Production & Design: Publishers Design and Production Services, Inc.

Designations used by companies to distinguish their products are often claimed as trademarks. In all instances where John Wiley & Sons, Inc., is aware of a claim, the product names appear in initial capital or all capital letters. Readers, however, should contact the appropriate companies for more complete information regarding trademarks and registration.

This text is printed on acid-free paper.

Three sections of Chapter 3 of this work are based on material published in *Using C in Software Design* by Ronald J. Leach. Copyright © Academic Press, 1993. Adapted with permission.

This publication is designed to provide accurate and authoritative information in regard to the subject matter covered. It is sold with the understanding that the publisher is not engaged in rendering legal, accounting, or other professional service. If legal advice of other expert assistance is required, the services of a competent professional person should be sought.

Library of Congress Cataloging-in-Publication Data:

Leach, Ronald (Ronald J.)
    Advanced topics in UNIX/Ronald J. Leach.
      p.   cm.
    Includes bibliographical references.
    ISBN 0-471-03685-4 (paper/disk). — ISBN 0-471-03663-3 (paper)
    1. Operating systems (Computers) 2. UNIX (Computer file)
    I. Title.
    QA76.76.063L398   1994
    005.4'3—dc20   94-10834
                                                                        CIP

Printed in the United States of America
10 9 8 7 6 5 4 3 2 1

Contents

About the Author

Ronald J. Leach is a professor of systems and computer science and the director of graduate studies in the department of Systems and Computer Science at Howard University in Washington, D.C. He came to Howard in 1969 as an instructor of mathematics. He has held his present rank since 1985.

Dr. Leach received his B.S., M.S., and Ph.D. degrees in mathematics from the University of Maryland at College Park and his M.S. degree in computer science from Johns Hopkins University. He is the author of more than 40 technical publications, including the recently published *Using C in Software Design,* published by Academic Press.

During his career, Dr. Leach has become knowledgeable in several areas. He has published in three areas of mathematics and in software engineering and software measurement, parallel computing, computer graphics, operating systems, symbolic computation, and algorithm analysis. His current research interests include measurement in software engineering, fault-tolerant and real-time computing, and program performance enhancement.

Dr. Leach has been a NASA/ASEE (American Society for Engineering Education) Faculty Fellow at the Goddard Space Flight Center in Greenbelt, Maryland, and he has participated in the Summer Faculty Research Program at Lawrence Livermore National Laboratory in Livermore, California. He has been the principal or coprincipal investigator on many research grants for the Army Research Office, Wright Laboratory, and other federal agencies, as well as on several grants from private companies such as AT&T and Hewlett-Packard.

Dr. Leach is the owner of a small company called AfterMath, which performs a variety of consulting and technical services. He met his wife, Mary, in graduate school, and they have three children, all of whom will have graduated from college (hopefully) by the time this book appears.

Preface

UNIX is currently the most common standard operating system in the world for workstations and minicomputers. It serves as the basis for many network-based software systems and is essential to an understanding of common networking tools such as `telnet` and `ftp`.

The rich set of utilities usually provided in UNIX systems also provides a rich set of programming tools. The common distributions of many other operating systems include utilities that are similar in usage and syntax to standard UNIX utilities.

The UNIX operating system is too large to be described in detail in any series of books, much less in a single book. There are more than 2,000 entries for common commands, system calls, and utilities in many online UNIX manuals. The associated online manual pages on a SPARC 2 running Solaris 1.1 require 7,234 megabytes for storage of 2,545 entries on disk. This is equivalent to more than 1,400 pages of text. Even after learning all this information, you would be able to learn only the syntax and common error codes associated with these commands, system calls, and utilities.

The software design and appropriateness of particular operating system features cannot be addressed fully by any manual. This statement is true for any modern operating system and for many software subsystems such as those for windowing or networking.

It is also true that students, users of application programs, and computing professionals bring different levels of knowledge to any book. Therefore, hard choices must be made in the selection of material to be included.

I have chosen topics for *Advanced Topics in UNIX* on the basis of what I wanted to know about UNIX. Observations about the difficulties many computer professionals had when moving to UNIX, as well as some observed gaps in the knowledge of even experienced UNIX system programmers, also have played a part in the selection of material.

For example, I included information about the physical layout of the i-nodes and file storage on a disk because I needed to understand the contents of a "superblock" to fix a disk with a hardware problem. Information about the structure of an a.out file was included because I wanted to understand the linking process for object files. Problems I observed in the improvement of program performance suggested the inclusion of information on the fast page frame array and memvad. Some of the discussion of shared memory was motivated by problems with the installation and operation of image processing software distributed by NASA. The comparison of interprocess communication was motivated by problems that arose in my research in real-time programming. Many of the other topics were similarly motivated.

Advanced Topics in UNIX describes the essential features of the UNIX operating system in varying levels of detail. Here I present an overview of each chapter and indicate the programming examples included.

Chapter 1 provides a high-level description of UNIX and should be read by all readers. The chapter discusses some of UNIX's most common implementations and its history. There are no code examples here.

The typical UNIX interface (the Bourne and C shells) is described briefly in Chapter 2. Several short examples of shell scripts are given. The technique of conditional compilation is introduced as part of a discussion of porting C programs to different compilers.

Chapter 3 includes a detailed description of the process and file subsystems of UNIX. There are six programming examples that show how to change the soft limits of a process, how to operate on files using both C and UNIX system calls for I/O, and how to use lock files for process synchronization. The use of the perror() function and external error numbers is discussed in this chapter, as are the new facilities for asynchronous I/O.

The interaction of the file subsystem with the organization of a physical disk is discussed in Chapter 4. Also included is detailed discussion of i-nodes and i-numbers, as well as System V Release 4 (SVR4) and ufs (Berkeley-type) file systems. There are four examples in this chapter that illustrate file and directory access. A detailed description of the ln utility is given, after which ln is applied to problems in porting C programs to different compilers and to problems in efficient library organization for C++ friend functions. Terminal I/O and device drivers are also discussed, briefly.

Chapter 5 includes an in-depth description of the techniques of process creation in UNIX. It describes the `fork()` and `exec()` system calls and appropriate ways to develop concurrent programs. The segments of a process, shareability of text segments among processes, the structure of a `.out` files, and COFF (common object file format) are discussed in this chapter, as are lightweight processes (threads). There are nine examples here, illustrating a wide range of topics in process creation.

Chapter 6 deals with the memory and process scheduling subsystems of UNIX. It describes commonly used scheduling algorithms and real-time schedulers, as well as use of the `nice()` system call for improving performance of a system of processes. The reader-writer and critical-section problems are introduced here, and an example of the use of monitors for synchronization of lightweight processes is given.

The technical details of interprocess communication (ipc) are presented in Chapters 7, 8, and 9. Programs in these chapters emphasize solutions to the reader-writer problem. Comparative performance of different methods and discussion of their appropriateness for some environments are presented in Chapter 10.

Chapter 7 is devoted to the simpler methods of ipc: files, shared file pointers, pipes, FIFOs, and streams. There are 11 programming examples illustrating the essential techniques.

Chapter 8 discusses three ipc methods—messages, semaphores, and shared memory—that are commonly called the System V IPC package. The required data structures are complex for each of these methods; and so they are discussed in detail. Nine examples are given.

Chapter 9 treats signals, sockets, remote procedure call (RPC) and the `rpcgen` utility. A variety of client and server examples are given, including connection-based servers (data stream) and connectionless servers (datagram). There are 18 examples in the chapter.

Some of the special facilities available in UNIX for support of fault-tolerant computing are discussed in Chapter 11. Techniques discussed include shell scripts to replace certain calls with those with more error information, the system calls `setjmp()` and `longjmp()` to implement roll-back techniques, and message queues for multiple processes that make up an N-version programming system.

Chapter 12 briefly discusses security, standardization (including POSIX), and the potential for rewriting the UNIX operating system in an object-oriented language such as C++.

Approximately 15 percent of the material presented in *Advanced Topics in UNIX* is not available in any other book.

As much as possible, the book is self-contained. The typical reader should have a good understanding of fundamental issues of multiprogramming operating systems designs (at least at high level), should be comfortable programming in the C language, and should have some experience as a UNIX user in editing files, using electronic mail, traversing directories, and running processes. A relatively new UNIX user will probably need to read the book in sequential order. One more experienced will probably wish to skip most of Chapter 2, referring to it only when necessary, and begin the detailed study of UNIX in Chapter 3. Computing professionals who already know most of the rudiments of UNIX systems-level programming will still be able to benefit from most of the later chapters.

This book has been used for three semesters as one of two texts in my graduate course in operating systems at Howard University (The other book is an advanced, general-purpose operating systems text.)

I would like to thank several people who helped in the learning that led to the writing of *Advanced Topics in UNIX*. My colleague at Howard University, Don M. Coleman, taught me about fault-tolerant computing. Some of the code used in the general exception handling and recovery block examples in Chapter 11 is based on ideas originally developed by Georgianna Marquez, Michael Stotts, and Michael Harrington while they were graduate students at Howard. My colleagues Robert L. Gault and William D. Craven at Howard allowed me to watch over their shoulders and helped me understand some of the issues in installing operating systems, installing updated software, and configuring device drivers. Jennette Hardy, a student assistant in the Software Development Laboratory at Howard, explained the methods of invoking C compiler options on the HP-9000, on which some of the programs were run. Two AfterMath employees, Anne Santos and David Leach, helped with the proofreading and copyediting of earlier versions of the manuscript. Anne also helped to verify the contents of the disk containing the source code in the book. The book team at John Wiley & Sons, Inc. Professional, Reference, and Trade Division (my editor, Diane Cerra, and Tammy Boyd, Maureen Drexel, et al.) and the reviewers (Nancy Fulton and Alan Southerton) were very helpful. Finally, thanks are due to several classes of students at Howard University who suffered through earlier versions of this manuscript.

To the Reader

There is a great deal of resistance to learning a complex operating system and its new set of commands, even among computing professionals. However, the current trend in computing is toward open systems, so that applications programmers can make proper use of appropriate features of an operating system using well-designed and well-documented interfaces. Proprietary code is unlikely to be as important in the future as it was in the past. For example, Digital Equipment Corporation's Ultrix group was much smaller than its VMS groups in 1983; the reverse is true today.

Advanced Topics in UNIX will help you understand the basic design philosophy of UNIX. It will explain most of the essential features of the operating system, emphasizing many important features by extensive discussion and several examples.

A 3.5-inch disk containing the source code examples in this book is available from the publisher at a cost of $15.00. The disk also contains all necessary makefiles and some other examples of code for interprocess communication. It is in IBM PC format and adheres to the eight-character filename limitation of DOS.

The disk can be ordered using the order form provided at the back of this book, or by calling 1-800-CALL WILEY.

A Macintosh-format version of the disk is available from:

AfterMath
10 E. Lee Street #2101
Baltimore, MD 21202

Checks should be made payable to AfterMath.

1

Introduction to UNIX

This chapter provides an overview of the UNIX operating system. In it we emphasize the two building blocks of UNIX: files and processes. We present the hierarchical nature of the UNIX file system and the typical nature of UNIX processes, and we discuss the limitations of UNIX as a real-time operating system. In addition, we present a brief history of UNIX, followed by a discussion of some of the more popular UNIX versions.

The fundamental features of UNIX will be introduced in this chapter. The UNIX operating system has become extremely popular for reasons that will become clear by the time you finish this book.

1.1 OVERVIEW OF UNIX

UNIX is designed to be a powerful general-purpose operating system that allows multiple users to use the computer at one time and allows each user to run many concurrent processes. It is currently implemented on a large variety of computers with different architectures, including personal computers, workstations, minicomputers, mainframes, supercomputers, and parallel computers. Many important software applications have versions that run on computers using the UNIX operating system.

UNIX was developed at AT&T Bell Laboratories by Dennis Ritchie and Ken Thompson. Their goal was a small but powerful operating system that could be ported easily to computers other than the one for which the system was initially developed. The original UNIX had several important features:

1

- It had an elegant view of an operating system in that every essential feature could be classified as either a file or a process.
- Files were streams of bytes; any other structure of the file was imposed by the application program accessing the file. No assumption about file organization such as database design, size of records, and so forth, was made by the operating system. Thus, there was a high level of portability of application programs because the high-level information about file organization was described in the application, not the operating system. The file system had a hierarchical, tree-like design.
- The software was written in layers, with only the lowest level of software, the *kernel*, able to access the hardware directly.
- It was written mostly in the C programming language, with about 10 percent written in the assembly language, instead of being entirely written in the assembly language of the host computer. (C was developed at the same time at AT&T Bell Laboratories.) Thus, most of the code was portable from one platform to another.
- The command interpreter used for the user interface was a powerful programming language called the UNIX shell. It included facilities for the execution of processes and the combination of processes into larger processes, as well as for the control structures and variables that are typically found in programming languages.
- The operating system allowed multiple users to run their processes by interleaving execution on the same CPU. The scheduling of processes was dynamic and intended to maximize throughput. A process that was I/O-intensive received ready access to the CPU when it needed it. A CPU-intensive process could not control all the CPU cycles, but was given reasonable access to computing resources.

UNIX was developed according to an extremely simple and elegant design principle: that two types of objects—files and processes—make up the entire system. This simplicity of design and the resulting computing power have made UNIX a popular operating system. It has also been the prime motivation for UNIX users and application programmers to follow the discipline of designing new software while keeping with the original philosophy of a layered software architecture. A layered software architecture is one in which lower-level details are hidden by combining them as needed into larger software units.

The layered software architecture of UNIX is described in Figure 1.1.

In UNIX, the simplicity of only processes and files allows small processes to be easily connected, making larger processes that are tailored to meet user needs. The layered approach means that a user need not

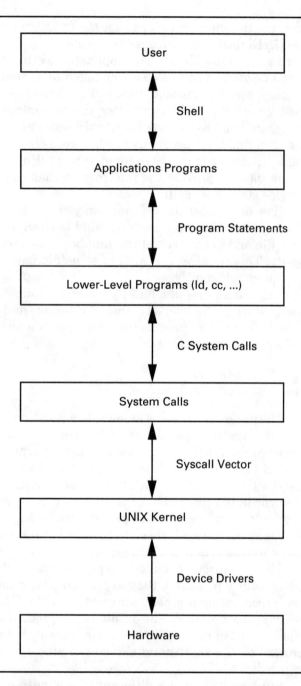

Figure 1.1.   UNIX software architecture

reinvent the wheel in order to use the operating system effectively. Instead, the UNIX user is encouraged to develop an application using existing software as building blocks. The application is thus tailored specifically to the user's needs and can be easily changed to do some other task.

Suppose, for example, that you wish to obtain an estimate of the accuracy of your typing by computing the percentage of misspelled words in a document you have typed. Most word processors have a spell-check facility that can find the incorrectly spelled words in a document, often by searching a dictionary for a match for each word. However, these word processors do not usually provide the information that you want—they usually don't provide counts of spelling errors.

How do you get the information you want? In most operating systems, you have to write a program by hand to check the spelling of each word in your file and keep track of the number of correctly and incorrectly spelled words. This requires a search of some dictionary and may not be easy to implement efficiently.

You can do this in UNIX by writing a simple program using the UNIX shell, which is the user's command interface and a programming language as well. The entire program can be written using two shell commands and looks something like this:

```
wc -w filename
spell filename | wc -w
```

The program works as follows. The first line counts the number of words that are present in the file named `filename`. The word count is invoked via the word count utility, `wc`. (A utility is a program that performs a commonly needed task; many utilities are provided in the standard UNIX software distribution.) It is used with the `-w` option since you want only the number of words in the file and not the number of lines and characters. The second line finds the number of misspelled words using the `spell` utility and sends the results of the spell check to the word count utility; each misspelled word is counted as it is found. One simple division and you are done.

The | character is called the pipe symbol and is used to connect the two UNIX utility processes that appear on either side of it. The connection of two processes by a pipe is automatic (in the UNIX shell) and requires no special programming. The output of the process on the left hand side of the pipe (the set of misspelled words) is transmitted directly to the input of the process on the right hand side of the pipe symbol (the set of words to be counted).

Suppose you want a different type of output. That is, you want a measure of the number of times that words are misspelled, but you want to ignore any duplications of words in the input file. If you wrote a program in a standard programming language to do this, a considerable effort would be required to change it.

In UNIX, you just use some additional building blocks. The new shell program looks like this:

```
cat filename | unique | wc -w
spell filename | wc -w
```

We used the UNIX utility `cat` that lists all the contents of the file on the terminal screen. We also used a user-written utility, `unique`, to produce a list of the unique occurrences of words in the file. As before, the pipe symbol connects utilities by sending the output of one utility directly to the input of another.

The user-written `unique` utility itself is made up of three standard UNIX utilities: `tr`, `sort`, and `uniq`. The steps in solving this problem are to organize the input so that there is one word per line, sort the lines of the file into alphabetical order, and output only one occurrence of each word. Each step involves an output that is a transformation of its input. The original input is not affected, since you are only using a copy of the file that was produced by `cat`.

The `tr` utility translates one set of characters as specified in its first argument into the set of characters specified in the second argument. With an input of

```
The frog and the dog went to study the compter at the dog
house.
```

(which has a single misspelled word), you want an output of

```
The
frog
and
the
dog
went
to
study
the
compter
at
```

```
the
dog
house
```

You want to specify that anything other than the set of alphabetical characters is to be changed, so you use the complement of this set. Doing so forces you to use the -c option. The code is somewhat different in the two most common versions of the shell. In the C shell, the tr utility is used in this way:

```
tr -c 'A-Za-z' '\12'
```

while in the Bourne shell, which is most common in System V UNIX, the usage is

```
tr -c '[A-Z][a-z]' '[\12*]'
```

(Another shell, called the Korn shell, will not be discussed in this book.)

The quotes are to ensure that the various shells interpret the ranges of characters correctly. The characters \12 refer to the ASCII newline character; the use of the backslash to denote special treatment of the next characters is similar to its use in the C language. Chapter 2 will discuss the differences between the two shells. For now, just note that we are providing solutions to the problem and that there is a difference between the two shells.

The next UNIX utility needed in this solution is sort. It is an extremely useful tool with many options. In this case, you need it only to produce a sorted list of the lines, which produces a sorted list of the words in the file, one per line, because of the previous use of tr.

```
The
and
at
compter
dog
dog
frog
house
study
the
the
the
to
went
```

The reason for using the `sort` utility is that the next utility, `uniq`, whose job is to remove multiple occurrences of an input line, works correctly only if the input is sorted, since it compares adjacent lines. Because the two utilities `sort` and `uniq` are connected by a pipe, the output of `uniq` is obtained by the action of `uniq` on the output obtained from `sort`. In this example, the output is

```
The
and
at
compter
dog
frog
house
study
the
to
went
```

You can finish the problem by using `wc`.

The pipe facility is a simple mechanism for solving a problem in a modular way. We can build up a solution using small software tools with well-defined interfaces. Our solution can be modified easily if our needs change. The apparent simplicity of the solutions to these two problems is a direct result of the fundamentally simple and elegant design of UNIX. The UNIX design allows the shell, which is a programming language as well as a command interpreter, to rapidly connect processes.

We stated previously that UNIX uses two fundamental objects in its design: files and processes. Thus, the two UNIX shell programs we gave are one or the other of these. The difference is that a file is a collection of bytes, and a process is an action that is taking place. When our program runs, it consists of the code for the utility programs `wc` and `spell` in the first example and the code for the utility programs `cat`, `uniq`, `wc`, and `spell` in the second example. When each of these utility programs is executed, it becomes a process. Simply put, a process is a running program; if the process is not executing, the code that generates it remains a file. This is an extremely oversimplified view of how processes are created and executed in UNIX.

A natural question is how the utility processes are linked to form a single process. After all, the processes do not know about one another and thus could not possibly have prearranged their connections. The secret is in the second fundamental UNIX building block—the file.

A UNIX process always writes its data to a file; there is no other choice. The term *file* is used in a specific sense here; the standard input (keyboard) and standard output (display) are considered to be files. Files are considered to be streams of bytes, with no special organization assumed by the operating system. Any special organization of the data is performed by the application program that uses the data and not by the UNIX operating system.

This powerful assumption about the lack of data formatting is the key to understanding the use of pipes in the two UNIX shell programs we just gave. Unless other specific actions are taken by the programmer, a UNIX process gets its input from what is called standard input (usually the keyboard) and writes its output to what is called standard output (usually the display screen). Since no assumption is made about the input or output organization of the data, we can get the entire application process to work if we can connect the standard output of one utility to the standard input of another. This connection is performed by the pipe, which is denoted by the | character. Note that this connection needs only to connect two files, standard output and standard input, of two processes. This connection is made using two "channels" with which UNIX attaches input and output to processes using a file descriptor. We will discuss UNIX file descriptors in Chapter 3.

You should be aware of what it means for the input and output to be in files. If we enter data from a keyboard, we are not immediately aware of the use of any files; however, many files are associated with this process. A UNIX process named `getty` determines if there is any keyboard activity before a user logs in on a terminal line. If so, the keyboard input is sent to a special file called a device driver whose contents (the keyboard activity) are in turn sent to another active UNIX process via that process's standard input, which is considered a file. This is true even though the keyboard input isn't permanently stored (unless we take some other action). A similar discussion holds for standard output. Don't worry that that standard input and standard output are not files that are permanently stored on a disk.

1.2   THE FILE SYSTEM

The term *file system* can be interpreted in two ways: as the way directories and subdirectories are used and as the way they are stored on the disks or other peripheral devices.

UNIX uses a tree-structured approach to its files. The root of the entire file system is the `root` directory denoted by `/` (slash), which contains various subdirectories such as `/adm` (for administration and associated files and utilities), `/bin` (for binary or executable files), `/etc` (for system databases and other miscellaneous files), `/usr` (for many system files directly associated with user activities), and `/home` (for user's home directories and data files). Most of the users of a UNIX system will have their files in one or more directories under the `/home` directory. (Different versions of UNIX have different places for user files and directories.) Since these files are subdirectories of `/home`, which itself is a subdirectory of the root directory `/`, these files may be accessed by their absolute paths using full names such as

```
/home/username1/file1
/home/username1/file2
/home/username2/file1
/home/username2/file2
/home/username2/file3
```

or, if we use the directory `/home/username1` as our starting point, by partial names such as

```
file1
file2
```

and so on.

The file system commands allow the user to navigate throughout a hierarchical file system. The parent directory is the directory one level higher in the directory tree. Thus, the directory `/home/username` is the parent directory of the files `file3`, `file4`, and `file5`, and the directory `/home` is the parent directory of the two files `/home/username1` and `/home/username2`, among others.

It is important to note that a directory file is treated the same way as other files for most purposes. This aspect of UNIX design was a precursor to the current notion of object-oriented design, in which most or all aspects of a system are abstracted into a collection of objects and transformations that can act on these objects.

The storage of files is also related to the notion of an instance of an abstract object. All permanent files are stored in the same way on disk regardless of whether they are ordinary files (such as text, a database, or executable code for some program), directory files, or special files (used as device drivers). There are only three types of files in UNIX: directory files, special files, and ordinary files. (There are several different types of special files; the term *special files* usually refers to device drivers or particular special-purpose files.) These three major types of files are all stored the same way on disk, regardless of their contents.

In UNIX, the file system is organized hierarchically. This means that there are directories and subdirectories so that files can be organized logically within a tree structure. The user can easily traverse the directory tree to find any file.

The root directory, denoted by / (slash), serves as the base for all directories. Mounted on the root are two file systems: the root file system, for general-purpose administrative activities, and the usr file system, for many utilities, users' programs and data, and other applications. Other file systems may be mounted also, depending on how the system was organized by the system administrator when the operating system was installed or upgraded. All file systems can be traversed hierarchically using a tree structure for directories and subdirectories.

Files in UNIX are found by the lookup of a number associated with the file in a directory file. This number, called an i-number, serves as an index into an array of i-nodes. An i-node contains information that allows us to find the owner and access permissions of the file and its location on disk. Other information is also included. There is some indirection in the location of the file on the disk because we first search the list of i-nodes before determining the location of the file. This indirection provides a high level of flexibility.

Files are always interpreted by the operating system as a stream of bytes. Any other interpretation is made by a process designed to use the higher-level logical organization of the data within the files.

Directory files consist of two-dimensional arrays of filenames and i-numbers. We will discuss them in detail in Chapter 4. Special files are the way UNIX allows processes to write data to devices such as printers, tape and disk drives, and terminals. These will be discussed in Chapter 3. All other files are called ordinary files. We will discuss them in detail in Chapters 3 and 4.

1.3 HIERARCHY OF PROCESSES

In UNIX, the term *process* indicates a program during the time of its execution. Suppose you log on to a computer that is running the UNIX operating system. These processes will always be active:

- Process number 0—swapper. This process moves blocks of data to and from disk in a virtual memory or sequential memory system (sometimes called the pager or sched process).
- Process number 1—init. This is the initialization process that aids in the creation of new processes.
- The getty process (the process number varies). This process checks a terminal connection line for an input event such as a key being struck or a mouse being moved.

- The `login` process (the process number varies). This process checks validity of a user's password while the user is logging in.
- The `shell` process (the process number varies). This process allows the user's commands to be interpreted and executed.
- Other user processes (the process numbers vary). These are the actual user's commands to be executed by the shell.

Thus, there are always at least three processes running whenever a user is logged on to a UNIX system. Other users on other terminals will have different `getty` and `shell` processes, but share the same `swapper` and `init` processes. Different processes may have the same name, but are identified by a unique nonnegative integer called the *process-id*.

It is important to understand how the design philosophy of UNIX affects the entire operating system's organization. Recall that UNIX was developed with two simple universal concepts: files and processes. The file system hierarchy is clear from the tree structure of directories, subdirectories, and so forth. The process organization is equally clear to the experienced user; however, it is not obvious to the user meeting UNIX for the first time.

A fundamental assumption about processes in UNIX is that they can be combined in any order, with their input and output connected via standard methods. We saw the method of combining processes using pipes before. The basic idea is that each process is made up of smaller processes that are joined together.

Thus, the process that compiles a C program appears to the user as a single process because he or she types a single command. But the process is actually made up of the following lower-level processes: loaders such as `ld`; preprocessors such as `cpp`; compilers such as `cc`, `pc`, or `f77`; assemblers such as `as`; and linkers. Of course, a user can access most of these lower-level processes directly by typing a command such as

```
ld filename
```

which allows the user to access a process that will be a building block in a computation, such as

```
cc filename
```

There is a limit to the level at which a user may access essential system routines. Users are prevented from damaging the operating system because their access to the fundamental routines and data structures is restricted to the interface provided by UNIX system calls. The easiest way to understand this hierarchy is from the hardware level up. Here is an example.

Consider the problem of sending a file's contents to the user's display screen. At the lowest, or hardware, level, we have to place the read/write head of the disk drive over the location of the file to be read and move the read/write head along an appropriate path so that data can be read. Once read, the data is sent by the read/write head to a channel that places it where it can be sent to the screen. From this place, all the data is sent to be displayed on the screen, which means controlling an electron beam that might turn on certain collections of light-emitting phosphors, allowing the user to see the contents of the desired file.

As complicated as this problem sounds, we have oversimplified it by glossing over some of the lower-level hardware questions, leaving out how to change the magnetic field to a digital signal and how to physically control the electron beam or the phosphors. It is not necessary to know these lower-level details if we are just moving a read/write head and changing the intensity of a magnetic field and converting a digital signal. Thus, we have a hierarchy: Higher-level processes control lower-level ones.

We can continue this level of complexity by hiding the details of lower-level complexity. For example, we can call a function to place the read/write head in the proper position and to read some number of bits from that position. We can go one step farther by having more abstraction and allowing the user to specify that a certain number of bytes is to be read from a file. This is a higher level of abstraction because it allows the user to specify a higher-level structure of a file and read in the data as bytes instead of as bits.

The sending of data from the file, which was stored on a disk, to memory involves another hierarchy of memory access functions. The channel in which information is read in from the disk is usually not the one that is used to send data to the screen. Therefore, some memory movement is also needed. This memory movement involves a process to control the use of fast memory buffers that can store and forward the data that is sent. These memory movement processes must also provide a mechanism for blocking the reading of data to the screen if there is no more data available from the disk or if the buffers are empty, and blocking the writing of data from disk if there is no more room in the allocated buffers.

A third hierarchy is involved in the display of data to the screen. We leave the details to the reader's imagination.

Clearly, there is a hierarchy of processes in the system. The lowest-level processes control the lowest-level hardware, the electronics. A process that directly controls devices like disks and performs actions such as controlling the movement of read/write heads is often called a device driver. A UNIX device driver is usually encoded in a combination of C and assembly language. On rare occasions, it may even be encoded in the UNIX shell, if only limited speed is needed from the device.

These device driver processes are themselves controlled by higher-level processes, and the hierarchy of processes continues until the top-level process is reached. Many of the lower-level processes are called *system calls*. Any process that interacts with a device driver or the hardware directly is either a system call itself or is called by a system call. We will see several examples of system calls in this section.

The observant reader will notice that little has been said about UNIX that cannot be applied to nearly any other operating system. Most modern operating systems have this so-called layered architecture representing a hierarchy in which higher-level processes can call lower-level ones. What, then, is so special about UNIX?

The difference is that UNIX explicitly allows a hierarchy, in the sense that processes can call other processes to do actions at lower level, and certain actions can be taken by the higher-level processes only through the appropriate system calls to lower-level processes.

Here is an example. Suppose we wish to read a stream of data from a file using the three standard C language I/O functions `fopen()`, `fgetc()`, and `fclose()`. None of these functions are system calls, as we will see. A call to `fopen()` allows two parameters: the name of the file and the mode, which is often one of the character strings "r," "w," or "a," to indicate reading from the start of the file, writing from the start of the file, or appending data at the end of the file, respectively.

Consider the appropriate use of the C function call used to read from a file named `toy`. This function returns a file pointer, which is a pointer to a structure called a `FILE` in C. To make things simple, assume that `toy` is a file in the same directory as the one we are in.

```
if ( (fp = fopen("toy","r")) != NULL)
    /* etc */
```

The function `fopen()` works as follows. The file is checked to see if it exists. Existence is determined by the presence or absence of an entry for it in the directory. If the file does exist, the access permissions are checked to make sure that the user's process can read the file. The current directory is consulted for the name of the file, which is used to find the i-number, which is used to determine the i-node, which in turn stores information about the access permissions. If this process works correctly, the i-node provides information on the locations of the physical blocks that make up the file on the disk. This works smoothly because the contents of directories are stored as collections of bytes and can thus be easily read. The result of a successful call to `fopen()` is that a file pointer is returned; an unsuccessful call returns a null pointer.

Once we have determined the locations of the file `toy` on the disk, we can simply read in the data from the disk using `fgetc()` in a loop such as this one:

```
while ((ch = fgetc(fp)) != EOF )
    putc(ch);
```

Of course, we can close the file with a call to the C function `fclose()` as in

```
fclose(fp);
```

It may appear that we did not make any use of system calls, but that is not correct. We made many system calls; they just were not immediately visible to us when we looked at the code fragments.

Let's examine the use of the directory more closely. We read the directory to determine if the file existed. We also read it to see if the file had the correct access permissions and to find the location of the disk blocks in which the file is stored. The directory is a file, and its contents had to have been read in order for us to see them. We made no explicit call to read this file, and hence there must have been a hidden one whose details were not available to us. The simple code example has quite a few lower-level calls.

Each reading of the directory involved an instance of the UNIX system calls `open()` and `read()`. These system calls are necessary whenever a file is to be read. In addition, the C functions `fopen()`, `fgetc()`, and `fclose()` will have to be broken down by the C compiler into a collection of calls to lower-level functions. That is, they need to be broken down into system calls. The call to the C function `fopen()` always incorporates a call to the system call `open()`. It also uses the system call `creat()` if the file to be opened does not already exist. The call to the C function `getc()` always incorporates a call to the system call `read()`, and a call to the C function `fclose()` always incorporates a call to the system call `close()`. The details of the use of the system call are hidden from the user. The hierarchy of system calls is always present even if it is not explicitly stated.

There are both higher and lower levels in this organization. High-level software, such as database managers or spreadsheets, routinely incorporate file handling functions like those represented here. As is common on most systems, these higher levels of software can be combined to form very high level systems. We will discuss lower levels of the process organization when we discuss the UNIX kernel in the next section. We will learn more about processes in Chapter 5.

There is an additional feature of UNIX system calls. In general, a C function can perform any internal computation, but can return at most one value. UNIX system calls are C functions that generally return a negative integer to indicate that an error has occurred. In addition, they can provide more information about the cause of an error in a system call by means of a predefined set of errors provided in the standard header file `errno.h`. These errors are accessed by the standard function `perror()`, which produces an error message based on the error found.

1.4 THE KERNEL, USER MODE, AND KERNEL MODE

The UNIX operating system has grown large over the years. In addition to normal operating system functions, the standard UNIX distribution includes editors, compilers, sorting utilities, games, and so on, many of which are not needed for normal operating system functionality but are expected by users and system administrators. This distribution is far too large to be placed in memory on most systems and would be a waste of resources even if there were enough room.

UNIX installations are usually configured to have a relatively small kernel of essential routines and data structures stored in memory and the rest of the operating system stored on disk. When running, the kernel is treated in a fundamentally different way from the way other UNIX processes and treated.

The kernel of the UNIX operating system is that portion installed in main memory when the system is running. The rest of the operating system resides on the disk, to be paged in as necessary. The contents of the kernel include those operating systems routines that have the most effect on response times: organization of memory, location of disk controllers, schedulers, algorithms for these operations and the associated data structures, and special device drivers for the hardware attached to the computer.

You should think of the kernel as providing the software interface between the hardware and higher-level system calls and user programs. The layered architecture of UNIX requires that a user process wishing to use the hardware must interact with the kernel. This interaction takes place by a change of "mode," which is different from the situation in which control of the CPU is switched from one user's program to another, as is typical in multiprocessing operating systems.

To understand the lower levels of system calls, it is necessary to understand the mode of a UNIX process and how it relates to processes. There are generally two classes of process in UNIX: user and kernel. (The superuser class has special rights in certain cases, but the general distinction is between user and kernel processes.) Thus, processes are executing either in user mode or in kernel mode.

UNIX uses system calls and kernel and user modes to limit access to the routines that should be reserved to the operating system and to the hardware itself. These modes are separated by means of system calls.

A system call is the only way that a process can access the hardware of a computer running UNIX. A system call to open a file might require, among other things, checking directories, reading the i-number and i-node to get information about the file, and moving the disk's read/write head to an appropriate location. All these activities are done by lower-level processes that can only be activated through the use of system calls, which are made up of these lower-level processes.

To prevent other processes from using these lower-level processes and thus compromising the security of the operating system, UNIX only allows these lower-level processes to be accessed when the calling process is executing in kernel mode. Executing in kernel mode means that the process is making use of the UNIX kernel's essential data structures, which are forbidden to user processes. Operating in kernel mode means that the rest of the process's activities are suspended until the kernel completes its actions, after which the process continues its execution in user mode.

Lower levels than the system call level are incorporated into UNIX. However, they may not be executed by any user's process on behalf of itself; they may only be executed by system calls in a special manner.

Here is an example of switching modes. A user's program has a statement involving the read system call

```
read(fd, buf, num_bytes);
```

where fd is a "file descriptor," buf is a pointer that represents the location of a buffer, and num_bytes is the number of bytes to be read. The statement is embedded in the user's C program. After the program has been compiled and is executing, the process is in user mode because all the instructions and data are in the user's area where program instructions and data are stored. When the read() statement is executed, the following steps occur:

- The call to read() is detected as a system call because the linker has already recognized it as one.
- The operating system switches to kernel mode.
- The processes' file description table is accessed using the file description fd.
- The kernel determines the location of the file and the offset that marks the location of the file pointer.
- The kernel controls the reading from the file of num_bytes of data and places this data in the buffer pointed to by the variable buf.
- The mode is switched back into user mode after the read is completed.

What is the purpose of this change of modes? It forces all the user processes to interact with the hardware through specially designed interfaces. It separates the user's memory space from the memory space in the kernel that is assigned to this process. It also means that a user's program need not be rewritten if the kernel changes.

Changes to the kernel are more frequent than you might imagine at first glance. A kernel is changed whenever new hardware is added to a system. For example, the addition of a disk drive, compact disk reader, or a tape drive requires reconfiguring the system design and thus reconfiguring the kernel. It is nice to know that the user's programs will work no less efficiently than before on the reconfigured kernel.

1.5   UNIX AS A REAL-TIME OPERATING SYSTEM

UNIX provides a powerful environment for software development because of its layered software architecture and its enforcement of a well-defined interface between user programs and the operating system's services through system calls. There is also a well-defined interface to the lower-level routines that control the hardware; these lower-level routines are invoked by the system calls.

UNIX's elegant design has several drawbacks, however. The first is that there is a considerable amount of overhead caused by these system calls and the resulting switches from user mode to kernel mode and back, which cannot be eliminated. The most common distributions of UNIX have a single kernel that performs all operations. The need for more predictable real-time performance may cause some UNIX implementations to replace a single, monolithic kernel that performs all essential operations with a small kernel with one or more "micro-kernels" that do some of the most essential operations efficiently. A major feature of AT&T System V Release 4 UNIX (hereafter referred to as SVR4) is that there is additional support for real-time performance in scheduling algorithms and the treatment of processes.

The second drawback is in the way UNIX improves its throughput. Since UNIX was designed to be portable, it was primarily written in C, with some penalty in performance compared to that of operating systems written entirely in assembly language. As part of the effort to improve the response to a large variety of user actions such as CPU or I/O use, the reading and writing operations on the disk are not performed directly but are done indirectly, using a set of software data structures in the UNIX kernel that are collectively called the *buffer cache*. Disk write requests are not sent immediately to the disk but are queued up in the buffer cache for later action by the disk scheduler. The purpose of this approach is to improve disk throughput.

The details of the internal organization of the buffer cache are not important to understand now; we will study some of them later.

The effect of the buffer cache on real-time performance is demonstrated when a user process requests that data be written to a file. The requested data is first written to a data structure in the kernel's buffer cache and then queued with all the other data in the buffer cache (from the same process or other processes) until the kernel synchronizes the disk. That is, the kernel arranges for the contents of the buffer cache to be written to disk. When this synchronization of the disk occurs, the contents of the buffer cache are written to disk in an order set by a disk scanning algorithm instead of in the order in which they were sent by the processes. This method provides high throughput for many processes. However, individual requests for reads and writes may be delayed as much as 30 seconds in some installations, since a period of 30 seconds is typical between disk synchronization operations.

Compare this with what happens in a real-time operating system. Real-time systems have priorities for actions; higher-priority actions are always compelled to execute before other processes with less critical needs are serviced. In a real-time operating system, the disk's read/write head immediately moves to the appropriate disk blocks, and writing of data begins as soon as the read/write head is in position. This activity occurs regardless of the activity of any other process, unless some other process has a higher priority.

The scheduling of processes is the job of the *scheduler*. In the latest release of one version of UNIX (System V UNIX), two schedulers are available: one that computes priorities dynamically and one with real-time features. Nearly all other UNIX systems have a non-real-time scheduler only.

The lack of real-time performance is a major problem in some instances and is a fundamental consequence of UNIX design. It cannot be overcome completely by clever applications programming. Improvements to real-time performance usually require extremely careful systems programming and redesign of the UNIX kernel.

1.6   THE HISTORY OF UNIX

The first version of UNIX was developed at AT&T Bell Laboratories by Dennis Ritchie and Kenneth Thompson in 1969–1970. They wrote a portable operating system in a new high-level language called C, which was developed at about the same time by Dennis Ritchie. The C code in the operating system accounted for over 90 percent of the operating system's size, with the rest of the code written in nonportable assembly language.

UNIX was originally available on the PDP-series minicomputer from

Digital Equipment Corporation, which is a tiny machine by today's standards. It was later ported to many other computers with different hardware architectures. Today, UNIX is one of the most popular operating systems in the world and the leading operating system in advanced workstations.

Current implementations of UNIX are much larger than the original 10,000 lines of code. Minimal UNIX systems have a kernel larger than 500 KB, with essential system files totaling more than 20 MB. Most UNIX implementations have 1 MB or more in the kernel and have over 100 MB of essential system files.

What caused the increase in size? The primary cause is that UNIX was originally given to universities for a tiny fee and source code was provided. Thus, university researchers and students had access to the source code so that they could fully understand the system and make enhancements to their own local versions of UNIX. Consequently, many useful enhancements and utilities were added.

A major change in the 1980s was caused by the breakup of AT&T. Under the terms of the court agreement, AT&T was no longer prevented from entering the computer business and, as a result, had been aggressively promoting UNIX. Advances from other sources have placed UNIX where it is today—in the forefront of multiuser operating systems and the operating system of choice for scientific workstations and computer networking.

1.7   VERSIONS OF UNIX

Because of the essentially free distribution of UNIX source code to universities, different versions of UNIX have evolved. Several important versions exist today, and they have many common features but some degree of incompatibility.

This continuing development has led to System V UNIX, which is one of the most popular UNIX versions. It is currently marketed and supported by a subsidiary of AT&T called UNIX Systems Laboratory. Novell recently purchased UNIX Systems Laboratory.

The University of California at Berkeley became a center for UNIX research and development. Its version of UNIX was known as BSD UNIX, a derivative of which was the most popular on Sun workstations. After the University of California Board of Regents decided not to support any more software products in this area, Sun and AT&T jointly developed a consistent version of UNIX, combining the best features of AT&T System V and BSD. This effort was aided by AT&T's purchase of 15 percent of Sun Microsystems.

A major UNIX effort by several other companies, among them Hewlett-Packard and Digital Equipment Corporation, resulted in the creation of a consortium called the Open Software Foundation, whose purpose is to develop nonproprietary versions of UNIX to provide open systems for easy software growth.

There are two popular versions of UNIX for microcomputers: XENIX from Microsoft Corporation and SCO UNIX from the Santa Cruz Operation. These versions have many more similarities than differences. They are both of extremely high quality and have adhered to the basic principles of UNIX.

All of this activity from different UNIX developers has caused a movement away from a single standard. There is only about a 70 percent overlap between some of the older BSD and AT&T system calls. The user who wishes to write portable programs should use only those system calls common to both versions.

UNIX standards are a moving target for several reasons. Several vendors have produced high-quality versions of UNIX-like systems for microcomputers. A major workstation vendor, Sun Microsystems, which developed a reputation for high-quality workstations running a version of UNIX based on BSD UNIX, has been partially purchased by AT&T. The two companies provide a "converged UNIX" containing the best features of each of the common flavors of UNIX.

Most applications software will run on all UNIX systems without substantial change. Fundamental differences in the different versions usually show up in interprocess communication. Software without this feature will have few problems. There are other, less serious problems caused by the renaming of certain files and the changing of certain constants in header files. Most of the other differences are enhancements made by manufacturers.

The Mach operating system, developed at Carnegie Mellon University, is the basis for an implementation that includes most of the higher-level UNIX utilities. Thus, to an applications programmer or a user of high-level software, it appears to be UNIX-like. It differs from other versions of UNIX in the way its processes are stored and executed in a multitasking environment.

POSIX is a UNIX-like system description that specifies the interface to hardware in a portable manner. It is an IEEE standard; the name stands for "Portable Operating System Interface for Computer Environments." POSIX is largely, but not completely, compatible with System V UNIX. There are some substantial differences between UNIX's lower-level descriptions and those in POSIX, particularly in real-time extensions to POSIX. Different UNIX systems have different lower-level real-time performance characteristics. For that reason there is a need for a consistent lower-level specification of hardware interface, which is precisely what POSIX provides.

POSIX is concerned with simplifying the programming interface to system calls across operating systems and across languages. It is a standards specification, not an operating system itself. The POSIX standard consists of a description of available services, real-time extensions to the common standard, and extensions to the standard for bindings to C and Ada.

The different versions of UNIX-like systems can cause major problems in carelessly written programs. Programs that follow the layered architecture of UNIX will have few difficulties.

We will emphasize portability in the programs that we present in this book. Any nonportable programs will be identified as such.

SUMMARY

UNIX is a multiprocessing operating system that is readily available on a wide range of hardware. It has a hierarchical directory structure for file storage and access.

The most important feature of UNIX is the elegant way in which essential system services and mechanisms can be classified as being either files or processes. This classification enables applications to be extremely flexible and readily combined into larger applications.

The user interface is via a text-based program called the shell, which is both a command interpreter and a powerful programming language.

REFERENCES

There are far too many publications on the UNIX operating system to include a complete list in a book of reasonable length. Instead, I will list only a few for each major topic. Several of the references in this chapter are taken from the papers directory provided in many standard UNIX distributions.

General Operating Systems References

Deitel, H. *Operating Systems*. 2d ed. Reading, Mass.: Addison-Wesley, 1990.
Silberschatz, A., J. Peterson, and P. Galvin. *Operating Systems, Concepts*. 3d ed. Reading, Mass.: Addison-Wesley, 1991.

General UNIX References

Bach, M. J. *The Design of the UNIX Operating System*. Englewood Cliffs, N. J.: Prentice-Hall, 1986.
Bourne, S. R. "UNIX Time-Sharing System: The UNIX Shell." *Bell Systems Technical Journal* 57 (1978): 1971-1990.
Crowley, T. H. "UNIX Time-Sharing System: Preface." *Bell Systems Technical Journal* 57 (1978): 1897-1898.

Johnson, S. C., and D. M. Ritchie. "UNIX Time-Sharing System: Portability of C Programs and the UNIX System." *Bell Systems Technical Journal* 57 (1978): 2021-2048.

Leffler, S., M. K. McCusick, M. J. Karels, and J. S. Quarterman. *The Design of the BSD UNIX Operating System.* Reading, Mass.: Addison-Wesley, 1989.

Ritchie, D. M., and K. Thompson. "The UNIX Time-Sharing System." *Bell Systems Technical Journal* 57 (1978): 1905-1929.

Ritchie, D. M. "UNIX Time-Sharing System: A Retrospective." *Bell Systems Technical Journal* 57 (1978): 1947-1969. Also in *Proceeding of the Hawaii International Conference on Systems Science*, Honolulu, January 1977.

Ritchie, D. M., S. C. Johnson, M. E. Lesk, and B. W. Kernighan. "UNIX Time-Sharing System: The C Programming Language." *Bell Systems Technical Journal* 57 (1978): 1991-2019.

Rochkind, M. *Advanced UNIX Programming.* Englewood Cliffs, N. J.: Prentice-Hall, 1985.

Stevens, W. R. *Advanced Programming in the UNIX Environment.* Reading, Mass.: Addison-Wesley, 1992.

EXERCISES

1. Obtain a list of commands from the UNIX commands manual. For each command, indicate if there is another command with a similar, but not identical, function. This will help you to understand the evolution of UNIX.

2. For any personal computer operating system, determine the degree to which it has a layered software architecture. Describe the ways in which the intent of the layered software architecture can be subverted to get access to lower-level routines.

3. For any operating system that supports multiprocessing, describe the fundamental objects of the system. Compare your answer to the existence of only two fundamental UNIX objects: processes and files.

4. Using the brief overview of UNIX presented here as a guide, indicate some of the ways in which the queue data structure might be used in the UNIX operating system.

5. Using the brief overview of UNIX presented here as a guide, indicate some of the ways in which the stack data structure might be used in the UNIX operating system.

2

The User Interface

The term *user interface* refers to the software and peripheral devices a user interacts with when he or she uses the computer. The user interface system contains software to

- Receive user input
- Interpret and execute user commands
- Channel input and output
- Provide error messages for improper commands

In UNIX, the user interface is called the *shell*. In this chapter, we discuss some features of the typical UNIX shell as the implementation of a user interface.

2.1   INTRODUCTION

There are many types of user interface and there has been considerable research and development aimed at making computers easier to use and standardizing the user interface. To understand the problems, consider the state of user interfaces in the early 1960s. Most computers allowed only one job to run at a time. The user had to provide special commands to the operating system, entering programs and data by typing them on punched cards. Minor errors in the punched cards led to incorrect programs, for which debugging was difficult because the error messages were hard to understand. There was no way to interact directly with an applications program.

Today, a user expects to have some helpful programs such as editors, compilers, linkers, and loaders to help with the programming process. The user interface is so much more powerful that computers are far easier to use than they once were. The most productive programmers often work in environments with multiple processes running in multiple windows, with easy transfer of data from one window to another.

Such environments often involve bit-mapped graphics systems, with graphical interfaces to many utilities. X Windows, Motif, and SunView are common window-based environments. For simplicity, this discussion is restricted to the traditional character-based user interface.

The UNIX implementation of the user interface is through an extremely powerful language known as the UNIX shell. There are actually several different dialects of the shell, the most popular known as the C, Bourne, and Korn shells. These shells are similar in their expressive power. We will concentrate on the Bourne and C shells; the Korn shell is much less common and will not be discussed here. "Shell" in this book, without a qualifier, means the C shell. We will frequently show the changes that are necessary for C shell programs to work in the Bourne shell.

Since UNIX was intended for use on many different terminals and workstations, the operating system itself assumes nothing about any input terminal. Unlike the MS/DOS operating system for personal computers, special function keys are not automatically associated with operating system actions in UNIX; instead, the use of function keys is determined by a "keyboard map" that assigns keys to specific actions. This assignment occurs after the shell variable TERM is set. We will discuss the TERM variable when we treat shell variables in section 2.2.6, on programming commands.

2.2   SHELL COMMANDS

In this section, we concentrate on some of the most commonly used commands that are available in the UNIX command interpreter known as the shell. The shell is both a command processor and a programming language. Commands fall naturally into several categories:

- Environment commands
- File system commands
- Process control commands
- Administrative commands
- Utility commands
- Programming commands

We will describe each of these categories of shell commands in a separate subsection. Some typical examples of each category of command will be presented.

2.2.1 Environment Commands

In UNIX, the most common use of the term *environment* includes those variables that are set up to allow the user to configure the terminal type, search paths, and utility functions that he or she wishes to have readily available. In short, the UNIX user can configure his or her programming environment to meet any special needs or preferences. Most of the environment is set up by the user in a file of shell commands. This file is executed at login time, so that the environment is automatically configured to the user's most likely needs. There is considerable variation in the initialization of these environment files. This variation is caused by different manufacturers' software distribution or by the local system manager's preferences.

The user can change the environment temporarily or permanently. The need for configuration of the environment will become clear to you if you use different devices to access UNIX systems. Suppose you must access a variety of computers on a network from many different devices. You might need to use simple character-based terminals; workstations running different versions of X Windows or other windowing systems, such as SunView or Motif; X terminals running only X Windows; personal computers using terminal emulation software, and so on. Being forced to use only character-based terminals on a graphics workstation might be annoying; requiring a mouse and bit-mapped graphics on a character-based terminal produces garbage.

The C and Bourne shells use different files for the initialization of the user's environment. For clarity, we will discuss the C shell first.

The C shell uses the files `.cshrc` and `.login` for initialization through what is known as environment variables. These files are normally in your home directory, which is the directory you are in when you log in.

The C shell first performs the actions specified in the `.cshrc` file. Here are some things that may be included in a `.cshrc` file:

- The search path, which is denoted by the variable `path`, will be initialized. This environment variable represents the set of directories that are to be searched for executable files and the order in which they are to be searched.
- Alias commands simplify the typing of shell commands. For example,

```
alias type cat
```

allows an MS/DOS user to use a familiar command, type, as well as the UNIX command, cat, to see the contents of a file.

- The variable history (a list of the most recent commands that have been run by the user) list may be set by something like

```
set history=32
```

There are many other possibilities.

You can see the values stored in your environment by running the setenv command. When run without any arguments, setenv will list all the variables that are part of your environment; when run with an argument that is an environment variable, it sets the value of that argument to 0 or NULL, as appropriate. Both environment shell variables and additional shell variables that are not included in the environment can be examined and set by use of the set command, as in the command to set the value of history.

After the commands in the .cshrc file are executed by the C shell, the commands in the .login file are executed. This file is used only when logging in and is especially useful when logging on to a graphical workstation from a character-based terminal. The .login file is used to set up terminal characteristics and to complete the setup of the user's environment.

Terminal characteristics are often set to a standard entry in a database; the termcap and terminfo databases are the ones most used. The setting of terminal characteristics to those of an entry in one of these databases is carried out by the tset command that is used with the eval command in a statement in the .login file, such as

```
eval `tset -s vt100`
```

which sets the shell variable TERM, which describes the terminal, to vt100, a common character-based terminal. This is a complex example, so we describe the steps needed to use it in detail in the paragraphs that follow.

The first shell command, eval, evaluates the shell variable that is its argument; this variable is the rest of the line of characters. The backquotes (`) are used to prohibit the shell from having eval evaluate the expression

```
tset - s vt100
```

as a group of shell statements, each of which is to be evaluated separately. The backquotes force the statement to be evaluated as an entirety.

The statement tset -s vt100 is then interpreted as a call of the command tset with the -s option (specifying that the setenv command be used to copy the entry from the terminal database into the environment) and the argument `vt100`. Sending this complex statement to `eval` forces the terminal type to be set by the `TERM` variable.

Additional statements can change the environment within the `.login` file. These include setting the characters that allow the user to terminate programs, log out, and control backspaces on the input device.

There can be many ways to perform the same operation. A user could simply type the shell command

```
set TERM=vt100
```

instead of using the `.login` file. This is a temporary change to the value of the `TERM` variable; the effect of this change disappears when the user logs off.

We now consider the methods for changing the environment in the Bourne shell. The two relevant files are `.profile`, which provides the same services as the `.cshrc` startup file, and `.login`, which behaves as it did in the C shell. There are two important differences between the two shells in the way the environment is treated. In the Bourne shell, the assignment to the shell variable `TERM` has the syntax

```
TERM=vt100
```

and does not use the set command for assignments (either to environmental or other shell variables). In addition, an assignment of a value to a shell variable does not automatically cause a change to the environment even if the shell variable is an environment variable; often we need to use the export command to allow the environment to have access to the variable, as in

```
TERM=vt100
export TERM
```

Most of the other differences in the treatment of the environment in the two shells are minor.

2.2.2   File System Commands

Most of the commonly used shell commands for file system management are available in both the C and Bourne shells and have the same syntax and semantics. We now describe some of these commands.

A user can change directories with the `cd` shell command, which has the syntax

```
cd optional_directory_name
```

(We use italics for optional shell command arguments.)

This is typical of UNIX shell commands. Shell commands are entered in response to a system prompt. They are character strings that are parsed as tokens that may be separated by blanks or tabs as long as the system-defined length of a command is not exceeded. The first token represents the command to be executed, and the other tokens represent options or arguments to the command to be executed.

For example, if we are working in the directory /home and wish to go to the subdirectory rjl, we type the command

```
cd /home/rjl
```

Since the shell understands and keeps track of what the current working directory is in the shell variable cwd, the shorter command

```
cd rjl
```

is sufficient. Here cd is the command and rjl is the argument. In the previous example, /home/rjl is the argument. To change to the directory /home/abc from the directory /home/rjl, we could type

```
cd /home/abc
```

or

```
cd ../abc
```

The ellipsis notation (..) means the parent directory of the current working directory. Thus, cd ../abc means to go first to the parent directory and then to the subdirectory abc.

The command

```
cd
```

by itself has a somewhat different meaning; it changes the current working directory to the user's home directory.

The shell keeps track of the current directory and the home directory in shell variables. We will return to this topic later in this section. For now, just remember that this information can change dynamically as a user moves around the directory tree. If you are unsure of what directory you are in, type the shell command

```
pwd
```

to print the current working directory.

Files are created and destroyed frequently in UNIX. The most common way of creating files is to use an editor such as vi or ed. (For a description of these editors, see your UNIX manual.) Files are also created by other programs such as compilers generating object files (whose names end in .o), linkers generating executable files such as the familiar a.out, graphics programs creating raster files for display, database programs creating data files, and so on.

One type of file cannot be created by this method—a directory file. A directory is created by the mkdir command, whose syntax is

```
mkdir directory_name
```

Files other than directory files can be removed with the rm command. A directory can also be eliminated by using the rm command if it is empty.

The directory name can be as simple as newdir if we are creating a new directory in our current directory. It can also be a more complicated relative pathname such as ../other_dir/newdir or a full pathname. The rm command unlinks the location of the file from its parent directory, which means that the file cannot be accessed from this directory any longer. It does not erase the data from the disk, and this lack of security is one reason some people feel that UNIX is not a "secure" operating system.

The rm command can lead to serious trouble because of two features. If the user types

```
rm file1
```

then only the file named file1 is removed, if it existed before the rm command.

However, the command

```
rm file*
```

removes not only file1, but also files named file, file3, file8, file_old, file_new, and so on, since the * (asterisk) means that zero or more characters will be automatically matched by the so-called wildcard. Adding a space before the asterisk changes the command to

```
rm file *
```

But this is a disaster—if the noclobber shell variable is not set in the .cshrc (or similar startup file), this command removes not only files with names beginning with file but all other files as well. Be extremely careful in using wildcards as part of an argument to the rm command. Setting the `noclobber` optional shell variable in a startup file can prevent disasters when removing files.

When `rm` is used with the `-r` option, which denotes recursion in this command, all files in the current working directory will be removed, including directory files. When a subdirectory file is detected by using the command `rm -r`, all the files in it are removed, as are the subdirectories of the current directory. The command

```
rm -r filename
```

is used to remove (recursively) the file named `filename` from the current working directory. Here `rm` is the command, `-r` is the option, and `filename` is the argument.

The syntax of `rm` is typical of UNIX commands. The command line begins with the name of the command, followed by the set of options, and finally by the argument list that is a set of files to be removed.

A related command is `rmdir`, which will remove an empty subdirectory from a directory; its syntax is

```
rmdir sub-directory-name
```

We now know how to create and remove directories and how to change them. The `ls` command is used to list the contents of a directory. It has the common UNIX syntax

```
command-name options arguments
```

There are many options available for the `ls` command. Here are a few of them:

```
ls
```

(produces a list of all files in the current directory in alphabetical order).

```
ls -l
```

(produces the long listing, including access permissions, ownership, and date of last modification). The access permissions are three sets of permissions to read, write, or execute for the owner, owner's group (to be discussed later), and others. Since each of these nine permissions is either allowed or not, the set of access permissions can be described by a three-digit octal number.

```
ls -al
```

(produces the long listing with all files whose name begins with a period added). We have already stated that the ellipsis symbol (. .) denotes the parent directory whose value is stored in the shell variable . . ; the period symbol (.) denotes the current directory whose value is stored in the shell variable cwd. This includes the output of the ls -l option and information on the current working directory, the parent directory, and files such as .profile **and** .login .

```
ls -t
```

(Lists the files in order of date of last modification.)

```
ls -x
```

(Lists the files, putting an asterisk next to all executable ones.)

The optional arguments can be the names of one or more files and may contain wildcards. To appreciate the range of options on a command such as ls, you should experiment with ls using many options, including upper- and lowercase letters. Invalid options will show you some of the shell's typical error messages.

2.2.3   Process Control Commands

In this section we discuss process control commands, which allow a process to run at various times. Recall that *process* is the term that UNIX uses to describe programs that are executing. The common UNIX shells are inter- preters that allow the execution of the processes that are described in the shell statements. The commands described in this section are the same for the Bourne and C shells.

We have already seen shell commands for use with processes. The pipe symbol (|) connects two processes and automatically sends the output of one to the input of the other.

There is another way of controlling the input and output of processes— we can redirect their input or output, using the symbols > and <. For ex- ample, we can send the output of a process named process_name to a file named outfile with the command

```
process_name > outfile
```

so that the output is sent to the file instead of to standard output. This example assumes that the process name process_name wrote its output to the standard output file (usually the output terminal). If the process writes its output to some other "file," the output can still be redirected using a slight variation of the above shell command, as in

```
process_name n > outfile
```

where *n* is a nonnegative integer that represents a " file descriptor " for the process that determines where its output is to be sent. File descriptors 0 and 1 generally refer to standard input (`stdin`) and standard output (`stdout`), respectively, unless some action has been taken by the programmer to change this. These are the defaults for process input and output. File descriptor 2 is similarly used as the default value of the place to write the standard error messages (`stderr`) from a process.

Thus, to keep an error log of the execution of the process called `process_name`, with all normal output going to the screen (or to other files if specifically set by the process), we use the shell command

```
process_name 2 > error_file
```

We can also obtain input from a file. For example, we can read in data from an input file named `infile`, instead of from standard input, with the command

```
process_name < infile
```

The use of other file descriptors is the same as with output redirection.

These redirections can be combined into shell commands such as

```
process_name < infile > outfile
```

An interesting process control command is the ampersand (`&`), which is used to run a process in the "background"; the process continues execution while another process, called the "foreground," executes. The background process is impervious to input from the keyboard; keyboard inputs are sent to the foreground process. Background processing is used for processes that need no user input and will continue without interruption. Background processing is ideal for compilation of a large program because it leaves the terminal available for other jobs such as file editing. On the other hand, editing a file in the background makes no sense because of the impossibility of entering keyboard input.

Suppose we type the two commands

```
cc file*.c &
vi book
```

The first command invokes the C compiler program `cc` on each of the files whose name is of the form `file*.c`, where * represents zero or more characters of any form. The ampersand, `&`, indicates that this is to be run in the background. The UNIX shell responds with a message something like

`[1234]`

The number `1234` represents the *process-id* of the process, which is a unique integer associated with the process. The process-id is assigned by the operating system, not by the user. (More information about process-ids will be given in Chapters 5 and 6 where we study concurrency.) We now execute the second command and invoke the `vi` editor even while the background C compilation is taking place. When the background process is complete, the shell reports something like

`1234 done`

indicating that the process with process-id number `1234` is now complete. This may appear to mess up the file `book`, but it doesn't; the message appeared on the screen because there was no place else to display it. The file you are editing has not been harmed; only the visual image was changed.

You can get a good look at the processes on your system by running the process status command

`ps`

which gives a listing of all running processes that are owned (created) by you for this login session on this system, while

`ps -a`

gives a listing of all processes running whether created by you, by other users, or by the operating system itself. Another command option, `-1` (for long), provides more detailed information about the status of the process.

The execution of any running process you own can be stopped with the `kill` command.

The `at` command can be used to begin a job at a particular time. Typical uses for `at` are system backups to tape or long compilations, which may take place late at night. The syntax of this shell command is

`at` *options* `time` *date week* `script`

and is interpreted by the shell to execute the set of shell commands called `script` at the specified time. The options include `-c` for executing `script` from the C shell and `-s` for executing `script` from the Bourne shell. If no option is specified, then the shell that was set in the variable SHELL will be used for execution control. An example of this is

```
at 3am week make project
```

which uses the UNIX `make` facility to create a (presumably very large) software system called "project."

2.2.4   Administrative Commands

Administrative commands include those to allow new users to log on to the computer, perform system accounting, and shut down the system. They can usually be found in the directories `/etc` and `/adm`. Since most of these commands require the user to have the highest level of system privileges— that is, to be able to log in as superuser or root—we will discuss them only briefly here.

Most systems are used by more than one person. Typically, one or two people are designated as system managers and are given special privileges and important responsibilities. Some of these responsibilities are: managing and avoiding crises, helping users, controlling access security, installing new software, upgrading old software, and providing backups of the file systems.

Crisis control means making sure that the system remains functional as continuously as possible and that any downtimes are minimized when an unexpected event happens. Backing up the system and keeping logs are extremely valuable in this regard. The most common backup utility is `dump`. Also important are the `halt` and `shutdown` commands, which are often found in the directory `/etc`; this directory is often included in the path of the system manager. (The path is described in section 2.2.6, on programming commands.)

Controlling access usually means creating logins for new users, which in turn means manipulating the password file in `/etc/passwd` and adding a desired home directory to the proper directory file system. Other actions might be needed on some systems. The process is aided by the existence of some utility programs for administration.

Installing new software and upgrading old software are specialized activities, and any good software includes an installation guide. A prudent system manager will keep a record of any entries made during the installation or upgrading of software.

The system manager must also control network access using tables indicating the name and network address of the computer.

Regular backups of the system are made with the `dump` command, which is found in the directory `/etc` on many systems. This utility allows the system manager to dump all of the contents of the file system to tape at one time. It also allows the use of incremental dumps affecting only files changed after a given date. All dumped files can be restored by the `restore` command.

2.2.5   Utility Commands

The term *utility* refers to programs that perform actions that are useful but limited in scope. Frequently, utility programs can be combined in UNIX to provide more powerful computing tools. There are far too many UNIX utilities for us to discuss in detail. Therefore, we will briefly treat only a small subset here.

Suppose that you wanted a listing of the files in your current directory with the output sorted by the size of the file. You might use the `wc` command, which has the syntax

```
wc options filename
```

and produce a count of the number of words, lines, and bytes in the file. The `-l` option prints the number of lines, while the `-w` option prints the number of words. This is a useful thing to be able to do, which is why `wc` is called a utility. The `wc` command can be connected to another UNIX utility called `sort` by the pipe (|) mechanism. This is similar to an example given in Chapter 1. The compound command to solve this problem using a pipe is

```
wc -l * | sort
```

Here, the `wc -l *` command counts the number of lines in each file in the current directory. As this utility finishes counting a file, it sends the information about the file and the number of lines in it to `sort`, which stores all data about the files and their sizes until `wc` has completed. Once all the data has been read by `sort`, the result is a complete list of files in the current working directory, sorted in order of the number of lines per file.

The syntax of the `pipe` shell command is

```
UNIX_command1 | UNIX_command2
```

where `UNIX_command` can also include a pipe. The idea is that the output from one end of the pipe is sent to the input of the next place in the pipe, and so on.

The existence of different processes in the pipe is not relevant; the sender will wait until the receiver is ready if the pipe is full. We will discuss this situation in more detail when we look at the pipe() system call in Chapter 7 as part of our study of interprocess communication. For now, think of pouring motor oil from a can into a funnel in your car's oil reservoir. The mouth of the funnel is wider than the base so that the rate of flow from the bottom (the end of the pipe) is slower than the flow into the mouth (the beginning of the pipe). Assuming that you pay attention and don't overfill or spill the oil, this process will work until there is no more oil in the pipe. (By the way, be sure to check your oil at least every other gas fillup.)

2.2.6   **Programming Commands**

The final aspect of the shell that we will study is its ability to be used as a programming language. Most programming languages have many dialects; in UNIX, the different shells should be considered as dialects of the same type of language. There are several differences between the C and Bourne shells in their programming syntax; where there are differences, we will provide programming examples for each concept in both shells.

Programming languages have variables; in the UNIX shell, they are called shell variables. To see some shell variables, log on to a computer running UNIX and type the command

```
set
```

which we saw previously. The output is something like this on one computer running the C shell; it will be similar (not exactly the same) on yours.

```
cwd      /usr/rjl/books/UNIX
history 12
home     /usr/rjl
path (. /bin /usr/bin /usr/local/bin /usr/ucb/bin
     /usr/VADS/bin)
prompt  faculty1-->!%>>
shell    /bin/csh
term     sun
user     rjl
```

This C shell output lists the values of 8 shell variables. The value of the current working directory is kept in the shell variable cwd, which in this case is the directory /usr/rjl/books/UNIX. Up to 12 of the most recent shell commands are stored for use by history. The home directory is /usr/rjl.

The C shell uses the `path` shell variable to describe the directories to be searched for executable files and the order in which they are to be searched. In this example, suppose that we enter the shell command

```
doit
```

The current directory is first on the search path, since the period (`.`) appears first in the `path` variable (other directories are separated by spaces in the C shell). Thus, we search the current directory for an executable file named `doit`, and if we find it, we execute it. If `doit` is not in the current directory, then we search for it in the directory `/bin`. We continue the search through the directories `/usr/bin`, `/usr/local/bin`, `/usr/ucb/bin`, and `/usr/VADS/bin` until we either find a file named `doit` or exhaust all possibilities. If we find the file in any directory, we stop the search and execute the file immediately. If the file is not found, an error message is printed by the C shell.

The syntax of the prompt output is interesting because of the embedded information in the `!%` characters. These characters allow the prompt to include the number of the shell command to be displayed in the prompt. For example, the prompt in the C shell login session in which the original version of this chapter was written is

```
faculty1-->409%>>
```

The meaning of the `shell` and user `shell` variables is obvious. The remaining C shell variable, `term`, is what was set up in the environment by the `.login` file initially, unless it was changed earlier in this login session. (Some of the other shell variables were set up in the `.cshrc` file.) It indicates a Sun computer.

The output of the `set` shell command is somewhat different in the Bourne shell. Here is some output from the `set` command on the same computer running the Bourne shell.

```
LOGNAME=rjl
MAILCHECK=600
PATH=.:/bin:/usr/bin:/usr/local/bin:/usr/ucb/bin
:/usr/VADS/bin

PS1=$
PS2=> PWD=/usr/rjl/books/UNIX
TERM=sun
USER=rjl
HOME=/usr/rjl
```

This output describes the values of nine shell variables; most of which clearly have the same function as in the previous C shell example. Note the use of uppercase for the standard Bourne shell environment variables such as HOME, PATH, and TERM, as well as the use of colons as separators in the PATH variable.

The two shell variables PS1 and PS2 in this Bourne shell example represent prompts to the user. They are used for different shells and help the user determine what environment shell (or even which computer on a network) he or she is using.

You can set shell variables yourself. Consider the example

```
wc -l
```

that we used earlier. We can assign this to a new Bourne shell variable by

```
shell_var="wc -l"
```

(use the syntax set shell_var="wc -l" in the C shell) and then use this command to get a listing of the number of lines in all the chapters in this book by typing

```
$shell_var chap*
```

which gives the same output in both shells. The dollar sign ($) should be typed in this example because it indicates the value of the shell variable, not just its location in the memory, which is what we mean if we type the shell command shell_var.

The Bourne shell program

```
for i in file*.c
do
   lpr $i
done
```

shows how to use the shell to program a loop of calls to lpr. The print utility lpr is available under that name on many systems. This program construction is typical of for-loops in the Bourne shell. Contrast it to the C shell program to do the same thing.

```
foreach i (file*.c)
   lpr $i
end
```

This program illustrates the difference in the control of for-loops in the C shell. The relevant reserved word in the C shell is `foreach`, and the delimiters `do` and `done` are replaced by the single ending delimiter `end`.

There is a potential problem with the two examples just given of the use of loops in UNIX shells. The `PATH` variable is almost always set to search the current directory first, so that the execution of shell scripts and executable programs developed by the user can be found quickly, without any other directories having to be searched. This can be a problem if an executable file with the name `lpr` is in the current directory. This problem actually occurred when a student electronically submitted source code to me for a programming assignment using the login name `lpr`, which happened to be the student's initials.

There are three obvious solutions to this problem. Use whichever one seems appropriate.

1. Rename the offending file in your directory.
2. Set the `PATH` variable to search `/usr/bin` and `/bin` before searching the current directory. (This can cause other problems.)
3. Use the full path name `/usr/bin/lpr` in the shell script.

The shell permits other control structures such as the while-loop and changes of control flow from the `if` and `case` (`switch` in the C shell) statements. We will see some examples of these structures in section 2.4, on shell programming.

Arithmetic can also be done with the UNIX shell, using the `expr` command. For example:

```
a=`expr 7 + 4`
```

(don't forget to use `set` in the C shell) assigns the sum of 7 and 4 to the variable *a* as we can see by using the shell output utility `echo`:

```
echo $a
```

The syntax of the statement with `expr` is slightly tricky. Shell assignments never allow spaces around the equal (=) sign. Moreover, the argument to `expr` is enclosed in backquotes (`` ` ``), not single quotes (`'`).

Multiplication and division present a small syntactical problem as well because the * and / symbols already mean wildcard and directory separator, respectively. The solution is the same here as in C—use a backslash. Thus, to assign to the variable *a* the value of $7 + 3 \times$ the value of $b + 8 \div c$, we write

```
a=`expr7 + 3\* (b + 8)\/ c`
```

2.3   THE BOURNE AND C SHELLS

There are several shell dialects in UNIX. The most common are the Bourne and the C shells. The Bourne shell is named after its inventor, Stephen Bourne, the C shell is so named because of some similarity in its syntax to that of the C programming language. The Bourne shell is part of nearly all standard distributions of UNIX, and the C shell is commonly added to systems based on BSD UNIX. Most systems provide both shells for programming use, so a user has a choice. (As was mentioned earlier, many systems also include the Korn shell.)

In this section, we will show the major features of both shells and their differences. It is important to note, however, that their similarities are greater than their differences, particularly their running of application programs, shell processes, and utilities.

The Bourne shell has the easiest facilities for loops, allowing the user to control loops using the simple for-loop syntax mentioned earlier. It is well-suited to running simple commands and simple programming. However, it does not allow the user to recover earlier actions such as recalling previous commands by referring to them by number. This facility is available in the C shell in the `history` variable, explained shortly. Much retyping is necessary when using the Bourne shell, unless you have a windowing system in which commands can be copied with the mouse and placed wherever needed.

The difference between the two shells that is most obvious to a casual user is the standard prompt. Unless the user changes the value of the prompt string, the prompt for the Bourne shell will be a dollar sign (`$`) and the C shell prompt will be a percent sign (`%`). Other differences are more fundamental.

There are some powerful and easily accessed program development features in the C shell that are not present in the Bourne shell. The most immediately useful such feature is the `history` utility, which is initialized by a C shell command that sets the size of a buffer that will store the last few commands entered by the user. The C shell syntax is

```
set history=some_integer
```

which fixes the size of the `history` buffer to the specified integer. The `history` command can be entered by the user at any time; however, it is commonly included in the user's `.profile` file so that it starts automatically when the user logs onto the computer. After the value of the history parameter is set, every command entered has a unique positive integer associated with it as an index. Assignments in the C shell are performed with the `set` construction.

The `history` utility eliminates the retyping of long commands. Suppose you have typed several long and complicated commands such as

```
ls $HOME/source_code/*.c |wc -l sort -n
```

and you are tired of retyping commands you have already run. If you know the number of the previous command you wish to retype, you can recall the command from the buffer and execute it simply by typing an exclamation point (!) followed by the command number, as in

```
!command_number
```

The exclamation point tells the C shell that it should search the `history` buffer for the command with the index that matches the integer following the exclamation point.

You may be unsure of the index of the command you wish to recall. Perhaps the current command number is 126 and the command number you want to use is 100 (which you have forgotten). You have three choices:

1. Get a list of commands in the buffer by typing `history`. Determine that the command is number 100 and then type !100 at the command line prompt.
2. Go backwards in the buffer using a command such as `!-offset` that recalls a command based on its offset index from the current command. In this case, the offset is 126 − 100, or 26.
3. Match by typing `!ch`, where `ch` is the first character or set of characters used in the command to be recalled. In this command, it is !l. This approach can be dangerous if there are other commands with similar starting characters between the current command and the desired command in the buffer.

As we have seen, the assignment of values to shell variables is different in the two shells. In the Bourne shell, a simple assignment statement suffices—

```
PS1="MY COMPUTER-->"
```

is adequate to change the major prompt string. Changing the prompt in the C shell involves using the `set` construction and looks like

```
set prompt="MY COMPUTER-->"
```

Each of the shells allows the automatic parsing of command-line arguments and the use of shell variables. For example, a command line such as

```
cp file1 file2
```

is automatically parsed into three separate tokens. These tokens are, by convention, separated into temporary variables named

```
$0
```

for the name of the copy utility `cp`,

```
$1
```

for the name of the first file `file1`, and

```
$2
```

for the name of the second file `file2`, and so on. The number of command-line tokens is denoted by `$#` in both the Bourne and C shells. These shell variables can be used in shell programs, as we will see in the next section.

2.4   SHELL PROGRAMMING

The shell is both a command interpreter and a high-level programming language. In this section, we focus on the shell as a programming language. The shell programming language is interpreted, and, ordinarily, an interpreted language produces programs that execute slowly. However, since the commands executed usually are already compiled into executable code, performance is generally not an issue.

The shell allows sequential execution of commands, with commands separated by carriage returns or semicolons. Branching and looping are also allowed.

Earlier we saw an example of the for-loop in the UNIX shell when we used a loop to print several files. We can also use a while-loop, although the Bourne and C shells treat the while-loop differently.

In the Bourne shell, the syntax of the while-loop is

```
while (list_of_expressions)
    do
        list_of_statements
    done
```

and the expected control variable is a list. The syntax of the while-loop in the C shell is

```
while (expression)
    list_of statements
end
```

and the execution of what we have called `list_of_statements` continues until the value of the expression becomes 0.

Branching is done with the `case` and `if` constructions. The termination of the block of statements in an `if` statement is with the characters `fi`, and the termination of a `case` statement is with the characters `esac`.

Equally important to shell programming are shell variables. We met one of them in the TERM variable in the Bourne shell (`term` in the C shell). Shell variables can be used in several ways.

Example 2.1 is a simple Bourne shell script that was used in a computer science course to evaluate a set of C programs for correctness. Note the use of the pound character (#) in the first position on a line to indicate that the line is a comment. The corresponding C shell program is similar but uses a percent (%) sign instead of a # sign. There are other minor syntactical differences, but the logical organization is the same.

Example 2.1: A Simple Bourne Shell Script

```
#
# doit program -- first version
#
$i=$1
rm a.out
echo $i
echo $i >> out
cc $i
for j in testfile*
do
    a.out $j < $j >> out
    echo "----------------------------" >> out
    echo $j "done"
done
echo "-----------------------------------" >> out
```

The script is stored in a file named `doit` that has its execute permissions set so that it can be executed. It is invoked on a student file named `abc.c` by the command line

```
doit abc.c
```

which replaces the formal parameter $1 by the file name abc.c. The value of the shell variable $1 is local to the file doit.

The symbol $1 always denotes formal argument number 1, with $0 referring to the name of the shell script being executed. Other arguments are referred to, in order, as $2, $3, and so on. The symbol $$ refers to the number of arguments. The similarity to the passing of command-line arguments in C is a result of the concurrent development of C and UNIX.

The execution begins with the replacement of the value of the local shell variable i with the value of the formal argument $1. The shell script, or set of shell commands, in the file doit then removes the file a.out. The script doit then echoes the name of the file abc.c to the screen and to the output file out. The next step is the compilation of the file named in $1, namely abc.c. The next for-loop uses a shell variable, j, to run through all files whose names begin with the character string "testfile." The program then terminates after some cleanup operations.

The file doit could have been invoked on an individual file such as abc.c or on many files within a loop by running the shell program

```
for i in [a-f]*.c
do
    doit $i
done
```

The two shells allow the use of multiple branches within a shell program. The Bourne shell uses the reserved words case and esac. For example, the improved version of the Bourne shell script doit, in example 2.2, uses the delimiter symbol ;; to indicate the end of a selection of code associated with an option in a case statement. Note the use of the right parenthesis to indicate the end of a specification of an option in a case statement.

Example 2.2: Improved doit Script

```
#
# improved version of the doit program
#
case $# i
0)
    echo "Usage: $0 requires other arguments" ;;
*)
```

```
i=$1
rm a.out
echo $i
echo $i >> out
cc $i
for j in testfile*
do
   $PWD/a.out $j < $j >> out
   echo "---------------------------" >> out
   echo $j "done"
done
echo "---------------------------" >> out
;;
esac
```

The use of $PWD in front of the call to the executable program a.out prevents the use of another file named a.out in any other directory on the search path, if the file named a.out is not present in the current working directory. There are many other possibilities for shell programming but we do not mention them here.

2.5   ADDITIONAL PROGRAMMING EXAMPLES

In this section, we will briefly describe some common programming problems and their solutions in the shell. The solutions will illustrate the use of some of the ideas discussed earlier in this chapter.

The first problem occurs when software is ported from one UNIX system to another and the compilers are different. Many older UNIX systems had C compilers that did not meet the ANSI standards. Some new compilers enforce ANSI standards and won't compile older code. There is likely to be a large investment in the existing code so that rewriting it is not feasible. This situation occurs often, even if there is no explicit use of UNIX system calls.

Many compilers have optional flags that allow easing of the ANSI restrictions. How can we incorporate these options into our environment efficiently, avoiding the typing of the (sometimes) complex options every time we compile a C program?

One solution is to define a new shell variable that incorporates the options. For example, in HP-UX version 9.0 on the HP-9000, we can set a shell variable called CCOPTS to obtain the value -Ae. This allows overriding of the strict ANSI C compliance enforced by the standard -Aa option.

There is another solution to the problem. If code is to run in several environments, we may want to keep the standard values of shell variables. We can still solve our problem using conditional compilation and the C preprocessor.

Conditional compilation can be performed by statements such as

```
main()
{
#ifdef _HPUX_SOURCE
printf("Hello HP\n");
#endif
#ifndef _HPUX_SOURCE
printf("Hello Other System.\");
#endif
}
```

in a source code file. These statements permit use of the same code in several different compilation environments. They also allow the use of libraries that may be in different places on different systems.

A third solution is to use shell variables within C makefiles. Instead of using the cc variable to denote the compiler within a makefile, we can define the compiler to be used in an initial statement, such as

```
CC=cc
CC=gcc
```

or something similar. The compiler is then invoked elsewhere in the makefile by referring to it as $CC. For example, the makefile

```
prog: file1.o file2.o
    cc file1.o file2.o -o prog

file1.o:file1.c
    cc -o -c file1.c

file2.o:file2.c
    cc -o -c file2.c
```

is transformed to

```
CC=gcc

prog: file1.o file2.o
    $CC file1.o file2.o -o prog
```

```
file1.o:file1.c
    $CC -o -c file1.c

file2.o:file2.c
    $CC -o -c file2.c
```

so that the Free Software Foundation (FSF) gcc compiler can be used.

The UNIX shell can also be used for software testing. Suppose we have a program under development and have obtained results from program execution on a collection of test cases. If we change the program in order to fix some error, we must make sure that no new errors are introduced. We do this by comparing the execution of the old and new versions of the program on a set of test files. This can be done automatically with the UNIX diff utility.

Here is an example of a shell script that will compare the output of two executable files named program1 and program2 on five test files named test1, test2, test3, test4, and test5. All of the outputs of the execution of program1 on these five test files are to be placed in a file named out1; the outputs of program2 on the same inputs are to be placed in the file out2.

```
# Bourne shell script to compare the output of
# two programs named program1 and program2
# on five test files.
for i in test*
    do
            program1 < $i >> out1
            program2 < $i >> out2
    done
# Now compare the output files.
# If they are identical we will produce 0.
diff out1 out2 | wc - l
```

Example 2.3 is a final illustration of the application of shell scripts. It shows a portion of an installation script for a (hypothetical) system. The program will install the binary files in a directory indicated by the user. Note the use of a shell variable to translate the user's input to the appropriate directories. If the directory already exists, a warning message is printed so that the user can avoid losing important files.

Example 2.3: Part of an Installation Script

```
echo "In what directory should the executable"
echo "files be placed?"
```

```
read DIRNAME
# Test for DIRNAME being the name of
# an existing directory.
if test ! -d $DIRNAME
      then
      ... Code to continue with installation
      ... would go here.
else
echo "Warning - directory already exists."
echo "Re-enter directory name."
      .. and so on
fi
```

2.6   THE USER INTERFACE

Historically, UNIX had a text-based interface. That is, a user would interact with the UNIX operating system via the shell by entering a command, with its options and arguments, at his or her terminal. The user was responsible for remembering the commands and the meanings of their options.

Unfamiliar options and commands could be checked by looking them up in a manual or by using the online help and manuals available on some systems via the

```
man command_name
```

command at the shell prompt. This command could often be confusing because the manuals appeared to be terse, at least to the novice UNIX user.

Some research has considered the replacement of text-based interfaces with graphics-based ones. We discuss one such interface.

Several user interfaces are based on "WIMP," an acronym that stands for "Window, Icon, Mouse, Pointer." The idea is that a user can select actions he or she wishes to take by using a mouse, which acts as a prompting and pointing device. The set of possible actions available at any one time is displayed on the screen. The user moves the mouse so that the cursor (which mimics the position of the mouse) is over the item desired. He or she then clicks the mouse, and the selected option begins execution. Many times the set of actions is displayed as an icon. The most familiar examples of window-based user interfaces are the Apple Macintosh and IBM PCs running Microsoft Windows.

Windows are portions of the screen devoted to specific applications. A word processing program, for example, might run in one window and a database management program might run in another. In older Macintoshes with limited memory, only one such program can run at a time, and multiple windows can be opened only if they correspond to directories, subdirectories, and a single application. In newer Macintoshes with more memory, special operating systems software, called the multifinder, allows several versions of an application to be open in different windows at once; these applications can even share data.

Only one application can be computing at any one time, however. The other application is suspended until the window in which it is running is selected to be the "active" or "listener" window. This idea is fundamentally different from that of multiprogramming. Multiprogramming allows the execution of different programs in such a short time period that many operations appear to the user as simultaneous.

There are several window-based interfaces for UNIX systems. The most common are X Windows, Motif, OPEN LOOK, NeXT Step, and SunVIEW. Each has features that make it desirable in a UNIX or UNIX-like environment. They all combine some features of menu-driven systems interfaces and text-based commands.

X Windows is a result of an MIT research project, called Project Athena, in the area of user interfaces and advanced workstations. The X Windows interface is based on the idea that the computer to which the display surface is attached need not be the one on which the computation is done. It is heavily network-based, but can also be used on standalone systems.

Running on top of X Windows are several window managers that control lower-level routines in the X library. Perhaps the best-known is Motif, which is produced by the Open Software Foundation. Motif has a high level of performance in terms of the quality of the user interface and the number of things that can be done easily and smoothly. SunVIEW, a product of Sun Microsystems, also gives a high performance level.

All these window systems perform well only when there is a large amount of local memory available. My experience is that for the local terminal or workstation, 16 MB are necessary, and 24 MB are highly desirable, if the systems are to perform quickly and not make undue demands on the network's capacity.

The subject of window-based user interfaces is far too complex to be considered here in any detail. For more information, consult the references.

SUMMARY

The UNIX user interface is a command-based program called the shell. It acts as both a text-based command interpreter and a powerful programming language. Programming constructions supported by all versions of the UNIX shell include looping and branching.

There are several variants of the UNIX shell. The Bourne shell is the most commonly available and is always included on versions related to System V UNIX. The other two shells, the C shell and the Korn shell, are similar, but not identical, in their power. There are differences in the syntax of the three shells.

Different shells perform environment control, process control, administration, utility, and programming actions. Window-based environments such as X Windows, Motif, and SunVIEW are becoming popular for UNIX systems.

REFERENCES

Arthur, L. *UNIX Shell Programming*. 2d ed. New York: John Wiley & Sons, 1990.

Bolsky, M., and D. Korn. *The Korn Shell Command and Programming Language*. Englewood Cliffs, N. J.: Prentice-Hall, 1989.

Kernighan, B. W., and R. Pike. *The UNIX Programming Environment*. Englewood Cliffs, N. J.: Prentice-Hall, 1984.

Kochan, S., and P. Wood. *UNIX Shell Programming*. New York: Hayden Books, 1990.

Nemeth, E., G. Snyder, and J. Seebass. *UNIX System Administration*. Englewood Cliffs, N. J.: Prentice-Hall, 1989.

Sobell, M. *A Practical Guide to UNIX System V Release 4*. New York: Benjamin Cummings, 1990.

Southerton, A. *Modern UNIX*. New York: John Wiley & Sons, 1992.

EXERCISES

1. How long does it take to learn simple tasks such as editing, compiling, printing, and so forth, on your favorite operating system?

2. How long does it take to do most tasks on your favorite operating system?

3. How long does it take to become an expert on your favorite operating system?

4. Which operating system interface do you prefer to use: menu-driven, command-driven, or some combination? Explain.

5. Design a grammar for a command-driven interface in BNF (Backus-Naur form) or extended BNF. Will the grammar be fully command-driven like UNIX, or will it, after receiving a command, prompt the user for additional options?

6. Implement a parser for a command processor based on the grammar you designed for exercise 5.

7. Look at the manual descriptions of any family of UNIX commands that perform a similar action, such as compiling (pc, px, cc, CC, f77), **tape manipulation** (cpio, tar, mt, dump, restore), **or editing of files** (vi, sed, ed, view, emacs). Determine the class of all command options for this family and indicate which ones use the same options with the same meaning.

8. Write a shell program to determine the number of users logged onto a system. You will probably need to use the finger shell command. Modify this program to determine the number of users logged on at midnight.

9. Write a shell program to determine the number of processes running on a computer. You will probably need to use the ps command with the -a option.

10. First, examine the options available in the ps command. You can do this by checking the manual, running the command

   man ps

   if you have online documentation, or by checking the error message you get after selecting an illegal option such as -Z. Then write a shell program that is an interface to the ps command. The program will check for command-line arguments and pass the options to ps if they are valid. The program will use a case statement and, in the event of erroneous input, will produce as output a message on the terminal indicating a correct call to ps with other options you think are related to what the user actually meant if there was no error.

3

Input and Output

In this chapter, we discuss the fundamentals of I/O, beginning at byte level and ending with the concept of a file. Higher-level file organization is given in Chapter 4.

The basic idea of file input and output is that a file is a sequence of bytes. The organization of the file's contents is up to the programmer. To perform the typical operations of reading and writing file data, we have to be able to set up a link between the program and the file, which is external to the program. The essential step is to "open" the file before any action of reading or writing is performed. After all the reading or writing is complete, the file should be "closed." This requires that we communicate with the operating system of the computer to be able to access low-level operations such as setting the correct date on the file, checking any access permissions, locating the file on disk.

All the I/O described in this chapter is based on the idea of file I/O, since UNIX treats everything as either a file or a process. We begin our discussion with a review of general I/O facilities in C that are not specific to the UNIX operating system. We then discuss the C language interface to UNIX system calls and file descriptors. The notion of an i-node is briefly mentioned. It receives more advanced discussion in Chapter 4.

Terminal I/O is then discussed followed by a discussion of device drivers. The chapter closes with a discussion of the operations that must be performed on a disk to use it; the discussion emphasizes a simulation of disk movements.

3.1   **FILE POINTERS**

In this section, we describe some standard C language functions for input and output that are not UNIX-specific. Our purpose is to set the stage for a more detailed discussion of UNIX I/O.

C uses a variable called a file pointer to connect the program to the actual data stored on the disk or in some other storage area. This file pointer must be initialized to point to the desired file. The C function `fopen()` takes two arguments and has a return value of the type "pointer to a FILE." The type FILE is defined in the header file `stdio.h` and has a predefined meaning in C. The technical details of what FILE means are something like this: A FILE is a structured data type whose fields represent a base address and an offset from the base address. The data type has a way of representing the size of any buffer in memory that can hold a portion of the file, reducing the number of disk accesses by bringing a block of data the size of the buffer into memory in a single operation rather than bringing in the data one byte at a time.

Figure 3.1 represents a *file*. Note the similarity to the structure of an array. We have shown a particular byte (the one containing the letter 'f') and suggested how it might be accessed. The file pointer initially points to the beginning of the file. To access the byte containing the f, the file pointer must be moved a particular offset value of 5 from the initial position. Both the initial and final values of the file pointer for this file access are shown. This linear view of how a file is stored is appropriate for any file I/O function in the C language. If a structure more complex than a linear array is needed, the applications programmer must implement it.

A data structure is needed for the storage of information about a file. One possible implementation of such a data structure is

```
extern struct FILE
{
int     _cnt;
char    *_ptr;
char    *_base;
int     _bufsiz;
/* other fields might be included */
} ;
```

Some of the fields in this FILE data structure are used as follows:

- The _cnt field represents the number of bytes.
- The _ptr field represents the value of the current file pointer.

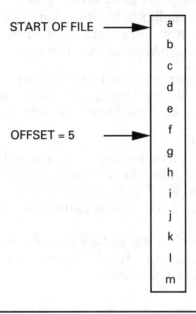

START OF FILE

OFFSET = 5

Figure 3.1.   Example of a file in UNIX   Reproduced from *Using C in Software Design*, Ronald J. Leach, © Academic Press, 1993. Used by permission.

- The _base field represents the value of the base pointer—that is, the start of the file.
- The _bufsiz field represents the size of the buffer used for buffered input and output.

An array of elements of type FILE is associated with a program. This array is called the *open file table* and has a fixed maximum size that corresponds to the maximum number of files that can be open at one time in a user's process.

The function fopen() provides a mechanism by which a C program can access a file using file pointers. The two arguments of fopen() are a character string that represents the name of the file to be opened and the *mode* (which is also a character string) that indicates how the file is to be used. The values of the mode accepted by nearly all C compilers are

- "a" for appending data at the end of the file
- "r" for reading data starting at the beginning of the file
- "w" for writing data starting at the beginning of the file

Some C compilers allow other options. The values "a+," "r+," and "w+" are somewhat similar in function, but are not universally available on C compilers. Their meanings are determined primarily by the first symbol with the following additional requirements:

> The programmer must be sure to protect the state of the data that is in the file at all times. Use of the + option requires certain function calls to move the file pointer after a switch from input to output.

The effect of mode "a" is that the value of the int _cnt is added to the value of the base pointer _base (using the C language's facility for pointer arithmetic) to get the location of the next byte in memory after the last byte in the file. The last byte is then used as the position of the current file pointer _ptr. The effects of the other modes in the function fopen() are similar.

Figures 3.2, 3.3, and 3.4 show the same file depicted in Figure 3.1 with the file pointer position if fopen() is called with each of the three sets of arguments given above.

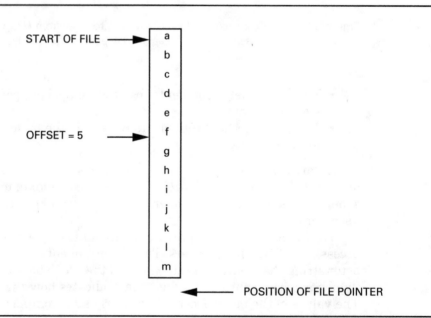

Figure 3.2.   The action of fopen("name","a"); Reproduced from *Using C in Software Design*, Ronald J. Leach, © Academic Press, 1993. Used by permission.

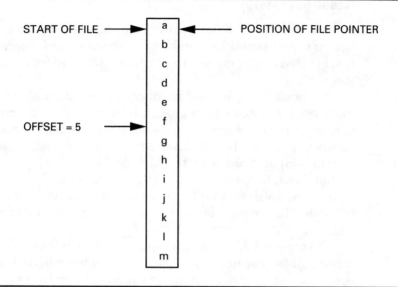

Figure 3.3.   The action of `fopen("name","r");` Reproduced from *Using C in Software Design*, Ronald J. Leach, © Academic Press, 1993. Used by permission.

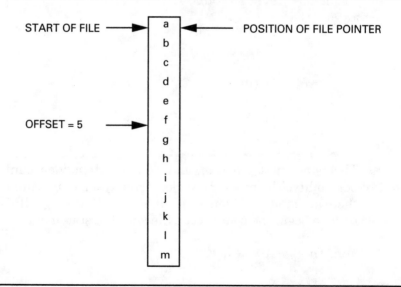

Figure 3.4.   The action of `fopen("name","w");` Reproduced from *Using C in Software Design*, © Academic Press, 1993. Used by permission.

3.1.1   Resource Limits

A limited number of file pointers can be used in any given program; you should expect portability problems if the number is more than eight, which is suggested as a minimum in the ANSI standard for C. Many systems allow more.

A process has a limited number of files that may be associated with it. Files are associated with a process by means of file descriptors. The default is now 64 files per user process on a Sun computer running Solaris; this number is called the *soft limit* and it can be easily increased to 256 via simple computations with the include file sys/resource.h. Other information is available in the file stdio.h. The number of file descriptors can be increased still further to the so-called *hard limit*, which is generally set to 2,048. This amount is most useful in larger database applications, especially those that are network-based.

Example 3.1 is a short program to change the soft limit to 100 for a process. It may or may not work on earlier versions of UNIX, depending on the value of the hard limit, or its equivalent, on the system.

Example 3.1: Changing the Soft Limit of a Process

```
#include <sys/resource.h>
main()
{
    struct rlimit buf;

    getrlimit(RLIMIT_NOFILE, &buf);
    buf.rlim_cur = 100;
    setrlimit(RLIMIT_NOFILE, &buf);
}
```

This is our first program, and we have already encountered a problem in portability. The program works correctly on a Sun running Solaris 1.1, but there are minor problems with it on an HP running HP-UX. On the HP, we have to begin the source code file with the statement

```
#define _HPUX_SOURCE
```

in order for the program to work properly. One indication that we are using the wrong constants for computation options is the program's failure even to compile, giving messages such as

```
structure : unknown size
```

On other systems, we have to use the name `rlimit` instead of `rlim_cur` in order to make the program work.

Use the suggestions given here if you encounter any portability problems. Note that other system resources for process can be determined in a similar manner.

Every C program has at least three files opened automatically when it begins execution: `stdin`, `stdout`, and `stderr`. These files respectively represent input from the terminal, output to the terminal screen, and error messages, which are usually sent to the terminal screen. (In this context, the word *terminal* means the computer's display device itself if you are using a standalone computer system without terminals.) Thus, you should not assume that you may have more than five $(8-3)$ files open unless you know the default limits for your system. These designations of the standard three files are compatible with the UNIX standards for file access, as we will see in section 3.2. The three files are described in the file `/usr/include/stdio.h` by statements similar to

```
#define stdin        (&_iob[0])
#define stdout       (&_iob[1])
#define stderr       (&_iob[2])
```

The attachment of special meaning of input and output devices to standard numbers in C is similar to the way unit numbers such as 3 for the tape drive unit, 5 for terminal input, and 6 for terminal output are typically reserved in FORTRAN.

Example 3.2 illustrates how the function `fopen()` opens files. Note the use of the mode. Also note that there is a total of eight open files (the five here plus the three from the standard files). The last statement in the program is a UNIX system call, named `system()`, whose argument is a character string whose contents, `ls - l f*`, are passed to the user's shell. The shell causes the contents of the directory to be listed in the long form, in which detailed information about the files is included.

Example 3.2: `fopen()`

```c
#include <stdio.h>
main()
{
    FILE *fp;

    fp= fopen("file1","a");
    fp= fopen("file2","r");
    fp= fopen("file3","w");
    fp= fopen("file4","a");
    fp= fopen("file5","a");
    fp= fopen("file6","r");
    fp= fopen("file7","w");
    system("ls -l f*");
}
```

Only that portion of the output of this program that concerns the files opened is presented in the table below. The important features of the output appear in the first, fifth, and ninth columns. The first column concerns permissions: rw means that the opener of the files, rjl, has permission to read and write each of the files, the dashes mean that no other people in my group, or in the rest of the world, have permission to read them (this was independent of the mode I included in the call to the function `fopen()`). The column of zeros means that the size of each file is zero bytes, as expected, since I have put nothing in them. The last column has the name of the file.

```
-rw-r--r--  1 rjl        0 Apr 27 19:29 file1
-rw-r--r--  1 rjl        0 Apr 27 19:30 file3
-rw-r--r--  1 rjl        0 Apr 27 19:29 file4
-rw-r--r--  1 rjl        0 Apr 27 19:29 file5
-rw-r--r--  1 rjl        0 Apr 27 19:30 file7
```

Notice that not all files were created. The files named file2 and file6 were not created because the mode given was "r". Since neither of these files existed previously, they were not opened for reading.

3.1.2   **Copying Files**

We now show how to copy from one file to another. The names of the files are passed as command-line arguments. A count of command-line arguments is given to ensure that there is a file for input and a file for output. The program in example 3.3 works correctly if the file to be copied from already exists; it exits smoothly if the input file does not exist.

Example 3.3: Copying from One File to Another

```c
#include <stdio.h>

main(argc, argv)
int argc;
char *argv[];
{
    int c;
    FILE *fp[2];

    if ( argc == 3 )
    {
      if ( (fp[0] = fopen(argv[1],"r") ) == NULL)
         {
         fputs("Error opening source",stderr);
         exit(1);
         }
      if ( (fp[1] = fopen(argv[2],"w") ) == NULL)
         {
         fputs("Error opening destination",stderr);
         exit(1);
         }
      while ((c=fgetc(fp[0])) != EOF)
         fputc(c,fp[1]);
      fclose(fp[0]);
      fclose(fp[1]);
    }
    else
       fputs("Error in number of arguments", stderr);
}
```

No UNIX system calls (other than the call to `system()` to print relevant directory entries) were used explicitly in this section, which is why the code will work correctly, even on non-UNIX systems. However, not as much fine control is available as there would be if UNIX system calls were used, as we do in the next section.

3.2   FILE DESCRIPTORS

In this section, we consider the I/O facilities available in UNIX using standard C compilers. The emphasis in this section is on the use of UNIX system calls.

The UNIX operating system uses a somewhat different philosophy for file access. Instead of a file pointer that controls a data structure called a `FILE`, UNIX has a *file descriptor* that is associated with a program while the program executes. When a program uses a file, the file descriptor corresponding to that file is in use; when the program ceases to use the file and cleans up properly, the file descriptor becomes available for use and may be associated with another file. In this way, a file descriptor can be thought of as an index into an array of files.

In general, a maximum of 20 file descriptors may be associated with any program at one time; that number may be smaller if a system administrator wishes to restrict the amount of resources a user has available. Three of these file descriptors are automatically opened for a running C program: `stdin`, `stdout`, and `stderr`. These three files are the same as those available in non-UNIX systems. This may be changed by increasing the soft limit.

Instead of opening and closing files using the `fopen()` and `fclose()` functions, which return pointers to a variable of type `FILE`, UNIX uses three system calls: `creat()`, `open()`, and `close()`, all of which are system calls because they deal directly with the operating system. The life history of a file will always have a call to `creat()` before the first call to `open()`; after the file has been created, `open()` and `close()` can be called many times. Because the function `creat()` is the most unusual of the three functions, we discuss it first. Note the unusual spelling of `creat()`.

The function `creat()` returns an integer value of 0 if the function call was successful, or –1 in the event of an error. Successful execution of the `creat()` system call also associates a file descriptor with the given file. The syntax of `creat()` is

```
int creat(file_name, permissions)
char *file_name;      int permissions;
```

The character string "file_name" is interpreted as follows. If a slash character (/) is present in the string, directories indicated by the path are searched. If no slash is present, only the current directory is used. The permissions are interpreted as an octal number representing the bits for the read, write, and execute permissions for the owner, group, and world.

The system call creat() behaves differently depending on the existence of the file to be created and also on whether the owner of the program that calls creat() is the superuser. Here we consider only the behavior for ordinary users (for more information on the use of creat() by superusers, consult your UNIX systems programming manual). We also assume that the user has the correct read and write permissions on the directory in which the file is to be created.

If the file does not exist, and assuming that the user attempting to create the file has access permissions on the directory in which the file is to be created, the system call creat() creates the file by forming an i-node, which links the file and the UNIX file system. The read and write permissions on the file are those specified in the second argument. The file has an initial length of 0, and the file is opened for writing even if the given permissions don't match. If the file to be created does not exist and the permissions are adequate, the creat() system call is presumed to be successful and the function creat() returns a file descriptor. Thus, the next file to be created will have another file descriptor that is larger than the previous one. This pattern will continue unless file descriptors are released or we run out of them.

If the file already exists, creat() takes one of two actions based on the write permissions of the person invoking the creat() system call. If the user has write permissions on the file, creat() ignores the permissions argument and changes the length of the file to 0, thereby eliminating all data currently in the file. This action requires only that the user have execute permission on the directory to which the file is linked. If the user does not have write permissions on the file, creat() returns a value of –1, indicating an error state. Clearly, creat() can cause many problems if used incorrectly.

Here is a summary of the actions of creat() for an ordinary user:

- File does not exist
    new i-node created, file size = 0, open for writing
    system call succeeds
- File exists
    if write permissions
        length is truncated to 0

    file is opened for writing
    system call succeeds
  if no write permission
    return −1 and system call fails

Example 3.4 is a simple use of `creat()` for alternatively correctly creating and removing a file named `creation`.

Example 3.4: `creat()` for Creating and Removing a File

```
#include <stdio.h>
main()
{
  if (creat("creation",0444) == -1)
    {
    fputs("Error in create",stderr);
    system("rm creation");
    }
  else
    fputs("No error in creation",stderr);
}
```

The output from six successive executions of the program is given below. The alternation of output corresponds to the existence or nonexistence of the file `creation` at the time the program is being executed. The UNIX system call `unlink()` removes the file given as its argument.

```
No error in creation
Error in create
No error in creation
Error in create
No error in creation
Error in create
```

Note that what we have really done is use an event, namely, the prior existence or nonexistence of a file, to signal information back to a program. Note also that this event is external to the program and thus can be used by many different programs at the same time, which provides a means for implementing semaphores for communicating between processes. We will learn about semaphores and more efficient implementations when we study interprocess communication.

Example 3.5 shows the proper use of `creat()` for the creation of mul-

tiple files. The names of these files are formed by using the sprintf()
function in order to include numbers in strings.

Example 3.5: creat() with Multiple Files

```
#include <stdio.h>
main()
{
  char name[10];
  int i, fd[10];
   for (i=0; i <= 9; i++)
      {
       sprintf(name, "temp_file%d",i);
       printf("%s\n",name);
       if ((fd[i]= creat(name,0644)) == -1)
          {
          fputs("error",stderr);
          exit(1);
          }
      }
    system("ls -l temp*");
    exit(0);
}
```

3.2.1   **The open() and close() System Calls**

The syntax of open() is

```
open(char *filename, int flags);
```

Here the character string filename can be the name of a file in the current
directory or an absolute or relative pathname ending in the name of a file.
The second argument, flags, is one of the symbolic integer constants (listed
below), the bitwise OR of two or more of these (note that the first three are
mutually exclusive), or the bitwise OR of any allowable combination of these
constants with any three-digit octal constant that represents the allowable
permissions for the file. (The integer values of these constants are chosen so
that they do not affect the three octal digit representation of permissions.)

```
O_RDONLY
O_WRONLY
O_RDWR
```

```
O_NDELAY
O_APPEND
O_CREAT
O_TRUNC
O_EXCL
O_SYNC
```

The meanings of these constant values for the `flags` argument are

- `O_RDONLY`: The file is to be opened for reading only.
- `O_WRONLY`: The file is to be opened for writing only.
- `O_RDWR`: The file is to be opened for both reading and writing.
- `O_NDELAY`: The file is to opened immediately, regardless of the other requests for file action.
- `O_APPEND`: The file is to be opened for writing with the file pointer at the end of the file.
- `O_CREAT`: The file is to be created if it does not already exist.
- `O_TRUNC`: The file is to be truncated in the sense that the existing data is effectively removed.
- `O_EXCL`: The file is created only if it does not already exist. In certain situations, this is safer than a call to `creat()` followed by a call to `open()`, since it is conceivable that some other process running concurrently might attempt to access the file between the calls to `creat()` and `open()`.
- `O_SYNC`: Delay the opening of the file until there is an attempt to write to the file.

In practice, the first three flags are used almost exclusively, unless there is a need for concurrent file access.

The `close()` system call has the much simpler syntax:

```
close(int fd);
```

3.2.2   The read() and write() System Calls

Now that we know how to create a file using the C functions that are available under UNIX, it is time to use UNIX file operations for something useful. Perhaps the simplest way to illustrate the UNIX file operations is to rewrite the file copying program of the previous section using `creat()`, `open()`, and `close()`, instead of `fopen()` and `fclose()`. As could have been predicted from their names, the two pairs of functions, `open()` and `fopen()` and `close()` and `fclose()`, have similar purposes. Once the files are opened, the functions `getc()` and `putc()` can be used.

It is customary, however, to use two other functions for the reading and writing of data from files. The functions fopen() and fclose() handle file pointers; the next set of functions needs a file descriptor to work. A file descriptor is an integer, which is different from a pointer to a FILE structure. These two new functions read() and write() are UNIX system calls and have the syntaxes:

```
read(file_descriptor, buffer, number_of_bytes)
int file_descriptor;
char buffer[buffer_size];
int number_of_bytes;

write(file_descriptor,buffer, number_of_bytes)
int file_descriptor;
char buffer[buffer_size];
int number_of_bytes;
```

They are designed to read and write at the low level of byte access rather than at the high level of data structures such as characters, integers, or floating point numbers. The first argument to both read() and write() is an integer that indicates the file descriptor for the proper file. The second argument is a buffer that indicates where the data is to be read to or from. The third argument is the number of bytes to be transferred during the read or write.

Note that the number of bytes we wish to read from a file is declared in the third argument of the function and thus this number is determined before the execution of the function read(). If the bytes indicated in the third argument to read() are fewer than the bytes remaining in the file, then the number of bytes read is the number remaining in the file and the value returned by read() is the number of bytes actually read. If we reach the end of the file, read() returns 0. Both read() and write() return the value of −1 if an error occurs.

The general structure of the copy program in example 3.6 is the same as that in example 3.3, but the functions fopen(), fclose(), putc(), and getc() have been replaced by their UNIX equivalents.

Example 3.6: `read()` and `write()`

```
#include <stdio.h>
#define BUFSIZE 512
main(argc, argv)
int argc;
```

```
char *argv[];
{
int n; /* number of bytes read */
char buffer[BUFSIZE];
int fd[2];

if ( argc == 3 )
    {
    if ( (fd[0] = open(argv[1], 0644)) == -1)
        {
        fputs("Error in open",stderr);
        exit(1);
        }
    if ( (fd[1] = creat(argv[2],0644)) == -1)
        {
        fputs("Error in creat",stderr);
        exit(1);
        }
    while ((n=read(fd[0],buffer,BUFSIZE)) >0)
        if (write (fd[1],buffer,n) !=n )
            {
            fputs("Error in write",stderr);
            exit(1);
            }
    close(fd[0]);
    close(fd[1]);
    }
else
    fputs("Error: number of arguments", stderr);
}
```

The program uses the functions open() and creat() in an obvious way. The interesting part of the program appears in the while-loop to read from the input file. The loop header

```
while ((n = read(fd[1],buffer,BUFSIZE)) > 0)
```

remains non-0 as long as there are more bytes to be read from the input. The comparison

```
if (write (fd[2],buffer,n) !=n )
```

checks to make sure that the number of bytes read from the input is the same as the number of bytes written to the output. Note also that the program closes the open files at the end of its execution, using explicit calls to `close()`.

A complex program with a large amount of error checking might have many such calls to `close()` depending on the program execution path. To avoid such complexity, many C programmers simply call `exit()` with an argument of 0. This function call closes each open file descriptor, as does termination of a program. The parameter of 0 in `exit()` indicates successful execution.

The value of `BUFSIZE` is the size of a buffer for storing data; a buffer is necessary for fast program execution, since the I/O devices may have different effective data transfer rates at different times, depending on other use of the computer by different users or operating system requirements. The use of buffers is especially important in operations such as animation that are both CPU and I/O intensive. For most uses, `BUFSIZE` is either 1 (for unbuffered I/O) or a multiple of the size of a standard disk block (usually a multiple of 512). One of the exercises at the end of the chapter is an experiment to determine the effect on program speed of changing the value of `BUFSIZE`.

You might have noted that the syntax of the `creat()` and other system calls was presented using the older Kernighan and Ritchie dialect of C rather than ANSI C. The ANSI C syntax for the function prototype of `creat()` would be

```
/* creat -- ANSI C syntax */
int creat(char *file_name, int permissions);
```

We will use both the ANSI C and Kernighan and Ritchie C syntax for system calls as appropriate. You can easily change from ANSI C to Kernighan and Ritchie C if you do not have an ANSI C environment. You will frequently have to use the older version of C on some systems, for example, the C compiler bundled with Solaris 1.1 for a Sun SPARC 2. In addition, nearly all ANSI compilers allow the use of the older syntax for purposes of backward compatibility with existing code. The gnu C compiler, which is in the public domain, allows easy upgrades to ANSI C. Unfortunately, with ANSI C and a few minor system calls, some problems will arise because of minor semantic differences between the versions. Fortunately, these differences are rare.

We used the simplest form of error action in the previous programs. Specifically, we printed an error message and exited the program when a system call returned a value indicating that the system call was not successful. (Unsuccessful execution of a system call usually results in the value −1 being returned.) As we indicated in Chapter 1, additional information can be obtained by looking at the value of the error code produced as a side effect of an unsuccessful system call, and relating it to a meaningful error message.

The way to access the error code is to use an external variable called errno. The most common usage is something like

```
#include < errno.h >
...
extern int errno;
...
if (system_call() < 0)
  {
  perror("SYSTEM_CALL_NAME");
  exit(1);
  }
```

if we wish to terminate after a failure, or,

```
#include <errno.h>
...
extern int errno;
...
if (system_call() < 0)
  perror("SYSTEM_CALL_NAME");
```

if we wish to try again (which we will want to do in some situations involving concurrent actions).

The function perror() used in these code templates reads the value of the variable errno set by the kernel and sends a message to stderr. The message includes the string given as its argument by the programmer and concatenates to this a : and some meaningful text message associated with the value of errno in the file errno.h.

Use of perror() may seem redundant in the simple examples presented in this chapter. The most common errors for the system calls given so far are usually due to mistyping the name of a file or the lack of proper permissions, in which case the programmer can easily determine the source of the problem. However, the use of errno can indicate such unusual situations as no more room in a file system, in addition to pinpointing a problem.

The function perror() is used primarily with UNIX system calls, since only system calls set the value of the external int errno. However, we can obtain additional information about failures of several functions other than system calls.

Suppose, for example, that we are using the standard I/O functions `fopen()` and `fclose()`. On a UNIX system, the function `fopen()` could fail because of a lack of write permissions on the directory. It could also fail if the number of file descriptors for the UNIX process attempting to open the file exceeds the maximum. Unfortunately, the user of a failed `fopen()` call is normally unaware of these potential problems. Thus, replacing the code fragment here with the one following it provides additional information in the form of a more meaningful error message.

```
if (fopen ("filename", "r") == NULL)
    fputs ("Error in fopen", stderr);

if (fopen ("filename", "r") == NULL)
    perror ("fputs")
```

3.3 ASYNCHRONOUS I/O

The `read()` and `write()` system calls are synchronous I/O operations. That is, a running UNIX process that attempts to read information from a file using the `read()` system call, or attempts to write data to a file using the `write()` system call, is essentially prevented from doing any other computation until the reading or writing of the desired amount of data is finished.

More precisely, a request to read data from an open file on the disk via a `read()` system call causes the operating system to attempt to read the data directly. Any later statements in the program are blocked until the reading of data is complete.

For efficiency, writing of data to a file on a disk may not happen immediately, but may be delayed because the data is temporarily written to an operating system data structure called the buffer cache, which will be described in Chapter 4. A `write()` system call means that the data is written to the buffer cache and that its actual placement on the disk may be slightly delayed so that the disk is used more efficiently. With both the `read()` and `write()` system calls, the process using them is blocked from further computation until the read or write is complete.

Both reading and writing can cause a considerable drop in efficiency in programs that allow a large amount of "simultaneous" access to files—files such as online database or transaction processing systems. For this reason, asynchronous I/O is available on many newer UNIX systems.

The two new system calls are `aioread()` and `aiowrite()`. They require that the statement `#include < sys/asynch.h >` be included in a program using them. The syntax of these two system calls follows.

```
int aioread(fd, buf_ptr, bufsize, offset, from,
            resultp)
        int fd;
        char *buf_ptr;
        int bufsize;
        int offset;
        int from;
        aio_result_t *resultp;

int aiowrite(fd, buf_ptr, bufsize, offset, from,
            resultp)
        int fd;
        char *buf_ptr;
        int bufsize;
        int offset;
        int from;
        aio_result_t *resultp;
```

In both, the type `aio_result_t` is defined in the header file.

The system call `aioread()` initiates one asynchronous `read()` and returns control to the calling program. The remainder of the data transfer using the `read()` continues concurrently with other process activity. The system call reads `bufsize` bytes of data from the file with file descriptor `fd` into the buffer pointed to by `buf_ptr`.

The system call `aiowrite()` initiates one asynchronous `write()` and then returns control to the calling program. The remainder of the data transfer using the `write()` continues concurrently with other process activity. The system call writes `bufsize` bytes of data from the buffer pointed to by `buf_ptr` to the file with file descriptor `fd`.

Asynchronous I/O can greatly improve program efficiency in some concurrent processing environments because it decreases the blocking of processes.

For portability, we will use the `read()` and `write()` system calls instead of the asynchronous I/O calls given in this section. In general, the calls are interchangeable, with the new header file incorporated into programs and the appropriate modifications made to the function arguments.

3.4   TERMINAL I/O

It is reasonable to think of a terminal as a file, in the sense that one stream of bytes is being written to the terminal display and another is being written from the keyboard to the computer. This section discusses those features of terminal I/O that are based on the concept of files. Some, but not all, of this discussion also applies to a window-based system running software such as X Windows. For more information on this point, see a reference for your type of window-based system.

When a user logs on to a system running UNIX, he or she is accessing the computer via a *login terminal*. The login terminal is used as the default I/O device.

The login terminal has certain characteristics that are used by editors and other software. Among these are the size of the display (in characters or pixels), the mapping of the keyboard to the ASCII or other character set, keys for moving the cursor left, right, up, down, for erasing, and so forth, and the availability of pointing devices such as a mouse. These characteristics are read from the `termcap` database entry for the device that is read from the `.login .cshrc`, or similar startup file. Usually, the startup file is reconfigured by individual users from a default file that is sufficiently general to allow most editing and display operations to work. (Many UNIX systems use the `terminfo` database instead of `termcap`. One of these files is usually present in the `/etc` directory.) The characteristics of a terminal may be changed if another login terminal is assigned, as in the shell commands `set term=term_type` in the C shell, and `TERM=term_type` in the Bourne shell.

The data structures needed for terminal I/O can be found in the files `termio.h`, `ttychars.h`, or similar files depending on the version of UNIX used. Each of the appropriate files contains a data structure (a C struct) with fields to indicate that characters are used to erase a character or an entire line, stop a process, mark end of file, and so forth.

The `ifndef` feature of the C preprocessor is often used to provide sufficient flexibility if some of the fields in the operating system are upgraded. A common syntax is

```
#ifndef _TTYCHARS_
#define _TTYCHARS_
struct ttychars
    {
    definitions of special characters go here
    }
#endif
```

A set of default values for these constants is provided. You can see the effect of these default characters on systems with different characteristics if you attempt to use the vi editor to edit a file without having a terminal type set (or if you try to use a terminal other than your standard login terminal and don't reset the terminal type).

This discussion of terminal I/O is adequate for a normal user or applications programmer using a terminal type that is either in the standard databases terminfo or termcap or is so close that its characteristics can be easily entered into the appropriate database.

3.5 SYSTEMS-LEVEL I/O

We now consider some of the issues that arise when programming terminal I/O at a systems level.

An important system call for terminal I/O in current UNIX systems is setpgrp(), which stands for "set process group." The idea behind the setpgrp() system call is that the process can be tagged to a particular input/output device. A data structure associated with a process has, among other things, a numeric field that contains a unique *process group id*. The process group id is given a numeric value that is identical to the number associated with the user's shell created when the user logs in. This unique number is the process-id. The important thing to know for now is that the process group id can be used to determine the login terminal.

The process group id allows identification of which processes arise from which logins. This is important if the user is logged onto a computer from several different terminals simultaneously, or from different windows that are running terminal emulation programs. Such information is kept for a terminal driver program that correctly directs input and output.

The system calls for the use of process group-ids have the syntaxes:

```
int setpgrp(pid, pgrp)
int pid;
int pgrp;

int getpgrp(pid)
int pid;
```

Here the arguments are all integers, and the argument pid is an integer used to index all processes running on the computer. We will discuss process-ids in more detail in Chapter 5.

The setpgrp() and the related system call getpgrp() can be used as follows in systems-level programming.

- First obtain the process group id of a process whose process-id is the number `pid`, by using either the call and the default value returned by `getpgrp(pid)` or the call `setpgrp(pid, pgrp)` to set the process group id to another, predetermined process group id.
- Then, send only output to the device specified by this process group id using the call `getpgrp(pid)`.

Programs that use the `setpgrp()` system call are more portable than those that use the much older and more complex `ioctl()`. The most readily available reference for portability of system calls is *Portable C and UNIX Programming* published by Rabbit Software. For more information on the `ioctl()` system call, see Rochkind or Egan and Teixeira.

3.6   ADDING DEVICES AND DEVICE DRIVERS

The design of UNIX encourages the addition of devices to the underlying computer system. The reason is, of course, that everything in UNIX is considered to be either a process or a file. To add a device to the system, we need to do three things: (1) physically attach the device; (2) write a piece of software known as a device driver (or use some existing software); and (3) inform the operating system that the device is logically attached to a particular place. (Egan and Teixeira [see the references] offer detailed information on adding device drivers.)

It is easiest to discuss adding devices to a computer system by separating the subject into two levels: initialization of a computer system that will eventually run UNIX but for which no operating system is installed, and adding devices to an existing system on which UNIX is running. Some of the information about installing UNIX is similar to the actions taken when the computer is booted (turned on). We will discuss each of these in turn.

3.6.1   Adding Devices to a Non-UNIX System

The first scenario is highly dependent on the complexity of the system to be installed and the computer vendor's degree of automation of the installation process. In a typical situation, a powerful workstation is to be installed on an existing network. The system includes a box containing a CPU, memory and ports for connections to a network keyboard, and serial and parallel devices; a monitor with cables; and a separate box containing a disk drive, tape drive, or compact disk, and a controller. The full operating system is to be installed from a tape or compact disk. For simplicity we assume that the installation medium is tape.

The first step is to make all physical connections and allow the hardware monitoring routines in the box containing the CPU to check the entire memory for possible errors. We will assume that the hardware functionality check and each of the following actions is successful in our discussion of this process.

We now have a CPU and memory combination that is correct from a hardware perspective but does not have any software installed other than what has already been installed in the read-only memory of the computer. The next step is to install the UNIX operating system on the disk. The problem is that frequently the software has not been loaded onto the disk but is provided on the tapes that are intended for the tape drive. We have to load the software from the tape onto the disk in a bootstrapping procedure.

Many people try to avoid this step entirely by purchasing preinstalled systems. This is certainly possible if the entire system (hardware, software, and peripherals) is purchased from a single source. However, many other people prefer to choose among computer hardware vendors in their selection of tape and disk drives to customize their system. Integrating disks and tapes from various vendors is much simpler than it was in the past because there is now a common method and protocol for their use and control. The Small Computer Systems Interface, or SCSI, is one example. We will briefly describe what needs to be done when using SCSI disks and tapes. Many UNIX systems hide the technical details of peripheral installation from the user; the activities described here are frequently automatic.

The hardware routines already in the system usually allow the use of an extremely simple set of commands for the initial booting of some portion of the operating system from the tape drive. The purpose of this is not to install the operating system directly but to enable the disk drive to be placed into full operation so that the entire operating system can be placed on the disk.

The first routines booted from the tape allow the software connection of the disk to the rest of the system. Typically, the routines prompt the installer for information about the disk to be connected. Such information includes determination of the address of the SCSI controller and the position the disk takes on the SCSI bus. After the location of the device on the SCSI bus is given, the next step is matching the disk to an entry in a predefined table of disks containing disk formatting information. If the entry is present, the information about the physical design of the disk (number of cylinders, number of sectors per track, number of read/write heads, etc.) is placed in an appropriate disk file. If the entry is not present, then the information must be entered by hand. The successful completion of this step allows the operating system to know about the disk. A check of the disk for format errors and bad sectors is also done at this time.

If there are multiple disks, multiple controllers, and multiple tapes to be installed, they are handled by the above process. The installer should keep a log of all data entered during the installation procedure. This is necessary if the hardware ever malfunctions or needs to be upgraded.

At this point, the disk can be read by the routines that were booted from the tape, but none of the UNIX operating system is installed. The next step is reading enough routines from the tape to have a small subset of UNIX installed. The portion that is installed at this time is the root file system, which consists of the essential files for an operating system that does not allow users other than the superuser or root to log in. After the root file system is installed, the installer loads the rest of the file system (the so-called usr file system) from tape. Decisions to be made at this time include which of several optional libraries and directories are to be loaded onto the disk. An executable version of the UNIX kernel is created at this time.

This procedure creates an operating system using the general information provided in the installation software. Since the operating system that has been installed is general, the kernel might need to be optimized to make effective use of the peripherals present in the system. For more efficient functioning, we should also remove device drivers from the UNIX kernel for those peripherals not physically installed. Reconfiguration of the UNIX kernel is also important if we wish to fine-tune the kernel in terms of the maximum size of a process, maximum number of processes per user and in the system, number of simultaneous users, and so forth.

We want to make sure that our system functions properly. The best way to do this is to keep a copy of the old operating system kernel in a file named unix.old or something similar. This copy will be used if the newly created operating system has a fault in its kernel.

Some installations of UNIX are much simpler. Many vendors perform these steps themselves, thereby delivering a "turnkey system" set up so that the user need only turn the computer on.

3.6.2   Adding Devices to a UNIX System

The most important thing to remember in enhancing an existing system is "first, do no harm." This means that a copy of the existing UNIX kernel be saved in a file named something like unix.old, which is the same strategy for reconfiguring the UNIX kernel. A log should be maintained by the system administrator to keep track of the peripherals installed and where they are located on a bus. Also to be checked is the existence of a device driver for the new device. The entry places for these device drivers can usually be found in the directory /dev .

The computer should be off before any hardware, such as disks, tapes, or controllers, is added. The system administrator follows a shutdown routine that includes informing users of the intended shutdown and synchronizing the disks so that no information is lost. Once the system is shut down, the hardware connection of the peripheral is made. Then the log is consulted to determine where on the SCSI bus the peripheral is to be attached; this number is known as the logical unit number of the peripheral.

The computer is now rebooted using the existing operating system kernel. After the system is running, a copy of the existing kernel is reconfigured to include the new device and its driver, using either the existing driver or a new one.

Some editing of other system files may be necessary at this time. For example, a printer is often attached to the computer via a serial port. Terminals also are usually attached via serial ports. Unless a serial port is dedicated to printers, a major problem arises because of the different nature of these devices.

Specifically, a terminal expects to have two-directional communication. Consider the typical situation after a user has logged on. The pressing of a key or the movement of a mouse must be communicated to the computer's CPU. The operating system receives input via a process called `getty`, which is placed on terminal lines by the operating system to permit logins from the terminals. It is reasonable to assume that the serial port has an active `getty` process. This is exactly what we want for a terminal line.

For obvious reasons, a `getty` process is exactly what we *do not* want for a printer. A printer and a terminal receive information for display, but a printer provides no input (other than errors or a report of a change in status). It is therefore necessary to disable communications from the printer to the computer along the serial line by which it is connected. This step is referred to as *disabling logins* and is carried out by the change of a 1 to a 0 in a particular entry in the file `/etc/ttys`, which changes the status of the serial line on which the printer is connected after future logins. To kill any active `getty` processes, we must enter a shell command such as

```
kill -HUP 1
```

(This `kill` shell command is an interface to the system call `kill()` that will be discussed in Chapter 5.)

When a device driver is written for a UNIX-based system, it must communicate smoothly with the kernel. This means that the writer of the device driver must understand the arguments and return values of the system calls. Of course, the basic source of technical information is the documentation for the system itself, and no general-purpose book can hope to provide more than a high-level description.

Here is an example of how this communication is done. Suppose that we wish to add a disk to an existing system. We already have a disk and disk controller (if not, our system would not be usable). If the new disk is a clone of the existing one, we can use the existing disk device driver and simply let the operating system know where the new disk is. The ioctl() system call has the syntax

```
ioctl(fd, command, argument list)
int fd;
int command;
/* third argument varies */
```

where fd is the file descriptor of the device (it must be an open file descriptor) and the other two arguments are driver-specific. The third argument is usually a pointer to a driver-specific data structure.

How do these device drivers behave? They are different from ordinary or directory files and thus are special files. Access to device drivers is created directly via the mknod() system call instead of creat().

The syntax of mknod() is:

```
mknod(path, flags)
char *path;
int flags ;
```

The path is a character string ending with the name of the file corresponding to the i-node to be created. The flags argument is the logical OR of the three octal permissions (read, write, execute), with an argument indicating the type of file. Allowable types of special files are character device drivers, block device drivers (which have a higher level of complexity than do character device drivers), links, sockets (depending on the system), and FIFOs. We will study FIFOs in Chapter 7 and sockets in Chapter 9.

To see the effect of such a call, examine some of the entries in the /dev directory using the ls shell command. A terminal—say, tty number 7—might have an entry such as

```
cxxxxxxxxx          /dev/tty7  2      7
```

which means that this is a device with a major number of 2 and a minor number of 7. A major number of 2 indicates that this device has its driver places at entry number 2 in a character device switch table, and a minor number of 7 says that this is the seventh entry in a table of units of that type, which is to be expected because of its name. The initial character, c, indicates that this is a character device, transmitting data one character at a time. Other device drivers allow physical devices to be considered as block devices, which buffer data in a data structure called the buffer cache for transfer in blocks. Disks and tapes usually have both types of driver and can be used as either character or block devices.

Many other issues must be considered when a device driver is added to a system. In addition to the initial setting up the system and providing the links to the appropriate code, we must make sure that the device's runtime system is integrated into the UNIX kernel, and that no problems occur because of incorrect protocols, incorrect bus addresses, or similar complex problems.

3.7   USE OF FILE POINTERS FOR RANDOM ACCESS

A file in UNIX is considered a collection of bytes, with any additional file structure determined by an applications program rather than by the operating system. One easy way of reading the data stored in a file is to use the sequential order appropriate for reading a stream of data. However, there are other file access methods. In this section, we discuss the use of system calls to allow random, or direct, file access.

The terms *random access* and *direct access*, which are interchangeable in this context, refer to a method of file access that allows the reading of bytes in nonsequential order. For simplicity, we will only use the term *random* in this section.

The essential part of any random file access system is being able to move the read/write head of the disk forward and backward, without having to read or write the intermediate data. This is a slightly tricky concept and needs to be pursued further. Moving the read/write head past intermediate data does not necessarily mean that the intermediate data does not pass under the read/write head; it might, depending on the head's movement. This random access means that the intermediate data is ignored in the case of a read, allowing the movement of the read/write head to be much faster. From the programmer's perspective, the actual object being moved is the file pointer. In the write() system call, the intermediate data is not read into the software buffer cache in the kernel for later entry on the disk.

The system call used for random access is lseek(), whose syntax is

```
long lseek(fd, offset, mode)
int fd;
long offest;
int mode;
```

The file pointer is set by this system call for use by the next `read` or `write` command. Initially, the position of the file pointer is at the start of the file, with `offset` having the value 0.

The return value and the second argument are long ints because the file size, and hence the largest possible value of the file pointer, may be larger than the largest value that can be stored in an ordinary int.

The actual movement of the file pointer is controlled by the third argument, `mode`, with the following interpretation:

- `mode` = 0. The value of `offset` represents an assignment of a value to the file pointer that represents the actual position of the file pointer.
- `mode` = 1. The value of `offset` represents actual movement of the file pointer from its current position.
- `mode` = 2. The value of `offset` represents an actual movement of the file pointer from the position of the end of the file.

Thus, if the current file pointer value is 0 (meaning that we are at the start of the file), then the following pairs have equivalent meanings.

```
lseek(fd, offset,0);
```

```
lseek(fd, offset,1);
```

Suppose that the size of a particular file is `FILE_SIZE`. If the value of the current file pointer is `FILE_SIZE`, which indicates that we are at the end of the file, then these statements also have equivalent meanings:

```
lseek(fd, offset,1);
```

```
lseek(fd, FILE_SIZE + offset,2);
```

The most common uses of the `lseek()` system call are with a mode of 0 to find an absolute file position, with a mode of 2 to find the end of the file, and with a mode of 1 to determine the value of the current file pointer.

There are two extreme cases to consider. When the value of the file pointer becomes greater than the size of the file, the next `write()` command allows the file to increase its size to the amount necessary. A corresponding value of the file pointer is usually an error, although not all systems catch it.

3.8   SIMULATION OF DISK OPERATIONS

In this section we describe disk movement when writing data to and from computer memory. We describe the situation in general terms by a simulation. The material in this section will be especially useful to those readers who do not have access to the source code for their version of UNIX so that certain changes cannot be made to the UNIX kernel for purposes of experimentation. The material also serves as a guide to disk performance for those who do have source code. Readers who are knowledgable about the principles of disk operation may omit the remainder of this chapter.

The simulated system will have to be able to move blocks of data from memory to the disk and from the disk to memory. The input commands will allow for data to be entered into memory directly. Data can be entered into memory directly, sent from memory to disk, or sent from disk to memory in units called blocks. Our system will be able to move data in blocks that are accessed in memory by identifying a starting memory location; it will also be able to access blocks of data on the disk by the track and sector numbers identifying this block. We will concentrate on the actions that our program will perform and on how we will communicate our wishes to various portions of the program.

We interpret memory as a two-dimensional array of data elements whose type is the same as we considered earlier; that is, the data is of type int. The contents of memory locations are addressed by simply giving their location. Since we will be moving blocks of data from memory to disk and from disk to memory, we also want to think of memory as being composed of blocks that can be accessed by knowing the starting location of a block and the number of elements in the block. Hence, we will also want to be able to view memory as a two-dimensional array of blocks of data.

A disk is a more complex system, since it is inherently a two-dimensional object. We access elements on the disk by determining the disk block in which they occur. A disk block has its position determined by two parameters—the track and sector of the block. Think of a disk as being a set of concentric rings. Each ring is assumed to have the same capacity for storing data even though the rings of smaller diameter have the data packed more densely. By analogy to a phonograph record, these concentric rings are called tracks. There is another division of the disk into sectors. Each of the tracks is considered to be divided into the same number of sectors.

In actual disks, there is a read/write head that moves relative to the disk. The head can move along a particular track through various sectors, or can move to different tracks while remaining along the same sector. For our purposes, it doesn't matter if the read/write head is fixed and the disk spins or the disk is fixed and the head moves. In most larger computers, there are many read/write heads and many "platters" making up a disk system; for the sake of simplicity we consider only one platter and one read/write head.

On most computer disks, movement of the read/write head in and out while staying in the same sector is slower than changing sectors while staying in the same track. Therefore, we will access a block of data by reference to the pair (track, sector) instead of the pair (sector, track). An element of the disk is then found by knowing the track and sector numbers that tell which block the element is in and the offset of the element from the start of the block.

We can consider a disk to be a three-dimensional array of data, with the data indexed by three numbers: the track, sector, and offset from the start of the disk block.

The header file of constants looks something like

```
/* header file for disk simulation */
#define NUM_MEM_BLOCKS 10
#define NUM_TRACKS 50
#define NUM_SECTORS 10
#define BLOCKSIZE 10
```

The header file will be included in each source code file used for the disk simulation. Some of the functions that we will need are:

- `put_in_memory(data)`
  Parameter is of the type of data that we will enter into memory.

- `mem_to_disk(mem_loc, track, sector)`
  Parameters are of type int. The first parameter represents a memory location in the range `0..MEMSIZE - 1`, the second parameter represents a track number in the range `0..NUM_TRACKS -1`, and the third parameter represents a sector number in the range `0 .. NUM_SECTORS - 1`. This function will move a block of data that is specified by a memory location to a disk block that is specified by a track number and a sector number.

- `disk_to_mem(mem_loc, track, sector)`
  Parameters are of type int. The first parameter represents a memory location in the range `0..NUM_MEM_BLOCKS - 1`, the second parameter represents a track number in the range `0..NUM_TRACKS -1`, and the third parameter represents a sector number in the range `0.. NUM_SECTORS - 1`. This function will move a block of data that is specified by a track and a sector number to a memory location specified by the parameter `mem_loc`.

- `print_disk()`
  Prints the contents of the array simulating the disk.

- print_mem()
  Prints the contents of the array simulating memory.

This is the organization for the simulation. The global declarations are:

```
int data
int track, sector;    /* track, sector parameters */
int mem[NUM_MEM_BLOCKS][BLOCKSIZE];
int disk[NUM_TRACKS][NUM_SECTORS][BLOCKSIZE]
int mem_loc;
```

An element in memory is found by directly specifying the block_number and the offset from the start of the block. For example, if the value of BLOCKSIZE is 10 and the value of NUM_MEM_BLOCKS is 10, then the last element in memory can be found by specifying a value of 9 for the block_number and a value of 9 for the offset. The next to last element has a block_number of 9 but an offset of 8, and so on.

We can relate the value of the variable mem_loc to the values of the block_number and offset by the formulas

```
mem_loc = block_number * BLOCKSIZE ;
block_number = mem_loc / BLOCKSIZE;
offset = mem_loc % BLOCKSIZE;
```

Note that the values of MEMSIZE or NUM_MEM_BLOCKS do not figure into these formulas. Note also that the location of a particular memory element is found by adding the offset of the element from the starting position in the block to the value of mem_loc.

What about the three remaining functions put_in_memory(), mem_to_disk(), and disk_to_mem()? In each case, we need to make a decision about where the block of data should be placed. There are several ways of doing this. We will use the "first-fit" method since it is the simplest to code.

We still have to consider the disk. We will use the same method of first-fit to find available blocks, but with a slight difference. We will choose to fill up the disk by filling up all blocks on the first track, then all blocks on the second track, and so forth. On each track, we will fill up the sectors in increasing numerical order. This is the first-fit method applied to both the tracks and sectors, in order.

This takes care of the situation when there is room in memory for the storage of the desired data. If there is no room, then we have three choices.

First, we can terminate the program with an appropriate error action. Second, we can continue the program execution by swapping the block of data from memory to the disk and thus freeing up the memory block. The third option is unacceptable: We continue execution of the program in an error state. Options 1 and 2 are used in many computer systems. We will arbitrarily choose the second option if memory is full; that is, we write a memory block of data onto the disk.

A similar problem occurs when the disk is full. In this case, we have no place to put extra data, and so we select the first strategy of terminating execution of our program with an appropriate error action.

Everything looks fine from the point of view of how to access blocks of data on the simulated disk or simulated memory. However, there are some things that we have overlooked. For example, we need to have some mechanism of determining if a block of space in memory or on the disk is available. We have to store such information somewhere and access it somehow. Finally, we have to know the state of the simulated disk and memory initially; that is, we have to initialize the system.

Most operating systems store information on what space is available in memory, in what is historically called a *free list* or *free vector*. We will use an array to store the information for memory; this array will contain as many entries as there are blocks in memory, NUM_MEM_BLOCKS. Recall that the dimension of the simulated memory is MEMSIZE, which is the product of NUM_MEM_BLOCKS and MEMSIZE. Similarly, the availability of blocks on the disk is kept in a two-dimensional array. Thus, we need the two new data declarations

```
int free_mem_list[NUM_MEM_BLOCKS];
int free_disk_list[NUM_TRACKS][NUM_SECTORS];
```

in order to keep a record of the available blocks. If a block is available, then we should have a 0 in the corresponding "list"; if the block is in use, then we should have something else, such as a 1, in the appropriate place.

The algorithm is simple:

```
mem_block_number = 0
do
    {
    test free_mem_list[mem_block_number]
    mem_block_number ++
    }
while free_mem_list[mem_block_number] != 0
```

This works perfectly if there is a free block. If none is available, then we would continue searching until we exceed the amount of memory allotted to our running program. The correct algorithm tests for failure also:

```
mem_block_number = 0
 do
     {
     test free_mem_list[mem_block_number]
     mem_block_number ++
     }
while (free_mem_list[mem_block_number] !=0) &&
          (mem_block_number < NUM_MEM_BLOCKS);
if (mem_block_number == NUM_MEM_BLOCKS)
  puts("Error-no available memory blocks");
```

We need a similar search for free blocks on the disk. For the disk, the algorithm is

```
track_num = 0;
sector_num = 0;
do
   /* search each track, one sector at a time */
   do
   {
   /* search a complete track */
   test free_disk_list[track_num][sector_num];
   sector_num ++;
   }
   while(free_disk_list[track_num][sector_num] !=0)
             && (sector_numb < NUM_SECTORS)

   track_num ++;
   sector_num = 0;

while (free_disk_list[track_num][sector_num]!=0)
             && (track_num < NUM_TRACKS)
if (track_num == NUM_TRACKS)
  puts("Error - no available disk blocks");
```

We can use bit operations for finding free memory space by implementing the free list of unused memory as a single bit vector instead of as an array or list. A bit vector is a memory unit that is used to simulate the contents of a Boolean array. The bits are either 0 or 1, and this means that the memory location corresponding to the position of the bit is either empty or full. The only function that we have to change is the one that manages the free list. The way that this function should work is simple—each bit represents a specific memory block. We can access a bit directly by using a mask to obscure all the other, unwanted bits.

One way of using the masks is as follows. To test the rightmost bit, we simply take the bitwise AND of the bit vector with the octal number 0001. A value of 0001 means that the value of the rightmost bit is 1, and a value of 0000 means that the rightmost bit is 0. All other bits can be selected by using a similar procedure with other masks. This method clearly involves the creation of as many masks as there are bits to be tested; that is, as many masks as there are possible entries on the free list.

Another method is to determine the first bit that has a value of 0. We can use a function to select the bit by shifting the input until the bitwise exclusive OR of the number and the octal number 0000 have the value xxx1, where we have used the x to indicate that we don't care about the first three octal digits. The exclusive OR operator will return a value of the form xxx1 if the rightmost bit is a 0, which is the situation that we want. This is the preferred method since it doesn't require the creation of a large number of masks and keeps the program simple.

The function header for the new function `find_free_block()` should be of the form

```
find_free_block(list_vector)
double list_vector;
    {
    /* body of find_free_block goes here */
    }
```

with the free list passed as a parameter named `list_vector`. The reason for this is that the shifts would only change a copy of the input parameter while we are testing and the free list would not have to be reset to the correct order. The value that is identified as needing to be changed because of a memory insertion or deletion is determined by this function. The actual change to the free list should be made elsewhere in the program.

SUMMARY

Input and output are relatively simple in UNIX because of the simplicity of file design. A UNIX file is merely a collection of bytes, and any organization of the file is imposed by an application rather than by the UNIX operating system.

Files can be accessed from C programs using file pointers and functions such as `fopen()` and `fclose()`. These functions are in turn built upon file descriptors and system calls such as `creat()`, `open()`, and `close()`.

File reading and writing can be done from C programs with the `fgets()` and `fputs()` functions, among others. File reading and writing can also be done directly with the `read()` and `write()` system calls. All C functions for file reading and writing are implemented through these system calls. If asynchronous I/O is required, the system calls `aioread()` and `aiowrite()` can be used. All UNIX I/O is carried out through system calls as far as the operating system is concerned.

Files can be accessed either sequentially or randomly. Random access is performed via `lseek()`.

A device driver is a special process that aids the control of peripheral devices. It is itself a file and has no special importance when it is not being used. Two types of device drivers are character device drivers and block device drivers. All block device drivers use a kernel data structure called the buffer cache. Device drivers are always created with the `mknod()` system call, as are the other types of special files.

REFERENCES

Many books contain information on both general C I/O and UNIX-specific C I/O functions, including

Bach, M. J. *The Design of the UNIX Operating System.* Englewood Cliffs, N. J.: Prentice-Hall, 1986.

Egan , J. I., and T. J. Teixeira. *Writing a UNIX Device Driver.* New York: John Wiley & Sons, 1988.

Kernighan, B. W., and D. M. Ritchie. *The C Programming Language.* 2d ed. Englewood Cliffs, N. J.: Prentice-Hall, 1988.

Leach, R. J. *Using C in Software Design.* Cambridge, Mass.: Academic Press, 1993.

Rochkind, M. J. *Advanced UNIX Programming.* Englewood Cliffs, N. J.: Prentice-Hall, 1986.

EXERCISES

1. Design and implement an experiment to determine the effect of changing the value of BUFSIZE on the copy program for reading text data. Compare your results with those of a C program using the non-UNIX code for FILE pointers presented in this chapter. The precise determi-

nation of running time is difficult on a multiuser UNIX system because of system overhead and the effect of other users. Therefore, you should repeat your experiment three times to get an average time.

2. Repeat the experiment in exercise 1 using four different types of data: integer, floating point, double precision, or bit. Compare your results to the results you obtained previously.

3. Describe the system calls necessary to execute when the copy program of example 3.3 is executed.

4. Design and implement an experiment to determine the efficiency of the UNIX system calls read() and write() for file reading and writing as compared to that of the non-UNIX C functions described in this chapter.

5. Design and implement an experiment to determine the efficiency of the UNIX system calls aioread() and aiowrite() for file reading and writing as compared to the efficiency of the system calls read() and write().

6. Describe the differences between the open() and creat() system calls.

7. For each of the system calls in this chapter, examine the errors indicated in the file errno.h and determine which ones can occur for that system call. Write some small programs to generate several of these errors for different system calls and determine if the message printed is of any use to you. Use your results to determine when to use perror().

8. Encode the simulation described in the chapter.

4

The File System

In this chapter we consider a higher-level organization of data in UNIX – the file system. UNIX organizes files into file systems.

There are three types of files in UNIX: directory, ordinary, and special. Directory files contain information about other files and are part of a "directory tree." The designation "special file" includes device drivers, links, sockets, FIFOs, and similar operating system features. All other files are ordinary files in UNIX, and all types of files are stored the same way on the disk.

We begin this chapter with a discussion of lower-level disk organization and special disk blocks followed by a discussion of file creation. We then describe i-nodes and i-numbers and details of file system organization. The chapter concludes with a description of several UNIX file systems.

4.1   DISK ORGANIZATION

The UNIX file system makes few assumptions about the organization of the physical disks on which the system exists. To fix our terminology, we use the term *disk* in this section to mean a logical disk; that is, the term means that the file system is considered to reside on a single disk, even if many physical disks are available and a file system extends over more than one. There are four important sections of every UNIX disk. The first block is logical block 0 and is called the *bootblock*. It is used when the system is booted initially or rebooted after a system shutdown. The *bootblock* is never used during normal operation of the file system. It contains information used only when booting, and its data should never be corrupted.

The next block is logical block 1, which is where the *superblock* is stored. The superblock keeps track of the information that is essential for the file system to work properly. Information stored in the superblock includes

- Number of blocks used to store the list of i-nodes
- Size of the file system in blocks
- Number of free blocks
- List of free blocks
- List of free i-nodes
- A flag to indicate that the `superblock` has been modified
- Time of the last update of the `superblock`
- Count of the number of free blocks and free i-nodes
- File system name

The most common UNIX file system names are `/`, `/usr`, `/usr2`, `/home`, `/var`, and `/pub`; any name can be used, however, as long as it is not being used for some other purpose as well.

Most systems have multiple superblocks if there is a disk block failure. One of these (usually block 1) is the primary one used for checking a file system when the system is booted or for checking consistency. The alternate blocks contain the same information and are used only if there is a failure of the primary superblock, which can happen if a sector of a disk is bad. You can see the use of the superblock if you look at the system console for messages about the file system's integrity when rebooting after an unexpected shutdown such as a power failure.

Most manufacturers of UNIX systems recommend that the installer of the system write down the location of the alternate superblocks in case of failure of the primary superblock. If you keep a log with that information, you will be rewarded if a system crash occurs.

The next section of the logical disk is an array of `i-nodes`, usually stored as a contiguous set of disk blocks. The elements of the array are indexed by an int called an `i-number`. An i-node has the following contents:

- File type (ordinary, directory, or special)
- Number of links to the file
- File owner's user ID
- File owner's group ID
- File access permissions
- File size in bytes
- Time and date of last access
- Time and date of last modification
- Time and date of creation

- Pointers to logical disk blocks containing file data (or pointers) (There are typically a maximum of 13 such pointers in an i-node.)

There is one important thing to notice about the structure of i-nodes. An i-node associated with a file does not contain the name of the file. Access to a file by its name requires the use of directory files. This will be discussed in sections 4.2 and 4.3, on file creation and file access, respectively.

The final section of the logical disk is the collection of data blocks that actually make up the file system. These take up most of the room on the disk.

A physical disk may hold multiple file systems, such as / and /usr. A popular file system on a disk is /usr2, and there are many other commonly used file system names. What we have called a "disk" may in fact correspond to multiple physical disks. Each file system has a disk organization corresponding to what we indicated in this section. Organizing the user files on a disk into multiple file systems can greatly improve file system performance.

Here are some of the details of UNIX file system organization on a Sun SPARC 2 running Solaris 1.1. Many of the defined constants and data types can be found in the three include files

```
#include <sys/types.h>
#include <ufs/fs.h>
#include <ufs/inode.h>
```

A Solaris file system is divided into a certain number of blocks. Sectors 0 to 15 of a disk contain primary and secondary bootstrapping programs.

The actual file system begins at sector 16 with the superblock. The organization of the superblock is described in the header file ufs/fs.h .

Each disk drive contains one or more file systems, or portions of file systems. A file system consists of a number of cylinder groups, and each cylinder group contains both i-nodes and data.

The superblock is replicated in each cylinder group. This replication takes place at file system creation time, and the critical superblock data does not change.

Addresses stored in i-nodes are capable of addressing fragments of blocks. File system blocks of size at most MAXBSIZE can be optionally broken into two, four, or eight pieces, each of which is addressable; these pieces may be of a size that is some multiple of DEV_BSIZE.

Large files consist exclusively of large data blocks. The last data block of a small file is allocated only as many fragments of a large block as are necessary. The file system format retains only a single pointer to such a fragment, which is a piece of a single larger block that has been divided.

The root i-node is the root of the file system. The first i-node, 0, is not used for normal purposes, and bad blocks are linked to i-node 1 for historical reasons. Consequently, the root i-node is 2. The `lost+found` directory is given the next available i-node when it is initially created; this can be checked with the `ls -i` command.

Each file system has a fixed number of i-nodes. The i-node allocation strategy is adequate, and it is extremely rare for a disk to have space available for file storage but to run out of i-nodes.

The pathname on which the file system is mounted is maintained in the variable `fs_fsmnt`. `MAXMNTLEN` defines the amount of space allocated in the superblock for this name.

4.2   FILE CREATION

The UNIX operating system allows many types of operations to be performed on files, including creating, deleting, opening, closing, reading, and writing. Of course, such operations are commonly supported by programming languages and by nearly all operating systems. To demonstrate how these operations are handled in the UNIX operating system, we will briefly discuss some typical file operations at several different levels. The material in this section demonstrates again how UNIX's layered software architecture allows higher-level routines to access the functionality of lower-level routines through precise interfaces.

Recall that a file descriptor is an integer associated with a process during the period in which the process executes. When a process uses a file, the file descriptor corresponding to that file is in use; if the program ceases to use the file and cleans up properly, the file descriptor is available for use and may be associated with another file. A file descriptor is an index into an array of open files called the *open file table* ; each process has an associated open file table.

In attempting to open the file, the user process must check the open file table in the user's virtual address space for the availability to have another file associated with a process. This is actually a check on the availability of a free file descriptor for the process; a file cannot be opened by a process if there is no file descriptor available.

Each running process contains a table of open files as part of its runtime support system. When a file is closed by a process, its file descriptor is available for other uses by that process. The file itself may be opened by another process even if the file was opened previously by a different process. You can demonstrate this by editing the same file from different terminals or from different windows on the same terminal. Or you can run an editing processes in the background, as in

```
vi filename &
vi filename
vi filename
```

The results are interesting. Try this on a file that you don't care about messing up.

When a UNIX process is created, it always has at least three open file descriptors numbered 0, 1, and 2 and indicating `stdin`, `stdout`, and `stderr`. The process can have additional file descriptors when it is created; as we shall see later, every UNIX process inherits all file descriptors that were opened by its parent process. (The *parent process* is explained in Chapter 5.)

The maximum number of open file descriptors that can be associated with any UNIX process is usually 20. In general, we can open a file descriptor for each file we wish to access, as long as we stay within that limit. There are exceptions to this principle, however.

The use of the UNIX system call `creat()` when creating files was discussed in Chapter 3. The creation of the file is an action that is independent of the life or death of the process that successfully created the file. It merely means that the file is given an i-node and an associated i-number. The file can live on long after the termination of the user process that created the file.

The creation of a file implies an update of a directory. Thus, the user who created the file must have directory access. This is often not the case in different file systems. Also, a user who tries to create files in the directory of another user may be denied access permissions, which is appropriate from the perspective of file system security.

4.3   FILE ACCESS: I-NODES AND I-NUMBERS

There are three types of files in UNIX: directory, ordinary, and special. Special files can be subdivided into character special files, block special files, links, sockets, and FIFOs; we will discuss some of these special files later on. All of these files can be accessed in one of two ways: by name and by number. We will discuss these two methods of file access in order.

The UNIX operating system uses i-nodes and i-numbers. An i-number is a number assigned to a file that serves as an index into an array of i-nodes. As stated earlier, an i-node contains information about the file such as location on disk (track, sector) and size, as well as information about ownership, access permissions, times of modification, and so forth.

Directory files are grouped so that files can be organized hierarchically. Directories are logically organized as tables that contain two columns: the names of the files in the directory and the i-numbers. To access the files in a directory a user enters the `ls` command in order to print the names (but not the i-numbers) of the files in the directory. The `-i` option allows the i-number to be seen; `ls -i` prints the names of the files in the directory together with their i-numbers.

The only way to access a file by name is to read the contents of a directory file. A directory stores, in a form that is readable by both humans and computers, pairs of data related to the files in that directory.

On some older System V-based systems, a directory entry has 16 bytes, with 2 bytes for i-numbers and 14 bytes for names. Most varieties of UNIX now allow 32-byte character filenames. (BSD and POSIX systems allow both longer names and larger i-numbers, which in turn implies that more i-nodes are possible. System V Release 4 allows multiple file systems so that any of the common options are available.)

In any UNIX system, the pairs are of the form

```
(name of file, i-number)
```

and are the only way of accessing the file by its name. To find a file named `filename` we have to go through the following steps (including parsing the string presented to find the proper directory):

1. Get the request for file `filename`.
2. Find the location of the directory.
3. Use the array of i-nodes to find the directory.
4. From the directory, find the i-number.
5. Determine where the (i-node, i-number) pairs are stored.
6. Read the i-node and determine where on disk the file is stored.
7. Go to the place on disk where the file is stored.

Some of these operations need more explanation. Obtaining the name of the filename `filename` requires the UNIX kernel routine `namei`, which is called indirectly whenever a system call such as `open()`, `creat()`, or `mknod()` is given. This routine parses the complete string in "`filename`" and provides the proper movement from directory to directory if the string contains the slash (`/`) character that indicates subdirectories. Errors are returned if any directory or filename does not exist. The `namei` routine follows the command sequence

```
Repeat
      Read characters until either a '/' or end of
         character string is found.
      Store  temporary  string  in  a  string named
         directory
```

```
        If match found then get new i-number and make
            new i-node the current i-node
until either success (file found) or failure (file not
found).
```

There is a lower level of activity that is not obvious to the user. The namei routine is a kernel routine that lies between the level of system calls and the hardware interface. It is not accessible except by system calls, which is consistent with the layered software architecture of UNIX.

The action of going to the place on the disk where the file's data is stored may have several levels of indirection. Many UNIX systems allow three levels. We show how these levels of indirection work by an example.

Suppose that our system has a block size of 1,024 bytes and that each address can be stored as a 32-bit integer, each of which requires the use of 4 bytes. The 13 disk pointers stored in an i-node contain

- 10 direct pointers
- 1 singly indirect pointer
- 1 doubly indirect pointer
- 1 triply indirect pointer

The 10 direct pointers can directly access a total of 10 disk blocks that contain a total of $10 \times 1,024$, or 10,240 bytes, which is adequate for very small files. The singly indirect pointer points to a disk block that contains a maximum of $1,024 \div 4$ or 256 pointers, since each pointer needs 4 bytes. Each of these pointers can point to a disk block containing the 1,024 bytes of data in a block. Thus, single indirection increases the maximum possible size of a file by $256 \times 1,024$ or 262,144 bytes.

The use of double and triple indirection greatly increases the maximum possible file size at the expense of more time needed for file access because of the indirection. In double indirection, we have 256 pointers to disk blocks, each of which is a pointer to 256 disk blocks. Since each disk block can contain 1,024 bytes of data, a total of $256 \times 256 \times 1,024$, or 67,108,864, bytes is available. In triple indirection, we have 256 pointers to disk blocks, each of which is a pointer to 256 disk blocks, each of which is a pointer to 256 disk blocks, each of which can contain 1,024 bytes of data for a total of $256 \times 256 \times 256 \times 1,024$, or 17,179,869,184 bytes. The total amount of data that can be stored in a file on such a system is 17,247,258,432 bytes.

The maximum size of a file is a tunable parameter that can be set by the system administrator. Many systems do not allow such large files for reasons of performance and efficient use of storage. Most do not allow file sizes even close to this maximum limit. A limit of 1 or 2 MB is common for systems used primarily for teaching. Such systems have fewer than the 13 maximum possible pointers to disk blocks in an i-node.

We now consider the access of files without the use of their names. This is done by using the i-nodes of the files.

The i-node is located by using the associated i-number. You can see the i-number associated with a file by invoking the `ls` command with the `-i` option:

```
ls -i filename
```

The match of the i-number with the name of the file on disk can be found indirectly by the `ncheck` utility for checking i-nodes. When used with the `-i` option, this utility can find the name of a file with a particular i-number. Here are two examples from a computer running SunOS 4.0.1:

```
ncheck -i 10 /dev/sd0a
```

This example shows that the name of the file with i-number 10 is `/vmunix`. That the i-number of `/usr` is 1,664 is shown by the command

```
ncheck -i 1664 /dev/sd0a
```

Here `/dev/sd0a` is the name of the device on which the root directory is installed. On the system on which the `ncheck` utility was run, it indicates partition a of SCSI device 0. The corresponding information on your computer will probably be different.

Most UNIX systems use the concept of a *virtual node*, or *v-node*, as part of their implementation of i-nodes. A v-node has a structure similar to that of an i-node, but contains some additional information relevant to the location of the i-node's entries in the memory of the computer. Think of a v-node as an *in-core i-node*, that is, as a copy of the i-node kept in main memory to eliminate the constant need for disk access to locate files. The set of v-nodes is often called the *in-core i-node table*. It is slightly more volatile than the i-nodes on a disk. The relationships between v-nodes and i-nodes are observable in the two header files `i-node.h` and `v-node.h`.

4.4   LINKS

One of the fields present in an i-node is the "number of links." A link is a mechanism by which a file can be processed from a directory even if the file was not originally created within this directory.

A newly created file always has at least one link, which is to the directory in which the file was created. The file may be linked to other directories by the `ln` shell command or within a C program by the `link()` system call. There are three common reasons that a file might have several links.

The first situation in which a file might have several links occurs when applications software is installed. The installation subsystem for the software often makes an assumption about the location of certain library files. It is not reasonable to move existing libraries and directories from their current directories, which are the ones expected by most software already residing on the computer. Instead, we create a link to the new directory by the system call

```
ln olddir newdir
```

to provide access to the same files from two different directories. This increases by one the "number of links" field of the file's i-node.

A second reason to link files is to save room in certain file systems. If a file system is nearly full, some infrequently used files can be placed in another file system but can still be accessed directly from the original file system by a symbolic link

```
ln -s olddir newdir
```

which allows the freeing up of space on one file system at the expense of the other. The "symbolic link" is in fact a renaming of a file; it does not increment the "number of links" field of the i-node corresponding to the file.

The third reason for links is to allow backward compatibility with existing conventions of file placement in directories. The names `/usr` and `/var` are often symbolically linked on newer UNIX systems. It is important to allow applications programs to have access to the directories they were designed to use. Symbolic links allow the applications programs to work even if the directory organization has changed.

The command

```
rm filename
```

removes one link to the file from the current directory. When the number of links to a file becomes zero, the file can no longer be accessed by the UNIX file system (although the disk blocks containing the file's data are not erased from the disk).

To implement these linking and unlinking actions in a program, we can use the system call `unlink()` to remove a link to a file named `filename`, as in

```
unlink(filename);
char *filename;
```

On many UNIX systems, a link is a special file and may be created by using the `mknod()` system call with an appropriate set of arguments. An alternative method is to use the system call `system()`, as in either of the following:

```
system("rm filename");

system("ls -s file1 file2");
```

The `ln` utility can be used in the organization of C++ class libraries. Most languages and compilers encourage the organization of precompiled object code and header files into directories. The suggested use of the UNIX `ln` utility is to allow files containing friend functions to be linked to directories containing class descriptions for objects other than the original one.

We now describe the suggested use in more detail. Suppose that you have written a description of an abstract data type as a class and a set of functions to be applied to the class. You probably want to place the header file for this class in one directory and the object code for the compiled functions in another directory (or a random archive library). Call this class `class1`.

Suppose that you recognized that many of the functions used for `class1` could also be used for another class called `class2`. You could describe these functions or friend functions for `class1`. The header file containing the description of the class is not likely to cause a problem.

You can eliminate redundancy on the storage of the object code by placing all the friend functions for `class1` in a separate directory and linking the appropriate functions for `class2` to the directory for `class1`. This can be done with a command such as

```
ln old_dir new_dir
```

Note that the solution prevents a major configuration management problem in addition to reducing the disk space needed for the object code.

4.5   DISK SCHEDULING

Many users have a major misconception about the way that disk operations are implemented in UNIX. The natural supposition is that the response to a request to read from, or write to, a file on a disk happens instantaneously or at least at the next available cycle of the computer. This is frequently not the case because UNIX attempts to maximize throughput for a multiple process computer system.

Disk write access requests are queued up in a special, complex software data structure called the *buffer cache* that resides in the UNIX kernel. This is not to be confused with a hardware cache that is designed with extra-fast memory to improve performance. The buffer cache allows the storage of disk request data so that it can be processed at what the disk scheduling subsystem determines is the appropriate time. The disk scheduling scheme may be *C-SPAN*, an *Eschenbach scheme*, or any of the commonly used disk scheduling algorithms. Information about disk scheduling algorithms is available in any general reference on operating systems.

A request to write data to disk simply means that the data is written to the software buffer cache in the kernel's memory, and then written from the software buffer cache to disk as much as 30 seconds later. When the contents of the software buffer cache have been written to disk, the disks are said to be *synchronized*. Synchronization of the disk with the software buffer cache ensures that the disk is in a correct state, with the data requested actually getting on it.

Disk synchronization is always done when the computer is halted with the `halt` or `shutdown` utility commands. An unexpected problem, such as loss of power or a disk crash, could mean the loss of as much as 30 seconds of data from the buffer cache. Such loss is unimportant for most applications when compared to the possible loss of performance that would occur with immediate execution of disk write requests.

Reading data from disk is often much faster than writing data to disk because it generally bypasses the buffer cache.

The buffer cache improves throughput at the expense of the user knowing that a requested disk write activity takes place when requested, and completes within a prescribed time. Thus, there is a problem when using UNIX for real-time applications. We will discuss this point later in more detail. For now, you should be aware of some problems with the performance of UNIX in a real-time environment.

The buffer cache is complex, and its organization is different on different UNIX systems. Consult the reference by Bach, at the end of the chapter, for information about AT&T System V Version 2, and by Leffler et al. for information about the BSD version.

4.6 ALTERNATE VIEWS OF FILE SYSTEM ORGANIZATION

There are several perspectives from which file system activities can be viewed. At the highest level accessible to a programmer, a file is opened, data is read from or written to it, and it is closed. This is the level we would see if we were using high-level code in a language such as C, FORTRAN, Ada, or

Pascal. Of course, there is an even higher level in extremely high-level languages such as database languages, but we do not need to consider this level of abstraction here. At the lowest level is the interpretation of electric and magnetic fields by the hardware. Intermediate levels include the system call level by, which the process requests the services of the kernel, and the level where commands are sent to the disk and memory controllers. The lowest level comprises the actions of the disk and the memory controllers, which send, receive, and interpret signals to and from specific locations.

Figure 4.1 illustrates the levels of the UNIX file system, most of which are forbidden to user processes. Recall that a fundamental feature of UNIX is that processes can execute in one of two modes: user or kernel. When a process executes in user mode, it needs no interaction from the operating system other than for checking the validity of memory addresses so that it does not violate its address space limitations. When a process executes in kernel mode, it is accessing the hardware indirectly by system calls. Thus, whenever a process executes a system call, it is executing in kernel mode until the system call returns. Any routines used when the process is executing in kernel mode are unavailable to processes executing in user mode. This means that these lower-level routines called by system calls cannot be executed directly by user processes.

To fix the concept of the system levels, the following paragraphs and examples will deal with reading the contents of a file named `infile` and printing the output of the file on the display screen.

First, consider the highest level that is most insulated from the hardware and can be used by a process without explicit access to any system calls. Examples 4.1 and 4.2 show how our file reading problem might be handled in two high-level languages, C and Ada, respectively.

Example 4.1: File Reading in C

```
#include <stdio.h>
main()
{
   int ch;
   FILE *fp;

   fp = fopen("infile", "r");
   while ((ch = getc(fp)) != EOF)
      putchar(ch);
   fclose(fp);
}
```

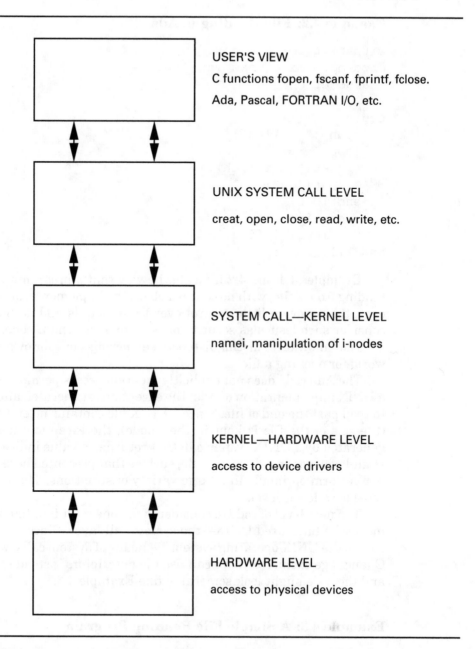

USER'S VIEW

C functions fopen, fscanf, fprintf, fclose.

Ada, Pascal, FORTRAN I/O, etc.

UNIX SYSTEM CALL LEVEL

creat, open, close, read, write, etc.

SYSTEM CALL—KERNEL LEVEL

namei, manipulation of i-nodes

KERNEL—HARDWARE LEVEL

access to device drivers

HARDWARE LEVEL

access to physical devices

Figure 4.1.   Alternate views of the file system

Example 4.2: File Reading in Ada

```
with text_io; use text_io;
procedure file_read is
character ch;

begin
   open ("infile");
   loop
      get("infle",ch);
      put("ch");
   end loop;
   exception
      close("infile");
end file_read;
```

Examples 4.1 and 4.2 indicate the way that a programmer might view reading from a file, with no concern about the implementation details. However, they provide little control over these details and do not allow us to consider such issues as security or performance. The C code, for example, does not allow us to distinguish between permissions for owner, group, and world for opening a file.

The Ada code does not explicitly mention access permissions, either. In a UNIX implementation of Ada, the exception is generated after an attempt to read past the end of file. Since a UNIX file contains no end of file marker (the size of the file is kept in the i-node), the exception must have been generated by a UNIX system call that returned a value indicating an error. High-level, general-purpose code, such as that presented here, usually does not perform optimally in a large variety of situations. Therefore, we must consider a lower level.

The next level of code to consider is the one most familiar to C programmers who have used UNIX—the system call layer. Since we now have access to the UNIX operating system by means of system calls, we will use the C language exclusively. We can use file descriptors instead of file pointers, and the code might look something like Example 4.3.

Example 4.3: A Simple File Reading Program

```
#include <stdio.h>
#define BUFFSIZE 1
main()
```

```
{
  int fd:
  char buf[BUFFSIZE];

  fd = open("infile", 0644);
  while (read(fd,buf,BUFFSIZE) == BUFFSIZE)
    putchar(buf[0]);
  close(fd);
}
```

This code is at a lower level than that in examples 4.1 and 4.2 in several ways. First, we now have more access to the operating system since we have explicit system calls within our program. Second, we have more explicit control over buffering. Instead of testing for the end of file marker, EOF, we compare the amount being read to the size of the buffer. Since the size of the buffer is 1, we are reading in one byte at a time. Thus, the only reason that the number of bytes being read in is not equal to the size of the buffer is that we have no more data to be read in; that is, we have reached the end of the file. We can provide much more control over the speed with which the input file is being read by varying the size of the buffer and delaying the printing of data until the buffer is filled.

A successful call to either the creat() or the mknod() system call always means that an i-node is created. The creat() system call generates i-nodes for ordinary or directory files, and the mknod() system call generates i-nodes for special files such as device drivers and links, and for certain constructions that need i-nodes but do not need space set aside for data storage. An example of the use of the mknod() system call was provided in Chapter 3 in the discussion of device drivers. Another example will be given when we discuss FIFOs in Chapter 8 on interprocess communication. Two different system calls create i-nodes, but the details of the created i-nodes are different.

The next lower level of the hierarchy of file operations consists of the routines accessed by system calls. No user, not even the superuser, can access these routines directly. All access must be arranged by the appropriate system call via the *syscall vector*.

The syscall vector is an array of pointers to lower-level routines that are run when a particular system call is executed. Thus, routines such as namei (which we discussed earlier), iput (which allocates and accesses space for i-nodes), iget (which acts on existing i-nodes), alloc (which allocates free disk blocks for storage of i-nodes), and many others are not available directly to the programmer if the UNIX source code is not available.

How can a user get information about such lower-level routines? A simple way is to take the previous two C programs and compile them with the -p option of the standard C compiler. This turns on the *profiler*, which then takes over the execution of the executable file. The method by which the profiler controls the execution of an executable file is called *process tracing*. After executing each of the programs on an input file of reasonable length, the profiler creates a file that contains detailed information about the routines in which the program spent its execution time. The file is named mon.out and probably can be read directly by the user. However, it is best to use the UNIX utility prof (or gprof on some systems) to get a listing of the time spent in these routines, sorted in decreasing order of total time spent.

Most of the routines mentioned in this output are unfamiliar; they are generally the lower-level I/O routines called by the system calls and include such things as device drivers as well as routines to send information about file contents and locations to queues for reading disk information.

Many operations must be incorporated into a single system call such as open(). The operations that are necessary when open() is called with one of its arguments as a string include

- Parsing the string to determine if the file is on some absolute or relative path or is in the current directory.
- Determining if the string contains the slash character (/), then searching the appropriate directories until the last substring without the slash is found.
- Reading the directory to find the i-number of the file.
- Checking the name of the file in the directory.
- Proceeding to the next step if the name of the file in the directory is found, which means that the file already exists. Returning with an error if the file does not exist.
- Looking up the i-node in the i-node table.
- Locating the i-node's permission fields.
- Checking the permissions for the user, group, or world.
- Determining if the disk block locations permissions match.
- Positioning the disk read/write head in the starting location of the file on disk.

Many of these operations involve the use of memory access routines, which we omit here.

The careful reader will have noted an apparent circularity in the previous discussion. We had to read the contents of a directory to determine if the file was present. However, it seems that a read() system call must be preceded by the system call open(), and we made no such explicit system call. How, then, was the directory opened for reading?

The answer is that the system calls themselves are composed of calls to these lower-level routines. The system call open() included routines to perform the lower-level operations discussed above. Even though we performed some of the same routines on the directory files, we did not need to make any other system calls. We mention again that these lower-level routines cannot be accessed except by system calls, since they can only be used while the process is executing in kernel mode.

The lowest level of operations involves direct access to the hardware. As before, the routines to perform these operations result from system calls and cannot be accessed directly by user programs.

There is another view of the process of determining if the name of a file is included in a directory file. We can read the directory using the read() system call after using the open() system call to access the file. This works because every UNIX file, even a directory file, is merely a collection of bytes, so it is possible to read a directory directly and determine its contents. However, though the reading of the contents of the directory is simple, their interpretation is somewhat tricky.

The structure of a directory is given in two different header files: dirent.h and sys/dirent.h. Both are in the standard UNIX header file directory /usr/include. The header file dirent.h has a statement including the header file sys/dirent.h, so the latter does not need to be included explicitly by the programmer. The first of these header files describes the structure DIR in example 4.4. The second, sys/dirent.h, describes the structure dirent in that example.

Example 4.4 uses a high-level interface to read directories. The functions opendir(), readdir(), and closedir() are defined in terms of the system calls open(), read(), and close(), and make it easy to determine the end of each entry in a directory. Note that the return value of opendir() is a pointer to the type DIR and is used as an argument to readdir(). Note also that the return value of readdir() is a pointer to the structured type dirent rather than to the type DIR. The types DIR and dirent are defined in dirent.h and sys/dirent./h, respectively.

We also used the stat() system call in the code of example 4.4. The purpose of this system call is to provide additional information about the entries in a directory. We used the st_mode and st_size fields of a structure called stat whose organization is specified in the header file sys/stat.h. The st_mode field is used with the S_IFREG constant to determine if the file is a regular file.

Example 4.4: Directory Reading

```
/* Program to read the contents of a directory. */
/* The directory name is specified as a          */
/* command-line argument. The size of each        */
/* ordinary file in the directory is given in     */
/* bytes.                                          */

#include <fcntl.h>
#include <sys/types.h>
#include <dirent.h>
#include <sys/stat.h>
#include <stdio.h>
#include <errno.h>

main(argc, argv)
int argc;
char *argv[];
{
    extern int errno;
    DIR *dir_ptr;
    struct dirent *temp ;
    struct stat *stat_buf = (struct stat *) malloc
                    (sizeof( struct stat ));

    if (argc != 2)
        {
        fputs("Error: not enough arguments", stderr);
        exit(1);
        }

    if ( (dir_ptr = opendir(argv[1]) ) == NULL)
        {
        perror(argv[1]);
        exit(1);
        }
    for(temp = readdir(dir_ptr); temp != NULL; temp =
                readdir(dir_ptr) )
        {
        if (stat(temp->d_name, stat_buf) == -1)
            perror("stat");
```

```
      if ((stat_buf->st_mode & S_IFMT) == S_IFREG)
        printf("%-14s %d\n", temp->d_name,
                        stat_buf->st_size);
      else
        printf("DIRECTORY FILE : %-14s\n",
                        temp->d_name);
      }
    closedir(dir_ptr);

}
```

The output of the program in example 4.4 for one directory is given below. Note the entries for both . and . . in the output.

```
DIRECTORY FILE  :  .
DIRECTORY FILE  :  ..
fork.c          238
count.c         117
create.c        96
process_table.c 486
prior.c         138
priority.c      25
awkfile         35
poll.c          691
inode_check.sh  274
lockfile.c      485
read.c          704
a.out           24576
multiple_wait.c 270
remove_ipc.c    411
directory.c     786
output          0
```

In the exercises you will be asked to read a directory without using these higher-level interfaces.

4.7   FILE SYSTEMS IN SVR4

We have previously discussed file systems in the context of the root and usr file systems that are used to partition a disk. Some optional file systems might be pub, local, usr2, and so forth. These systems are organized similarly to usr with regard to directories and means of access, although the names of the files in these directories and the file hierarchy might be different. In general, a user of such a directory would not be aware of any substantial differences between these additional directories and other directories.

System V Release 4 has a new organization for file systems. The file system hierarchy in some of the older versions of UNIX has a root file system for storing administrative and similar programs and files, and a usr file system for storage of commonly provided system programs such as editors, compilers, loaders, third-party application programs, user files, and user programs. The organization of SVR4 file systems includes a home file system for files and programs belonging to individual users that used to be stored in the /usr file system. Other commonly available directories and file systems in an SVR4 file system are var, share (for shareable files, usually architecture-independent ones), saf (for system accounting facilities such as log files), opt (for optional files, generally included in the original software distribution), export, news, and preserve. Most of these are of the same file system type as the root and usr file systems.

SVR4 allows file systems of different types to be mounted on the same disk or disks. Some of these new SVR4 file system types follow.

- ufs file system, which indicates that the file system is of BSD type, with names as long as 256 bytes and a blocksize as large as 8 KB.
- s5 file system, which indicates that the file system is of the earlier System V type, with filenames restricted to 14 bytes and blocksizes in the range of .5 to 2 KB.
- process file system, which indicates that another process may have access to the address space of the process simply by knowing the process-id. Names of files are replaced by ints, since these are valid for process-ids.
- Other file systems for NFS (network file system), RFS (remote file system), or similar.

The first two types listed, usf and s5, are important if two existing file systems are to be merged on a computer. Having the two types of file systems on the same computer allows the user to access both without having to truncate long filenames (and thereby cause confusion and the rewriting of some software that depends on the older filenames). Availability of several file system types encourages the reuse of existing software. The speed of access allowed by larger blocks is also important in some of these file systems.

The process file system allows a large amount of information sharing between processes. It is an important new tool in the interprocess communication method known as *process tracing*. Use of this system can simplify the writing of software development tools such as debuggers and profilers. However, its fine points are far too complicated to be included in this book.

The organization of the various network-based file systems will not be described in any detail here, since the topic properly belongs to a book on networking.

SUMMARY

UNIX files are accessed through i-nodes, which are stored in arrays indexed by i-numbers. There are three basic types of file: ordinary, directory, and special. The i-node table is stored on disk, and a smaller version of it is stored in memory. This smaller version is called the *in-core i-node table* or the *v-node table*.

A directory is an array of pairs of filenames and i-numbers. Files in the directory are accessed by determining the i-number from the directory and then using the i-number as an index to the array of i-nodes.

An i-node contains information about many things, including ownership, access permissions, times of last access and last change, and pointers to the disk blocks on which the file is stored. The name of the file is not stored in the i-node.

Special files include device drivers, links, sockets, and other system-level constructions. Special files are created by the mknod() system call.

Files are arranged in file systems. Many file systems can exist on the same physical disk, and, conversely, file systems can use many physical disks for their storage. Some of the common file system types new to SVR4 are ufs (BSD-type file system), s5 (System V file system), process file system, NFS (network file system), and RFS (remote file system).

REFERENCES

Bach, M. J. *The Design of the UNIX Operating System*. Englewood Cliffs, N. J.: Prentice-Hall, 1986.

Egan , J. I., and T. J. Teixeira. *Writing a UNIX Device Driver*. New York: John Wiley & Sons, 1988.

Kernighan, B. W., and R. Pike. *The UNIX Programming Environment*. Englewood Cliffs, N. J.: Prentice-Hall, 1984.

Lapin, J. E. *Portable C and UNIX System Programming*. Englewood Cliffs, N. J.: Prentice-Hall, 1987.

Leffler, S. J., M. K. McKusick, M. J. Karels, and J. S. Quarterman. *The*

Design and Implementation of the 4.3BSD UNIX Operating System. Reading, Mass.: Addison-Wesley, 1989.

Stern, H. *Managing NFS and NIS.* O'Reilly, 1991.

General Operating Systems References

Deitel, H. M. *Operating Systems.* 2d ed. Reading, Mass: Addison-Wesley, 1989.

Silberschatz, A., J. L. Peterson, and P. B. Galvin. *Operating Concepts.* 3d ed. Reading, Mass.: Addison-Wesley, 1991.

EXERCISES

1. Compile and run each of the programs for reading files (examples 4.1, 4.2, and 4.3) to see the effect of file size on system performance. In particular, note what happens if the file size is large enough to force the use of singly, doubly, or triply indirect disk pointers. You might expect a response time that is roughly linear in the size of the file. Is this the case when the file size becomes 10,241 bytes, 262,144 bytes, or 67,108,865 bytes? Use the profiler (compile with the -p option) to determine where the program is spending most of its time.

2. For each of the system calls open(), creat(), and close(), determine some of the lower-level kernel routines accessed via the syscall vector. Do this by writing simple programs such as

```
main()
{
int fd = open("filename",0666);
}
```

and running them after compiling with the -p option (for profiling). Which lower-level kernel routines are common to each program?

3. Write a program to print out all addresses of disk blocks used for storage of a file, using the file's i-node. Use a small file to reduce output.

4. Because of the indirection allowed for disk pointers in an i-node, disks can become quite fragmented. Many UNIX systems declare a file system to be full if it is at 90 percent capacity. Find out from your system manager what happens to file system performance on your computer if the file system approaches this limit.

5. List some of the lower-level kernel routines you might expect when using an archival device such as a tape with either of the UNIX utilities

`cpio` or `tar`. Test your answer by running a simple program such as that in exercise 2.

6. Examine the size of the bootblock and superblock on your system. (You may need permission from the system manager to bring down the system first.) What percentage of the total disk capacity is used for storage of these two objects? What percentage can be used for the storage of i-nodes?

7. As an alternative to the method suggested in exercise 6, you can compute the maximum possible number of i-nodes using the `df` utility and multiplying the value returned by the size of an i-node. Compare this with the answer you got in exercise 6.

8. Does the use of symbolic links slow down program execution when you attempt access to a file (either an executable file or a data file)? Explain your answer. Test your hypothesis by performing an experiment.

9. Write a program similar to the program in example 4.4 that uses the three system calls `open()`, `read()`, and `close()` to print the contents of a directory. After writing this program, compare the output obtained by running a profiler on it with the output obtained by profiling the program in example 4.4. Are there any major differences?

5

Introduction to Processes

In this chapter, we will discuss a fundamental concept in the UNIX operating system. Recall that in UNIX the term process means a running program during its execution. A high-level description of UNIX would include just two types of objects: processes and files. The high-level description would further divide the full UNIX operating system into the process and file subsystems that interact with hardware via the kernel and with users via the shell. The process subsystem controls the creation and initialization of processes as well as the interaction with other parts of UNIX. All these features of processes will be described in this chapter.

Consider what happens when the computer is booted. After the diagnostic checks of the memory, disk, and peripheral devices, two processes are created. The first handles the mapping from physical memory to the virtual memory of a disk. This first process is called by the names sched, pager, or swapper on various UNIX systems. It is controlled by the kernel and in turn controls the virtual memory system and scheduling of the CPU.

The second process created is called init and has a special place in the process subsystem. It serves as a dividing line between the boot-up activities that are needed to start the system and that frequently appear, to a casual observer, to be disconnected with the rest of the UNIX, and a situation of complete regularity in which all processes are created the same way using an action called a fork. We will see later that init has a special role when a process creates one or more "child processes," but the process "dies" while these child processes are still active.

115

This chapter is our first look at the structure of processes in UNIX. It will introduce the essential system calls `fork()` and `exec()`, and it will describe the structure of executable files produced by a compiler and discuss the scheduling of processes using a typical UNIX scheduling algorithm.

5.1   PROCESS CREATION AND `fork()`

Consider the simple C program in example 5.1.

Example 5.1: The Count Program

```
#include <stdio.h>
main(argc, argv)
int argc;
char *argv[];
{
    int i, limit;

    if (argc == 1)
        {
        puts("Error");
        exit(1);
        }
    limit = atoi(argv[1]);
    for (i = 0; i <= limit; i++)
        printf("%d n",i);
}
```

This program reads its command-line arguments, converts the second command-line argument from a character string to an integer, and then prints all integers from 0 to the interpreted argument, one integer per line. For clarity, we will call this program count when it is compiled and linked to create an executable file named count. A command line of

```
count 10
```

produces, as expected, the output

```
0
1
2
```

```
 3
 4
 5
 6
 7
 8
 9
10
```

We will return to this example later in this section.

The term *fork* has long been used in concurrent programming terminology to denote a time when a new branch of some software system begins execution concurrently with other branches. The UNIX system call fork() does essentially the same thing by creating a new process.

There are always precisely two of the user's processes involved in each use of the fork() system call: a parent process, which creates the new process, and a child process, which is the process newly created. The two processes continue to execute and have equal rights to the process scheduler.

Example 5.2 is a simple illustration of the use of fork():

Example 5.2: fork()

```
#include <stdio.h>
main()
{
  puts("Begin fork test");
  fork();
  puts("End fork test");
}
```

A reader unfamiliar with the fork() system call would expect exactly two lines of output to be printed. What actually happens when this program gets executed is this. A new process is created by the fork() statement; this new process is the child of the original, or parent, process. Each of these processes will execute. The parent process has already passed the first print statement when the fork() system call occurs. After the fork() system call is executed by the parent, the parent executes the second print statement. Thus, the output of the parent process is

```
Begin fork test
End fork test
```

The child process is also busy. After its creation, it begins execution as soon as the CPU scheduler gets around to scheduling it. The child begins executing statements after the point where the fork occurs and thus has the output

```
End fork test
```

Hence, this program has a total of three lines of output, with the

```
Begin fork test
```

as the first line.

This program has been run more than one hundred times; each time the three lines printed nicely. If you repeat the experiment, you are likely to have similar results and would believe that each of the processes, parent and child, would produce their output in sequence. This is easy to believe; however, it is completely wrong!

To understand what is happening, look at example 5.3, where the count program has been modified by the inclusion of a fork() system call.

Example 5.3: `fork()` System Call

```c
#include <stdio.h>

main(argc, argv)
int argc ;
char *argv[] ;
{
    int i, limit ;

    if (argc == 1)
        {
        fputs("Error", stderr);
        exit(1);
        }
    limit = atoi(argv[1]);
    fork();
    for (i = 0; i < limit; i++)
        printf("%d\n",i);
}
```

Run this program with an upper limit of 100 or more, given as a command-line argument. The output will be confused. We will observe integers in increasing order, and then another count begins. Some of the numbers may even appear jammed together on the same line. All integers from 0 to the upper limit will be printed twice, but the order will be garbled and will probably be different if execution of the program is repeated.

The reason for the difference in the output of the different runs of the `count` program, and the occasionally garbled output, is that the CPU scheduler will give each process access to the CPU when the process is scheduled for execution, not necessarily when it has completed its count to 100.

To summarize, the `fork()` system call creates a new process and allows it to execute. The order in which the original parent process and the child process execute their instructions depends on the CPU scheduler and appears to be random. (The scheduling of processes and the details of one UNIX process scheduling algorithm will be discussed in detail in Chapter 6.)

There is one other fact that is essential about the `fork()` system call: A child process inherits all open file descriptors, and hence all open files, from its parent. This means that the same file can be used for communication between the parent and the child processes. This will be an essential point in the discussion of interprocess communication in Chapters 7, 8, and 9.

5.2   PROCESSES

We now turn to a discussion of the technical details of the `fork()` system call and how UNIX treats processes. The two special processes `swapper` and `init` have process-ids 0 and 1, respectively. Every other process gets a process-id when it is created by a `fork()`. Our discussion of processes will ignore `swapper` and `init`.

A UNIX process can be created in only one way—with the `fork()` system call. The call to `fork()` creates a new process whose executable code is the same as the creating process. The executable code of this new process can be changed only by an `exec()` system call from within the thread of execution of the process itself. (We will study the `exec()` system call later in this chapter.)

Every UNIX process has an entry in a kernel data structure called the *process table*. The process table is accessed by the process-id, which is a unique integer assigned to the process on its creation and removed when the process terminates normally. The process table is organized as an array of structures with a fixed size dependent on the specific hardware of the computer. This means that there is an upper limit to the number of processes that can be active in the system at any one time.

A user can get a high-level look at the process table by running the `ps` command from the UNIX shell. This command produces a list of the processes that are currently active, including those currently executing as well as those whose execution has been suspended. The exact form of the output obtained from a ps command depends on the arguments given to the command. For example, a call to ps with no arguments produces as its output a list of processes that are running within the shell in which the user is executing his or her programs; the output is abbreviated and consists of the process-id and the name of each process.

More detailed output can be obtained with the ps command with the long option,

```
ps -l
```

Information about all processes running in the system, including operating system processes and other users' processes, can be determined with the

```
ps -a
```

command.

It is easy to determine the number of processes running at any one time. Piping the output of the ps - a command to the wc -l command, as in

```
ps -a | wc -l
```

produces a count of the entries in the process table and hence a count of the processes that are in the system at the time of the count. This method involves a high-level use of the output of the ps command and will always report a number at least three higher than the actual number of active processes. The three factors that each produce an error of one in the count obtained by this method are as follows:

- The method includes a call to ps as a process because the ps process was active when the count was made.
- The count includes a call to wc.
- There is a header line given as output by the ps command, and this is counted by the wc command.

The count will be four higher than the actual number of processes running at any one time if we run it from within a C program using the C statement

```
system("ps | wc -l");
```

This is because the call to system() causes a fork in the calling process (the executing program in which the statement is executed). This call to fork()

creates a new process and thus increases the count of processes by one. The new process is a shell process (because of the call to `system()`) within which the command `ps -a | wc -l` is executed.

After the command completes its work, the newest shell dies and control returns to the original program. This behavior is summarized by saying that the process represented by the original program is the parent of the shell process generated by the call to `system()`, which in turn is the parent process of the `ps -a | wc -l`. As each child process dies, its parent resumes its execution until we have the original process running.

The contents of the process table can also be read by utilities such as `w`, `perfmeter`, `pstat`, and `vmstat`.

5.3 THE SEGMENTS ASSOCIATED WITH A PROCESS

The memory allocated to a UNIX process is considered to be broken up into three segments. Each of these three segments has its own portion of memory assigned to it and the three segments are used in different ways.

The first segment that we consider is the *text segment*. This is occasionally called the code segment, but we will not use that terminology here. The purpose of this segment is to store all the executable code for the process. The term *executable code* means that portion of the process that can perform an operation on data. For example, a program to print the integers from 1 to 100 would include the machine translation of the source code for the loop and for the linkage with the library routine to print the output.

The other segments that are associated with a process are the *data segment* and the *stack segment*. The stack segment is frequently called the system data segment. In the case of a program to print the integers from 1 to 100, the value of the loop control variable would be stored in the data segment, and the environment of the process, among other things, would be stored in the stack segment. The data segment of a process is ordinarily controlled by instructions in the text segment of the process; the exception is that variables that are automatic, as in the C language, are part of an activation record stored on the stack.

A parent and a child process share the same text and data segments after the creation of the child by a `fork()`. The stack segments are similar, but not identical, since the processes are different and therefore have different process-ids. After an `exec()` system call, the segments are generally different, since the `exec()` reinitializes the text, data, and stack segments. After the `exec()` system call, the parent and child processes do not ordinarily share any information in their text or data segments, although there are a few exceptions to this. The data segment is initialized by the exec() system call, and the information in the segment is changed as the process runs.

Consider a process resulting from a program that initializes and modifies an array, as in example 5.4.

Example 5.4: A Simple Program

```
main()
{
  int i;
  int arr[1000];

  for (i = 0; i < 1000; i++)
     arr[i] = i*2;
}
```

Figure 5.1 shows the various segments of this process.

Every UNIX process has these three segments, and all processes other than those with process-id 0 or 1 are created with the fork() system call.

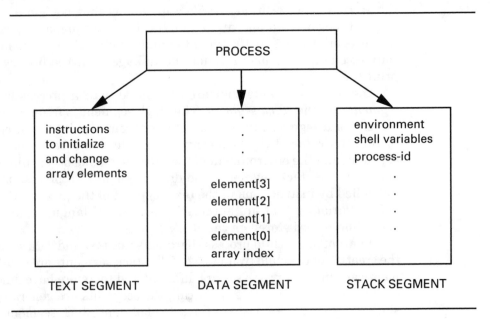

TEXT SEGMENT   DATA SEGMENT   STACK SEGMENT

Figure 5.1.   A typical process

5.4   INITIALIZING NEW PROCESSES WITH exec()

The purpose of an exec() system call is to overwrite the text and data segments of a process with those of some other executable file. In a program without an explicit call to exec(), the normal behavior of a data segment is to be modified only by the process itself. If there is a call to exec() within the program, then the normal behavior of the data segment is to be modified by the process that owns the segment after the data segment has been initialized by the exec that created it.

There are six different UNIX system calls that perform execs. We consider the simplest call, execlp(), first, which is shown here in example 5.5.

Example 5.5: execlp()

```c
#include <stdio.h>
main()
{
    puts("Hello");
    execlp("./exfile","exfile",0);
    puts("Goodbye");
}
```

Suppose that the executable file obtained by compiling and linking this program is named doit. When doit is executed, the text segment contains the executable part of the code. The data segment contains the strings "Hello" and "goodbye." It also contains the values of the arguments to execlp(), "./exfile", "exfile", and 0. The stack segment contains appropriate shell variables and an indication that execution begins in main(). The system is described in Figure 5.2.

Now execution begins. The call to puts(), which is in the text segment, sends the string "Hello," which is in the data segment, to stdout. The arguments to execlp() are read from the data segment, and the stack segment gets the return address for a potential return from execlp(). If we had any other function but an exec() or similar system call, after completion of the function's execution, we would return to the address that is popped off the stack in the stack segment, and execution would continue.

The system call execlp() is different—it never returns to its calling routine. The call to execlp() overwrites the segments of the process. The data segment is overwritten, and the strings "Hello" and "Goodbye" and the arguments to execlp() are now gone. The executable code in the text segment of doit is overwritten by the executable instructions in the file

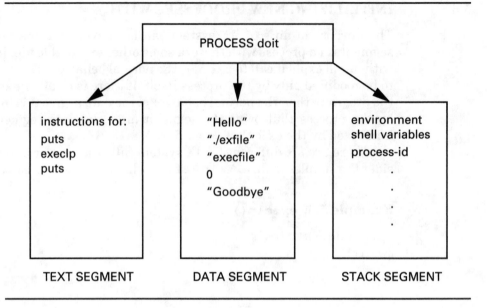

Figure 5.2. Before the call to `execlp()`

exfile in the parent directory, and thus the second `puts()` is never executed. The stack segment is changed to eliminate references to the return address for `execlp()`. See Figure 5.3.

This seems to be an unusual program construction. Why overwrite the segments of a process? The answer is that `exec()` by itself is not especially useful. The effective use of `exec()` is with a `fork()`.

The `fork()` system call has an important feature we have not used yet—`fork()` has two return values. The return values are possible because the system call creates a new process (the child process) while keeping the parent process alive. The two processes can be distinguished by their process-ids. The child process gets the value 0, and the parent gets the process-id of the child. As usual in C, a return value of –1 indicates an error.

Example 5.6 is a simple illustration of the use of `fork()` and `exec()`.

Example 5.6: `fork()` and `exec()`

```
main()
{
  int pid;
```

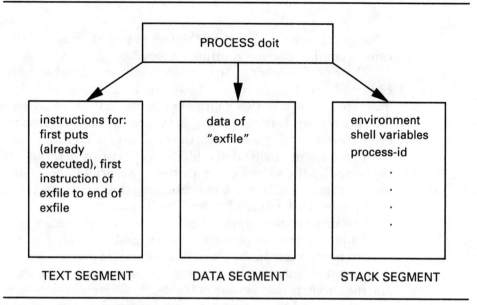

Figure 5.3.   After the call to `execlp`

```
switch ( pid = fork())
{
   case -1: puts("Error");
      exit(1);
   case 0: printf("In child, pid = %d\n", pid);
      break;
   default: printf("In parent, pid = %d\n", pid);
      break;
   }
}
```

Since the value returned by a successful call to `fork()` is a valid process-id, it can never be 0, since 0 is reserved for the process that is named `pager`, `sched`, or `swapper` on various UNIX systems.

Recall the discussion of the statement

```
system("ps -a | wc -l");
```

The fork is followed by an `exec()` system call that overwrites the text segment of the process in the forked branch by the executable code for

```
ps - a | wc - l
```

After termination of this code, the forked process dies and the process that came from the program continues execution.

There are five other exec() system calls: execle(), execlp(), execv(), execve(), and execvp(), which are used much less frequently than execlp(). The last two characters in the names of all six system calls indicate certain features: The l indicates that the arguments are in a list that is terminated by 0 or NULL, the v indicates that the arguments are to be given in an array instead of a NULL terminated list, the p indicates that the search path as indicated in the appropriate shell variable is to be searched, and, finally, the e indicates that the environment is not automatically passed to the exec'ed process by its parent.

A common construction using the fork() and exec() system calls is to have a parent process perform some computation, after which it forks and exec's a new process in the child. While the child process executes, the parent is suspended and resumes its computation only after the child process dies and the parent is made aware of the death of the child process. After the child process dies and the parent process is informed, the parent process resumes its execution. This is exactly the mechanism used by the shell to execute a command: The shell forks to create a copy of itself, suspends the parent until the child completes, exec's the command within the child process, terminates the child, and resumes control in the parent (which in this case is the shell). The mechanism is implemented with the wait() system call, which we will meet in Chapter 9. An example of this construction, using the count program of example 5.1, is shown in example 5.7.

Example 5.7: Use of wait() for a Single Child Process

```
/* Parent process forks and waits for child   */
/* process to complete execution of the count  */
/* program. The command-line argument argv[1]  */
/* is passed to the count program.             */

#include <stdio.h>

main(argc, argv)
int argc;
char * argv[];
{
   if (fork() == 0) /* in child */
      execl("./count", "count",argv[1], 0);
```

```
else /* parent process */
    printf("IN PARENT\n");
wait(NULL);
printf("IN PARENT, CHILD COMPLETE\n");
}
```

Note that we can have multiple processes executing as children of the same parent process, with the parent suspended until all children have completed execution. This is shown in example 5.8, where we have made use of the return value of wait(). This return value is −1 when all child processes have terminated and is nonnegative otherwise. In Chapter 9, we will learn how to obtain additional information from wait() in the form of its argument.

Example 5.8: Use of **wait()** for Multiple Child Processes

```
/* Parent process forks and waits for each     */
/* child process to complete execution of the  */
/* count program. The command-line argument    */
/* argv[1] is passed to the count program.     */

#include <stdio.h>

main(argc, argv)
int argc;
char * argv[];
{
  if (fork() == 0)
    execl("./count", "count", argv[1], 0);
  if (fork() == 0)
    execl("./count", "count", argv[1], 0);

  while (wait(NULL) >= 0)
    ;
  printf("IN PARENT, ALL CHILDREN COMPLETE\n");
}
```

5.5   **THE STRUCTURE OF AN EXECUTABLE FILE AND SHAREABLE TEXT SEGMENTS**

Several processes can share the same text segment. Sharing usually occurs when different system or standard application programs are used concurrently by different processes. A good example of sharing is the vi editor, which allows its executable code to be used by several users who are simultaneously editing different files. Before tackling shareability of the text segments of a process, we need to learn the structure of an executable file.

We need to be careful about some commonly misunderstood UNIX terminology. A file consisting only of ASCII text can be made "executable" if its permissions are changed. The ASCII text in the file is then interpreted by the UNIX shell as shell commands. If any of these commands are valid shell commands, they are executed. Commands that are meaningless to the shell are not executed and error messages are produced. This type of file consists of a collection of shell instructions and is interpreted. The file has no structure other than as a collection of bytes.

The other type of executable file is one created by a successful compilation and linking of a source code file. The result of such a compilation is a file whose instructions can be immediately executed, since the translation to machine-understandable instructions has already occurred.

In this section, the term *executable file* means one that is created by a successful compilation. You should assume that this is the structure of any file named a.out. In fact, the UNIX manuals generally title their description of executable files as the structure of an a.out file.

An executable file consists of a header and one or more sections. The header usually includes the following:

- The magic number
- The size of the text segment
- The size of the data segment
- Information about relocation of code
- The size of the symbol table for the process

Information about the shareability of the entire text segment is obtained in the header of the executable file and is stored in the value of the magic number. Many processes can share the text segment of a process, and no special use of the kernel's data structures are made except for the page tables used to map virtual memory to physical memory.

Options for the magic number, with common mnemonics on several UNIX systems, include those in the list that follows. The mnemonics are defined in the header file a.out.h.

- Normal process. The symbol is denoted by ZMAGIC or A_MAGIC1, depending on the system. The mnemonic OMAGIC is also used frequently; it differs from ZMAGIC in how the data segment is aligned to be contiguous with the boundary of the text segment. A magic number of ZMAGIC means that the data segment is aligned with the next available block boundary after the end of the text segment. A magic number of `OMAGIC` allows the text and data segments to be contiguous.

- Read-only text segment. The symbol is often denoted by `NMAGIC` or `A_MAGIC2`. Either is needed if two or more processes are to share the same text segment.
- Overlay segment (not used much on systems with large physical memory). The symbol is denoted as `A_MAGIC4`.

The header of an `a.out` file contains information about the size of the file's various sections. Some systems also include information about the relocatability of the object code within an executable file, in which case, the size of the relocation information is also part of the header.

Note that the shareability of the text segment is determined by the magic number. The magic number of utilities such as `vi`, `ed`, `ex`, and `sed`, which share the same text segment, would be either `NMAGIC` or `A_MAGIC2`.

The data segment contains two parts. The first part is used for storage of initialized data, the second part is used for storage of uninitialized data and follows immediately after the first part. This storage method explains how data can be corrupted by an array operation that exceeds the limits of the array as set by the program. Since arrays in C are essentially equivalent to pointers, it is easy to make this type of error and overflow array boundaries.

You can find more information about the structure of an `a.out` file on your system by examining the header file `a.out.h`.

Related to the structure of an `a.out` file is the *common object file format*, hereafter referred to as COFF. Its format is similar to that of an `a.out` file, as this list shows.

- File header
- System header
- Section headers (one per section)
- Data
- Relocation information
- Line numbers
- Symbol table

Some of the objects in the structure of a COFF file need explanation:

- The file header indicates the magic number, number of sections, time and date information, and global symbol table information.
- The system header contains information like that in a header for an `a.out` file, as mentioned earlier, and global relocation information.
- The data segment of a process's `a.out` file can be divided into two sections. The first section is for the portion of the data segment that

can be initialized from the information provided by the compiler. The size of this portion is measured in bytes and is denoted by `a_data`. The uninitialized portion of the data segment is denoted by `a_bss`, which is also measured in bytes. The value of `a_bss` is initialized to 0 and changes whenever the process requires dynamic allocation of memory. Programmers refer to the value of `a_bss` as the break value.

- The section header contains information about the physical and virtual addresses of the section, as well as pointers to data in both absolute and relocatable forms.

Note that an object file in COFF format does not have a magic number. This is obvious if you change the permissions on an object file to include execute permissions and then type the name of the object file. The common error message returned might be

```
object_file_name: bad magic number
```

More important, the object file does not contain any information about relocatable code. Therefore, unless the code is self-contained and needs no operating system or library support (which means that the code is trivial), an object code is not directly executable. The job of combining object files into an executable file belongs to the linker `ld`.

The significance of a standard format such as COFF is that it allows the dynamic linking of libraries of object code to runtime environments of processes. On some UNIX systems, COFF has been superseded by another standard called ELF, which stands for *extensible linking format*. (This facility for dynamically linking object code is not available on all UNIX systems). Dynamically linked object code can reduce the size of executable programs.

We now turn to the discussion of `a.out` files. At first glance, the information in an `a.out` file seems to be hidden from a user, since such a file frequently has many unprintable characters. Listing the contents via the `cat` command produces a mess and often causes the terminal to lock up and become unusable. Nevertheless, we can see the contents using the shell utility command `od`, which stands for octal dump. This allows us to see the contents of the file, byte by byte. When used with the `-c` option,

```
od -c filename
```

the contents of the file are listed in ASCII format. Piping the output of `od` through either `more` or `pg` allows us to see the contents one screen at a time. (The utility command `more` is common on BSD-based systems; `pg` is more common on System V UNIX.)

The octal dump allows us to see the magic number directly. You should experiment with it on some of your own executable files as well as some of the files in /bin and /usr/bin to see how the magic number of executable files varies.

For example, here is the executable file obtained from compiling the simplest possible C program:

```
main()
{
}
```

It creates an a.out file on one computer whose octal dump in ASCII format starts out this way:

```
0000000 001   p    004    +    206   y    x         203
0000020 034    b 003 001 013    002        002 260
0000040 020 200 200 330 200 200 320 200 210 002 374
0000060   . t  e  x  t  200 200  320 200 200     320
0000100      002    ,         320
0000120                            .    d    a    t    a
0000140 200 210 002 374 200 210 002 374 002 260 002
0000160                                           @
0000200 . b s s 200 210 005 254 200 210 005 254
0000220          020
0000240 200    .   c    o    m    m    e    n    t
0000260    003 314      005 254
```

Here the magic number is 1, which is the octal equivalent of the ASCII value 001. Note the start of the data segment. (The numbers in the left column are relative addresses given in octal. The file has been edited for clarity, and the printing of any special characters that are not among the normally printable ASCII characters has been omitted.)

The nm utility can also be used to examine a portion of a process that is obtained from an executable file—the symbol table. It is invoked with the simple syntax

```
nm executable_file_name
```

and produces a listing of the symbol table for the process. Different systems generate different output formats for this utility; consult your system manual.

5.6   **THE PROCESS TABLE**

There is a more accurate way to access the process table than using the ps command from within a C program. This method involves reading the process table directly. It is much faster because it avoids the overhead created by the switches associated with the calls to the system functions and it does not perform the extra fork.

This point cannot be emphasized enough: The only way that a UNIX process can be created is through the fork system call. The first process created on the system (usually called swapper, pager, or sched) and the init process are the only exceptions.

When a process is created (by means of a fork() system call), an entry is made in the process table for it. You can examine the processes active in the system by using the ps command to read those entries in the table that pertain to your own processes. This is a high-level view that is good for obtaining a quick check of the processes active in the system.

In addition to the information provided by the ps command, we can examine the structure of the process table by using the file process.h, which can be found in the directory /usr/include/sys on some UNIX systems and in similar directories with similar functionality on other systems. (On some systems the file is called proc.h.) The contents of process.h include the structured data type that is used for the individual entries associated with different processes in the process table, and the names of the various fields of this data type.

There are many fields in an entry in a process table; on a Sun SPARC 2 running Solaris version 2.1, there are 55 separate fields, including:

- The process state (running, blocked, waiting, etc.)
- Process flags (currently in memory, being swapped in or out of memory, etc.)
- Dynamically computed priority
- The process-id of the parent process
- A pointer to a linked list of running processes
- All signals pending for the process
- The address (in physical memory) and size of the process
- A pointer to the user's data
- The process group-id

Can we, as ordinary users, access the process table entry for a process directly by writing to the appropriate data structure? Of course not. Such an action would change the accounting statistics for the process and might even change the ownership and other access permissions. The reason is that the information about the process can be divided into two categories: the kernel's portion and the portion controlled by the user process itself.

We can only change the process table by having the kernel perform the desired actions so that we do not change the status of the system. Any process other than the kernel can be preempted, thereby leaving the process table in an inconsistent state.

We have discussed some reasons for not allowing an ordinary process to write directly to the process table. It is natural to ask about the possibility of having an ordinary process read the process table directly. However, we should note that there are entries from other users' processes in the process table. In general, we cannot access their private data, even for reading only, unless our process is executing in kernel mode. The only way to read the process table is to use a standard utility function such as ps.

One field in the process table is used to designate a *zombie process*. Such a process does not require any more CPU time; it is effectively doing nothing but taking up space in memory and in the process table. It is also taking up a small amount of time in the execution of the scheduling algorithm that we will study in Chapter 6. One instance in which a zombie process is created is when a child process wishes to report to its parent that it has completed its computation, but the parent process has died. In this case, the child process becomes a child of the init process. An excess of zombie processes may clog a system and force it to be rebooted to clear out these useless entries in the process table.

5.7   THE KERNEL PROCESS

The kernel has an entry in the process table and gets access to the CPU by a scheduling algorithm. Moreover, it has physical memory allocated to it, and it can run other processes as well as make use of devices. Even so, there are some fundamental differences between it and other UNIX processes.

The kernel keeps track of fundamental UNIX data structures within its own address space. It keeps much of this information in physical memory at all times and does not permit this information to be swapped to disk by a paging or segmentation process. In this way, the kernel gets special treatment from the memory management processes.

All executable code and data structures of the kernel reside in physical memory whenever the operating system is running.

The kernel also gets special access to the scheduling process. For example, the disk is synchronized to be consistent with the buffer cache every 30 seconds. (Different parameters might be used on other systems, but 30 seconds is common.) This synchronization requires the disk scheduler to read from the kernel's buffer cache, which requires that all user processes be suspended during this interval. Therefore, the kernel gets special treatment from the standard UNIX scheduler process.

Any ordinary process can be interrupted by receipt of certain signals invoked by the UNIX `signal()` system call, which we will study in Chapter 9. These signals often can abort the process if they are from the kernel or the process's parent. The kernel cannot be aborted by any user process (at least if the kernel is bug-free).

The kernel is the most interesting, and the most complex, UNIX process.

5.8   LIGHTWEIGHT PROCESSES

There is a large amount of overhead associated with the creation and destruction of a UNIX process. Consider the necessary background activities:

- An entry must be made in the process table for the new process. All the static fields in the process table must be filled in.
- In addition to the creation of an entry in the process table, each process has three segments associated with it.
- The process table entry should be removed when the process dies, and the memory used for storage of the segments associated with the process should also be made available to other processes.

These activities are relatively time-consuming if a lot of process creation and destruction activity is going on. In an extension of UNIX to a multiprocessor environment, this overhead makes programs extremely inefficient, since there is much distribution of computational tasks among multiple processors.

Thus, there is a reason to attempt to have a new form of UNIX process available, if the new type of process can have less overhead associated with its creation and destruction. This is now done by what is known as a *lightweight process*. Lightweight processes are the basis for the UNIX-like operating system Mach, which was the first easily available operating system to use threads and lightweight processes.

The idea is fairly simple: Create the minimal set of placeholders for the essential segments, but do not attach these segments to a process unless the process needs it.

A simple situation in which this idea is desirable occurs when a shell process is running in a window on a workstation on which there are many other open windows and running processes. An application program is to be run in this window. This means that the shell process has to call the system call `fork()`, which means that there is a copy of the shell running. The copy of the shell running in the child process and the original shell running in the parent process have different stack segments, and have pointers set to the memory area where the common portions of the text and data segments are stored. The child's access to these segment pointers and the child's stack segment are overwritten when the `exec()` system call reinitializes the child process to execute the application program. This is wasteful, and the elimination of this waste of CPU cycles is the purpose of lightweight processes.

A lightweight process contains the minimum amount of information necessary for it to execute—the stack segment, a pointer to a function whose code is to be executed, and a small amount of data to initialize it. There is no entry for a lightweight process in the process table. In general, many lightweight processes can reside in the same address space of a process.

Several new concepts come with lightweight processes. A *thread* is an execution path within a process that can execute concurrently with other threads within the process. A *pod* is a collection of threads.*

New function calls are needed for lightweight processes on many UNIX systems. On Sun SPARC computers running Solaris, they can be made available to programs by compiling the programs with the `lwp` library. These new function calls are not considered system calls in Sun's implementation, since the protection of separate memory for each lightweight process is not supported by the kernel.

The new function calls include

- `lwp_create()`, which creates a new lightweight process.
- `lwp_destroy()`, which destroys an existing lightweight process.
- `pod_setexit()`, which sets the exit status of an existing lightweight process, but does not exit the thread of execution.
- `pod_getexit()`, which gets the exit status of an existing lightweight process, but does not exit the thread of execution.
- `pod_exit()`, which exits the execution of an existing lightweight process.

The most complicated of these is `lwp_create()`, whose syntax is

```
int lwp_create( thread_t thread_id,
        void (*func) (),
        int priority,
        int flags ,
```

---

*The reader should be aware that some of this terminology is nonstandard in the operating systems literature.

```
                        stkalign_t *stack,
                        int num_args,
                        int arg1 .. argn
                        )
```

(We used the ANSI C syntax to illustrate that a variable number of arguments is allowed in the call of this function.) The types `thread_t` and `stkalign_t` are found in the header files `lwp/lwp.h` and `lwp/stackdep.h`, respectively, on Sun computers.

The first argument to `lwp_create()` is the `thread_id`, which is a structured type whose fields are used to identify the thread.

The second argument is a previously compiled function whose execution will be the primary reason for the execution of the thread.

The third argument is the priority for the thread. Unlike the typical UNIX scheduling algorithm, scheduling of threads with the same priority is nonpreemptive. Recall that normal UNIX process scheduling is by a dynamically computed priority.

The fourth argument is an integer that indicates appropriate actions for the thread. The default value of the argument `flags` is 0, which indicates that the thread is to begin execution in a running state and have a default treatment upon termination.

The fifth argument to `lwp_create()` is a pointer to the stack associated with the thread. This stack generally is the same as the stack segment, or system data segment, that is one of the three segments associated with a standard UNIX process. The only exception is when the value of this pointer is NULL, in which case the thread is suspended and has no program counter associated with it.

The sixth argument, `num_args`, is an int describing the variable number of arguments of type int that may be given to the thread.

There is no direct way to communicate between a lightweight process and the process that creates it, since lightweight processes are not created by a `fork()`. Thus, the parent, or creating, process cannot receive the process-id of the child, as is the case with standard UNIX processes. Lightweight processes can only be created with the `lwp_create()` function and the `lwp` library.

Here is a simple example of the use of the lightweight process library and threads. In example 5.9, we (1) create the mechanism for a thread using the appropriate header files and libraries, (2) set a priority for the thread, (3) create the thread with minimum priority, (4) attach a function `f()` with no arguments and void return type (the function `f()` is assumed to have been compiled elsewhere), and (5) destroy the thread. This model will work for any function `f()` with void return type and no arguments.

Example 5.9: Thread Mechanism

```
/* code to demonstrate creation and destruction   */
/* of a lightweight process.                        */

#include <lwp/lwp.h>
#include <lwp/stackdep.h>

main()
{
    thread_t *tid;
    void (*f)();
    int prior = MINPRIO;
    int flags =0; /* default value */
    stkalign_t *stack = (stkalign_t * ) 0:
    int nargs = 0;

    tid = (struct thread_t *)
                    malloc (sizeof(struct thread_t);
    tid->thread_id = (caddr_t) getpid();
    tid->thread_key = getpid();

    lwp_create(tid, f, prior, flags, stack, nargs);

    lwp_destroy(tid);
}
```

Notice that the stack for this thread was initialized to NULL and thus the lack of initialization of the pointer to the function f() caused no problems. Changing the function pointer to point to the simple function f() defined by

```
f(void)
{
    printf("IN THE FUNCTION\n");
}
```

also caused no difficulty.

Notice also that the priority was set to MINPRIO, which is defined in the header files.

Example 5.9 used a single thread of execution. It is clearly more realistic for lightweight processes to express multiple threads of execution, but this is much more complex for several reasons. We restrict ourselves to one example involving multiple threads within a single UNIX process.

The first problem with multiple threads is that if they are to execute the same code in the function attached to the stack of the lightweight process, the code must be re-entrant. That is, any attempt to use the code must not cause problems for other threads using it. This is not a problem for ordinary, heavyweight processes, since users have the protection of a context switching mechanism. However, context switching is not done currently (Solaris version 1.1 among others), and thus no I/O can be done by multiple active threads. Note that there was only one active thread of execution in the code in example 5.7, which is why placing a `printf()` statement in the function `f()` caused no problems.

There is also a problem if two or more threads access the same data. This is a typical instance of the mutual-exclusion problem, which we will meet in Chapter 6. We will present a solution of the mutual-exclusion problem for threads in Chapter 6.

The problems indicated in the previous two paragraphs are common to most implementations of threads at this point. Additional problems are caused by the lack of kernel support for threads, at least in current implementations. One serious problem is the lack of protection for multiple stacks used in threads within a single process. Without a careful analysis of the amount of space actually needed, a thread must take the safe path of declaring a relatively large stack for a process.

Another problem occurs when threads are rescheduled. Consider what happens when a typical UNIX process releases the CPU because another process has been scheduled for CPU use. The context, or state, of the current process, including register contents, must be saved. This involves some overhead and might cause unsatisfactory performance if the same methods are used for switching CPU access for lightweight processes. For this reason, some implementations of lightweight processes use the default action of not saving and protecting the contents of the memory space devoted to each thread running within the same process, and not saving the contents of most machine registers.

Clearly, a programmer must be extremely careful about preserving the integrity of the stack memory used by each lightweight process. Most implementations of lightweight processes bypass the kernel and leave the responsibility for checking with the programmer. The determination of the space needed for the stack of a lightweight process cannot be made easily unless the lightweight process has a simple, predictable execution with limited stack size and data.

There is some help in saving register contents on some systems. For example, the implementation of lightweight processes in SunOS version

4.1.3 (Solaris 1.1) requires the use of the `lwp` library and specific calls to the functions `lwp_ctxinit()` and `lwp_ctxset()`. These two functions have the following prototypes:

```
int lwp_ctxinit(thread_t tid,
                int type_of_context);

int lwp_ctxset( void (* save) (),
                void (*restore)(),
                uint ctxsize,
                int optimize);
```

These two functions are generally used together in programs. The first step is to define the two functions `save()` and `restore()`. Each should have three arguments: the context, which is of type `caddr_t`, and the ids of the old and new threads. The function pointed to by the `save` argument is invoked automatically when an active thread is blocked. The function pointed to by the `restore` argument is invoked automatically when a blocked thread is restarted. (It is occasionally necessary for the `save` and `restore` arguments to refer to `NULL` pointers.) These two function pointers are then used as arguments to the function `lwp_ctxset()`. After the context is set by `lwp_ctxset()`, we call the function `lwp_ctxinit()`, with the two arguments specifying the id of the thread and the type of the context.

The related function calls `lwp_ctxmemget()` and `lwp_ctxmemset()` are used to control specific memory for a thread. If the function pointers `save` and `restore` are `NULL`, the memory associated with a thread will be used for data storage only.

A special call to the function `lwp_fpset()` is necessary to save the context of the thread if the program uses floating point registers.

In the remainder of this book only standard, heavyweight (non-light-weight) processes will be considered, unless otherwise indicated.

SUMMARY

Processes are one of the two fundamental building blocks of UNIX; the other is files. Every running process gets an entry in a kernel data structure called the process table, which is indexed by the process-id. The process table contains dynamically computed priorities, so the kernel can use it alone to determine CPU scheduling. (The kernel is the most important part of the operating system and is itself a process.) Other portions of a process table entry include a set of pending signals for the process and the process state (running, asleep, etc.).

Processes have three segments: a text, or executable, segment; a data segment; and a stack, or system data, segment. The three segments are generally protected from other processes by the operating system, although the text segment of a process can be easily shared by another process. The shareability of a process is determined by the value of the magic number of the executable file for the process.

Common formats for executable files are COFF (common object file format) and ELF (extensible linking format).

Except for the processes first created when the operating system is booted, all processes are created by the `fork()` system call. The executable code of a process can be replaced by the executable code for another process via the exec family of system calls. A child process inherits copies of all open file descriptors from its parent.

Lightweight processes are an attempt to create processes without the high overhead of the `fork()` system call and frequent access to the process table for scheduling. Lightweight processes typically are not part of the UNIX kernel.

REFERENCES

The `fork()` and `exec()` system calls are described in many books, including

Deitel, H. *Operating Systems*. 2d ed. Reading, Mass: Addison-Wesley, 1990.

Kernighan, B. W., and R. Pike. *Advanced Programming in the UNIX Environment*. Englewood Cliffs, N. J.: Prentice-Hall, 1984.

Rochkind, M. *Advanced UNIX Programming*. Englewood Cliffs, N. J.: Prentice-Hall, 1985.

Stevens, W. R. *Advanced Programming in the UNIX Environment*. Reading, Mass.: Addison-Wesley, 1992.

General operating systems references that discuss fork abstractly include

Silbershatz, A., J. Peterson, and P. Galvin. *Operating System Concepts*. 3d ed. Reading, Mass.: Addison-Wesley, 1991.

Little information is available on lightweight processes in book form. Helpful information can be found in the original Mach-based reference listed below and in other sources.

Accetta, M. et al. "Mach: A New Kernel Foundation for UNIX Development." *Proceedings,* Summer 1986 USENIX Conference, June 1986.

EXERCISES

1. Write a program to determine the number of processes running on your computer and how many are suspended. This can be done in several ways. One way is to use the ps command with the -a option. Another is to read the process table directly, as shown in the chapter. Read your system manual to find out how to tell if a process is suspended.

2. You are allowed to have three uses of the fork() system call in a program. What is the maximum number of processes you can create at any one time? How does the answer change if there are four forks? How does the answer change if there are five forks? Is there a simple expression for the maximum number of processes that can be created with an arbitrary number, n?

3. This exercise is the same as exercise 2, except that you are to find the minimum number of processes that can be created. Assume that each process runs for at least a day, so that all of them can be assumed to be running after they are created.

4. Describe the number of fork() and exec() system calls used implicitly during the execution of the following three programs:

   a.
   ```
   main()
   {
   system("ls");
   }
   ```
   b. ls

   c. toy

   Here toy is the name of a file whose contents are the character string "ls" and whose permissions include "execute."

5. Describe the behavior of the file descriptors (not file pointers!) in the following program.

   ```
   #include <stdio.h>
   main()
   {
     FILE *fp;
     int ch;

     fp = fopen("infile","r");
     fork();
   ```

```
while ((ch = fgetc(fp) ) != EOF)
    putchar(ch);
fclose(fp);
}
```

What is the output of this program if "infile" consists of the integers 1 .. 100 in increasing order, one per line?

6. Repeat exercise 5 with the fork() and fopen() statements reversed.

7. Write a simple program that executes correctly on two different types of UNIX system. Then use the od utility with the -c option, as indicated in the chapter, to determine the differences in the a.out files.

8. Compile and run a simple C program of your choice and then edit the a.out file and change the magic number. Then run the program and tell what happens. You can edit the file easily by editing the octal image using od and then converting back to the original format.

9. Design and execute an experiment to determine the maximum number of threads that can exist within a single UNIX process.

10. Lightweight processes do not require the same structure as standard, heavyweight UNIX processes. Examine the file proc.h (or process.h on older systems) to determine which of the fields in a process table entry are needed for storage in a hypothetical "lightweight process table."

11. What happens if a lightweight process calls fork()? Is the new process a standard or a lightweight process?

Memory and
Process Management

In this chapter we consider the fundamental operating system concepts of memory and process management. The chapter is divided into two major portions describing the features of each of these topics.

Memory allocation is the subject of the first two sections, in which we describe virtual memory and the allocation of physical memory in typical UNIX environments. The remaining sections emphasize the process hierarchy, process scheduling, and the UNIX system call interface. The different scheduling algorithms available in newer versions of UNIX are discussed, with particular focus on some of the features of System V Release 4.

Concurrency in UNIX is treated in detail, with emphasis on process scheduling and on the classic reader-writer and critical section problems. We describe a method for the solution of the critical section problem for lightweight processes using the monitors available in the lightweight process library in several versions of UNIX.

6.1   VIRTUAL MEMORY

All modern UNIX installations use some form of virtual memory. We assume that the reader is already familiar with the basic concepts of virtual memory and some of the page replacement strategies that are needed for its implementation. For more details on virtual memory, consult the references given throughout this book or other standard texts on operating systems.

Virtual memory can be implemented as a paging scheme using demand paging or as a segmented scheme; other arrangements are possible but are infrequently used. (The term *segment* is used here in a different sense from its meaning in the terms *text segment*, *data segment*, and *stack segment* in Chapter 5.) Usually, virtual memory is implemented by the operating system at a lower level than that available to system calls, and such code is usually proprietary. Therefore, we will not provide any of the implementation code, but will discuss instead the algorithms that control virtual memory and the appropriate data structures.

Virtual memory allows a process to be located anywhere in physical memory. Nearly all UNIX systems use disk space as additional memory so that the address space of a process is not limited by the amount of physical memory available.

In a paging implementation of virtual memory, the logical address space of a process is broken up into frames, which are mapped into pages that are placed into physical memory. The pages are of equal size, and the number of pages associated with a process is fairly large. A segmented implementation uses larger sizes of memory for processes. Therefore, a process in a segmented environment uses fewer segments than the number of pages the same process (or one of equal size) would use in a paging environment.

The runtime performance of many programs can be greatly improved if the data is reorganized to minimize the amount of overhead caused by virtual memory. Consider the code fragment

```
float arr[N][N];
for (j = 0; j < N; j++)
   for (i = 0; i < N; i++)
     arr[i][j] = 2.0 * i + 3.2 * j;
```

This code initializes the elements of a square two-dimensional array. For simplicity assume that the value of N is the size of a page and that the array starts on a page boundary.

C stores two-dimensional arrays in row-major form. Thus, the elements of the array arr are stored as shown here:

```
arr [N-1][N-1]
   .
   .
   .
arr [N-1][0]
   .
   .
   .
arr [1][0]
```

```
arr [0][N-1]
         .
         .
         .
arr [0][0]
```

Since the inner loop variable changes much more frequently than the outer variable, it is clear that we are computing addresses of memory locations on different pages. This is a more complicated computation than is adding the constant value `sizeof(float)`.

The speedup obtained by changing the code fragment as shown below is even more pronounced if we must resort to paging because not every page is in memory. Obtaining speedups of 90 percent by restructuring such loops is not uncommon.

```
float arr [N][N];
for (i = 0; i < N; i++)
   for (j = 0; j < N; j++)
      arr[i][j] = 2.0 * i + 3.2 * j;
```

Most of the workstations, minicomputers, mainframes, supercomputers, and parallel computers that run the UNIX operating system use paging, and that is what we will discuss primarily; segmentation will be discussed only as necessary. We have already dealt with the segments associated with a UNIX process. We now describe how they are related to the kernel's storage of information about a process.

A fundamental data structure in the kernel is the page table. This table has the following information about the physical memory in the system.

For each process:

- Pages in virtual address space
- Mapping of these pages to pages in physical memory

To fully explain the page table, we will review some of the features of a related data structure, the process table. Recall from Chapter 5 that there is entry in the process table for each process and that each process table entry includes many different fields. Ordinary users cannot directly access a process table entry. Doing so would change the accounting statistics for the process and might even change the ownership and other access permissions.

Also recall that UNIX processes can execute in either user mode or kernel mode and that only processes executing in kernel mode can directly access kernel data structures. In user mode, we can access a copy of the process table and examine its contents, as we did in Chapter 5.

Sending information to the process table involves the writing of many pieces of data, since a process table entry has many fields. It seems that the reading or writing of the process table would occasionally be interrupted by the CPU scheduler so that the rest of the operation would complete in the next time slice of the process. However, this is not the case. These process table operations are performed by the kernel and are assumed to be atomic. That is, they complete whenever they start, and no other process can overwrite their data during a period of interruption.

The information needed for virtual memory for a process includes the process's page table entries. The atomicity of process table operations also holds true for operations on the page table and for the region table we discuss later in this section.

A page table entry consists of the following entries.

- A page frame number
- The date the page was created
- Page protection bits indicating that pages are readable or writable in user and/or kernel modes
- Bits to indicate if the page was modified on the last read or if the page is valid within the address space of a process

The *page frame number* refers to the physical memory page to which the page in virtual memory is mapped.

The placement of the page table information is different on different UNIX systems. On older versions of System V UNIX, it can be found in the header file `immu.h`. The typical page table entry on an AT&T 3B2/1000, for example, consists of a single 32-bit word. The high-order 21 bits of this word determine a physical page frame number, and the other 11 bits indicate if the page is to be locked in physical memory (not swapped out), if the page is already present in physical memory or needs to be swapped in, and so forth.

Since this particular implementation of UNIX uses segments, the file `immu.h` also includes a 64-bit segment table entry. The high-order 32 bits are divided into 8 bits for protection of a segment, 14 bits for the length of a segment, 2 bits in reserve for future use, and 8 bits for various flags. The lowest 32 bits are reserved for the segment address. A 14-bit segment length forces a maximum segment size of 16 KB bytes per segment.

On newer UNIX systems, some of the page-related data can be found in files such as `vmmac.h`. The organization is similar to that of `immu.h`.

A region table is a higher-level organization of memory than a page. An entry in a region table itself contains many entries, some of the most important ones are:

- Pointers to i-nodes of files stored in this region
- Type of region
- Region size
- Pointers to page tables storing the region in physical memory
- Bit indicating if the region is locked
- Number of processes accessing the region

As expected, a header file is associated with access to the region table, generally named `region.h`. The header file defines a set of fields of a structured data type called a region and a set of flags indicating how the region can be used.

These are the most commonly used flags and their meanings:

- `RT_UNUSED:`   Region not being used
- `RT_PRIVATE:`   Private, nonshared, region
- `RT_STEXT:`   Shared text region
- `RT_SHMEM:`   Shared memory region

Of course, these flags are used consistently with information about the virtual memory for the segments of a process determined earlier. For example, `RT_STEXT` is only possible for a region associated with a process if the text segment of that process is shareable.

Each process has a number of data structures that describe the regions attached to it. The types of regions that can be attached to a process and some common definitions follow.

- `PT_TEXT:`   Text region
- `PT_DATA:`   Data region
- `PT_STACK:`   Stack region
- `PT_SHMEM:`   Shared memory region
- `PT_DMM:`   Double mapped memory
- `PT_LIBTXT:`   Shared library text region
- `PT_LIBDAT:`   Shared library data region

In a region-based system, several lower-level system functions are needed. Typical names and their uses are:

- `*allocreg();;`   Allocate a region
- `freereg();;`   Free up memory in a region
- `*attachreg();;`   Attach region to process
- `detachreg();;`   Detach region from process
- `*dupreg();;`   Duplicate region in a fork
- `growreg();;`   Increase size of a region

- `*findreg();:`   Find from virtual address
- `chgprot();:`   Change protection for region
- `reginit();:`   Initialize the region table

All of these functions are accessible to the kernel only, not to processes executing in user mode. In particular, they are not system calls.

The virtual memory space of a process is divided into text, data, and stack regions. Some newer versions of UNIX also separate the detailed information about the shared memory regions. A virtual address includes three things: a byte offset, a virtual page number, and a region. The region table stores separate information about the three segments of a process (and the number of shared memory regions on some UNIX systems). Each region is stored as a contiguous collection of bytes.

6.2   MEMORY ALLOCATION

The UNIX kernel is designed to support multiple processes and always allows multiple users. Therefore, some memory protection scheme must be used. Protection is achieved via the page table referencing algorithm, which checks the validity of memory references. This means that the process itself cannot write directly to its own stack or system data segment, in order not to violate memory protection. Also, reading from or writing to particular locations that are assigned special memory addresses is usually troublesome because the mapping of a virtual memory address to physical memory, such as in the code fragment

```
x = * 0 ;
```

generally leads to a violation of the accessible physical memory after the mapping of virtual memory to physical memory.

Two important data structures for physical memory allocation are the free list structure and an array called `memvad`. The elements of `memvad` are bits. The array index of the bit array represents the number of a page frame. The bit is set to 1 if the page is in use and to 0 otherwise.

The free list structure contains many components. Some of the most important ones are these:

- A count of the free memory pages in an array of fixed size. This array is used for the storage of a small set of page frames and the associated information; the purpose of this small array of fixed size is to have fast access to the page frames that are most likely to be needed. This small array is called the *fast page frame array*.

- A pointer to the first free page frame in the fast page frame array.
- A pointer to the last page frame in the fast page frame array.
- A pointer to the last physical memory location allocated.
- The total number of free page frames available.
- The small array of numbers of page frames, called the fast page frame array.

The astute reader might ask two questions: Why have these separate arrays when a single array of more complex structures might suffice, and why use a small array of page frames when we could include an array for the entire set of page frames in the computer? The answer to both questions is the same: speed of paging access. The free list of page frames stored in the bit array memvad is accessed linearly, and thus the size of the array affects the performance of the search. Using a small array for a subset of the set of page frames, instead of the entire set, means that this set can be accessed faster. If the fast page frame array is full, more page frames can be added by choosing an available one from the complete list of frames stored in memvad.

Using a small subset of the page frames has the additional advantage of not requiring a major change if more physical memory is added to the system after operating system installation.

We present a set of examples, (examples 6.1, 6.2, and 6.3) with increasingly larger data segments, showing how such a two-tiered memory system might be used in practice.

Example 6.1: Two-Tiered Memory System (a)

```
main()
{
  int i;
}
```

Below is some assembly language file for an HP-9000 series workstation generated by this source code, which was obtained via the -S option on the standard HP-UX C compiler, ignoring any linkage to C library routines.

```
#9
    global _main
_main:
    link.l  %a6,&LF1
    movm.l  &LS1,(%sp)
    fmovm.x &LSF1,LFF1(%a6)
```

```
L11:
      unlk      %a6
      rts
      set       LF1,-4
      set       LS1,0
      set       LFF1,-4
      set       LSF1,0
      data
      version 2
```

Example 6.2: Two-Tiered Memory System (b)

```
main()
{
  int arr[10];
}
```

Here is the assembly language file generated by this source code, ignoring any linkage to C library routines, obtained via the -S option on the standard HP-UX C compiler.

```
#9
        global   _main
_main:
        link.l   %a6,&LF1
        movm.l   &LS1,(%sp)
        fmovm.x  &LSF1,LFF1(%a6)
L11:
        unlk     %a6
        rts
        set      LF1,-40
        set      LS1,0
        set      LFF1,-40
        set      LSF1,0
        data
        version 2
```

Example 6.3: Two-Tiered Memory System (c)

```
main()
{
```

```
    int arr[100000];
}
```

Next is some assembly language file generated by this source code, ignoring any linkage to C library routines, obtained via the -S option on the standard HP-UX C compiler.

```
#9
        global  _main
_main:
        link.l  %a6,&LF1
        movm.l  &LS1,(%sp)
        fmovm.x &LSF1,LFF1(%a6)
L11:
        unlk    %a6
        rts
        set     LF1,-40000
        set     LS1,0
        set     LFF1,-40000
        set     LSF1,0
        data
        version 2
```

The executable codes in each of the three examples will be similar, since the object codes are so similar. In fact, the executable a.out files were identical on one non-HP system running the same three programs. The HP code was presented to illustrate the discussion because its assembly language is easy to understand. Acceptable performance of the codes in most environments means a fast compilation and leaving the operating system to determine performance. Other compilers may attempt to optimize such features as the use of fast frame memory.

We could have used the octal dump utility od with the -c option to view the executable files in ASCII character format. We did not do this here for reasons of space.

There are two basic memory allocation routines: one for allocation of physical memory and one for deallocation.

Memory allocation involves the passing of two parameters: one for the base, or starting page frame address, and one for the size, or number of page frames to be allocated. If the parameter size is greater than the amount of page frames available, the allocation fails. Otherwise, we examine the small fast page frame array, and hence the free list, for available frames. As we find them, we allocate them and decrement the parameter `size`. This process continues until either the number of page frames is allocated or the memory allocation fails. If the fast page frame array is empty, we add new page frames from the free list as necessary.

Memory deallocation is similar except that frames are added to the fast page frame array instead of deleted from it.

It is often important to control the movement of large portions of virtual memory in and out of physical memory in order to improve performance by reducing paging. This control is generally called memory locking on UNIX systems.

Several forms of memory locking are available in SVR4. Their purpose is to increase performance of a program in a runtime environment that has many simultaneous users of virtual memory. These facilities are

- `mmap` allows all or part of a file to be mapped into the memory address space of a process and to be placed into physical memory.
- `munmap` destroys any maps between files and the memory address space of a process. Any such mapping was created by an earlier use of `mmap`.
- `msync` synchronizes the storage of information on disk with what is residing in buffers in the buffer cache.

6.3 PROCESSES AND THE UNIX SYSTEM CALL INTERFACE

We have already discussed the layered software architecture of UNIX. Higher-level processes and applications are typically made up of smaller subprocesses. The higher-level processes interface with the subprocesses through function calls. The same principle holds for processes accessing the UNIX kernel or the underlying hardware through system calls. Recall that the kernel lies between the hardware and other, higher-level processes. Thus, we need to study only two interfaces: between system calls and the kernel, and between the underlying hardware and the kernel. We describe the system call interface first.

System calls interact with the kernel by what is known as the *syscall vector*, in which each UNIX system call is given a fixed slot or position. The various versions of UNIX have different numbers of system calls, so the syscall vector is different for each one.

A user's program that had an instance of the system call `fork()` would be interpreted by the kernel as

```
syscall fork_number
```

where `fork_number` represents the position of the entry for `fork()` in the syscall vector. Other system calls would have different positions within the syscall vector, and hence the last integer in the command would be different.

Recall that a process can execute in either user mode or kernel mode. The use of a system call is slightly different from a function call in a user's program because of the change of mode in a system call. All system calls execute in kernel mode.

The kernel attaches the effective user id to the system call to obtain the appropriate permissions for things like file access. (The effective user id is the same as the user id unless the user's process has previously executed the `setuid()` system call.) This allows it, after executing the system call via the syscall vector, to return control to the user process.

The execution of a system call comprises the following seven steps:

1. Arguments (if any) for the system call are determined.
2. Arguments (if any) for the system call are put on a stack.
3. The state of the process is saved in a data structure known as the user structure.
4. The process switches from user mode to kernel mode.
5. The syscall vector is used as an interface to the kernel routine.
6. The kernel services the system call request. The returned value is obtained from the kernel service routine.
7. The return value is converted to a C version (usually an integer or a long integer), which is then returned to the process with the effective user id, and the process switches its execution to user mode.

Several lower-level kernel routines are only available to system calls via the syscall vector. For example, in Chapter 4, we met the `namei` routine, which is used with file operations such as opening and creating. Other lower-level routines mentioned previously are `iput`, `iget`, and `alloc`, and there are many more that are available only through the kernel's service routines. Here are some from a simple program to read data from the keyboard and use as parameters to a system call for process synchronization:

```
_findbuf
_doscan
_filbuf
_fwrite
_flsbuf
```

These lower-level routines are used for such actions as scanning the input, reading from buffers, and writing to buffers. They are among those the kernel needs to service system calls. They are also present in device drivers.

A device driver can be considered to have two parts: a higher-level part that frequently interacts with the system calls and a lower-level part that interacts directly with the hardware. The higher-level part interacts with the `termcap` and `printcap` databases, for example, and appears in a listing of routines accessed by the system calls used. It may interact indirectly with the kernel, since it may use some library routines.

The lower-level portion of a device driver is similar to the interface between the lower levels of other kernel routines and the underlying hardware. It is generally nonstandard and must be one of the first things written when UNIX is ported to a new hardware platform. Most, but not all, of these lower-level routines are written in assembly language rather than C.

6.4 CONCURRENCY

Concurrency is a difficult topic to understand completely. The basic idea is simple enough: Concurrency allows two or more computer activities to occur at what seems to users to be the same time; if several people are logged onto the same computer and are running their programs, they view the computer as doing their work simultaneously. The fact that there may be only a single CPU available and that the users' jobs are switched so that each gets some use of the computing cycles of the CPU is not immediately obvious because the computer is so fast. Allowing some degree of multiprogramming greatly increases the flexibility of a computer, yet, at the same time, it greatly increases the complexity of the operating system.

One problem that might have to be solved in an operating system that allows concurrency (or at least the appearance of concurrent execution if the system has only a single CPU) is the need to switch tasks. Switching involves the following:

- There must be a mechanism for stopping the CPU.
- Once the CPU is stopped, the intermediate state of the program must be stored.
- There must be a scheduling algorithm to choose the next job to access the CPU.
- There must be memory protection for the jobs in the system.
- There must be some way of restoring the state of execution of a suspended process.
- The system must be fair, or at least avoid starvation of processes.

- There must be extra memory for the multiple processes.
- There must be memory allocation for the operating system itself.
- Additional protection schemes must be created and implemented if virtual memory will be used (in which case a process may have some of its executable code or internal data on disk brought into and removed from physical memory as needed).
- Additional protection schemes must be created and used if the processor can read data from, or write it to, peripheral devices.
- Other processors, such as separate I/O processors, graphics display processors, and multiple CPUs in a parallel computer, must be synchronized to avoid the loss of data, and data must be buffered.
- A level of priority must be established for processes.

Peripherals such as tape or disk devices are generally much slower than the speed at which the CPU can access main memory. Therefore, commands to use these peripheral devices will be executed by the computer at a slower rate. This presents a timing problem for the operating system. Printers cause a similar problem because of their slow data rates. Adding more screen resolution to a bit-mapped graphics display can also cause timing problems because of the large number of bits to be written to the screen.

Typical priority levels for UNIX processes (with a low number meaning that the process is more likely to gain access to the CPU) are

> clock—0
> keyboard—1
> serial I/O—2
> disk—3
> tape—4
> printer—5

UNIX has all these features for memory scheduling and management. After we discuss scheduling of processes in section 6.5, we will discuss some of these features in more detail in the context of the classic reader-writer and critical section problems.

6.5   SCHEDULING OF PROCESSES

In a multiprocessing system, processes must be scheduled. UNIX uses a priority-based algorithm intended to provide good throughput for processes that need extensive use of the CPU while being fair to those processes that do I/O primarily. Priorities are computed dynamically so that no information about the future needs of the process must be predicted by the user of the process or the operating system.

What are the needs of an algorithm that computes and then assigns a dynamic priority? All other processing in the system must be stopped at regular intervals so that data needed for the scheduling algorithm can be selected. The data must be analyzed, which requires additional time. After the compilation, new priorities must be computed that will be used by the scheduler. The timing intervals for computation, the method of computation of priorities, and the use of the priorities by the scheduler must all be determined.

What we are describing is a non-real-time scheduling algorithm. It is not acceptable for real-time systems because it cannot accommodate a process that needs a fixed interval of uninterrupted access to the CPU, since another process might get the CPU. We will study real-time scheduling algorithms in section 6.6.

It is probably easier to describe one non-real-time scheduling algorithm in detail than to discuss algorithms generally. Different algorithms have different performance characteristics, but their general behavior is similar.

The algorithm we consider here assigns to each process both a static and a dynamic priority. [The priority is the sum of the dynamic and static priorities.] In an unusual terminology, the lower the value of this combined priority, the more likely the process is to get access to the CPU from the scheduler.

Here is a commonly used algorithm for the computation of the dynamic priority. For simplicity, assume that we start processing at time $t = 0$.

- Stop the CPU every 10 ms. At this time, measure the amount of CPU usage of each process that is active on the system. An active process is one either running or ready to run. At the same time that the CPU usage is computed, determine the number of active processes. Store this information.
- Every 100 ms, stop the CPU and total the amount of CPU usage for each active process. At this point, for each active process, we have a chart of CPU usage at time $t = 0$, $t = 10$ ms, $t = 20$ ms, ... $t = 90$ ms, $t = 100$ ms. We also know the number of processes that were either running or ready to be run at each of these times. Note that it is possible to take averages of the data collected. In particular, we can compute the average number of active processes over any time interval.
- Continue this process of data collection as processes run, are suspended, die, or are created.
- Recompute the dynamic portion of the priority of a process at time t by looking backward at the previous $5N$ seconds and ignoring much of

the CPU usage outside of that interval of 5*N* seconds. The number *N* that we use is the average over the last minute of the number of active processes.

For the first minute of the operation of this algorithm, starting from time $t = 0$, we look at everything that makes up the average. As time increases, we imagine a 1-minute window that moves along the chart of CPU usage and number of active processes. This is how *N* is computed.

We said that we would ignore much of the CPU usage after 5*N* seconds. In one algorithm, we would ignore 90 percent of the usage after the 5*N* seconds. Suppose that we have precisely two processes active in the system. A CPU usage chart for the process is shown in Figure 6.1. Also suppose that the two processes have the same base priority, which we take to be 0 for simplicity.

The value of *N* in our simple example is always 2. The series of values in Figure 6.1 refers to the CPU usage in the last interval, the cumulative CPU usage, and the dynamically computed priority, respectively. The priority

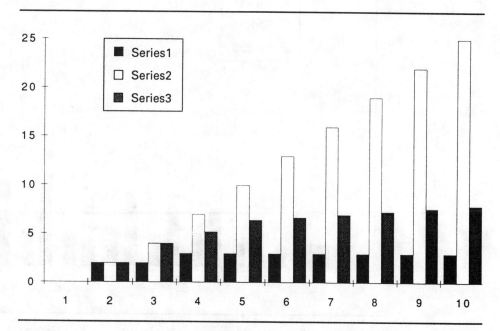

Figure 6.1.   History of one process (series 1 = most recent CPU use, series 2 = cumulative CPU use, series 3 = priority)

after each 10 ($= 5 \times N$) seconds is that both process 1 and process 2 have 10 percent of their CPU usage added to their individual base priorities, which we assume to be 0 for each process.

It is easy to see combinations of CPU usage that allow two processes to alternate in their CPU access. For example, Figures 6.1 and 6.2 illustrate two processes for which the total CPU usage is the same.

Each process will get access to the CPU after an appropriate interval. If, for example, a process was starved for the CPU during the most recent interval, its dynamic priority would eventually be lower since it had had little CPU access. The next computation of the dynamic priority would result in a lower number and thus a higher precedence after the next computation done by the scheduling algorithm.

On the other hand, if a process accounts for a large amount of the CPU

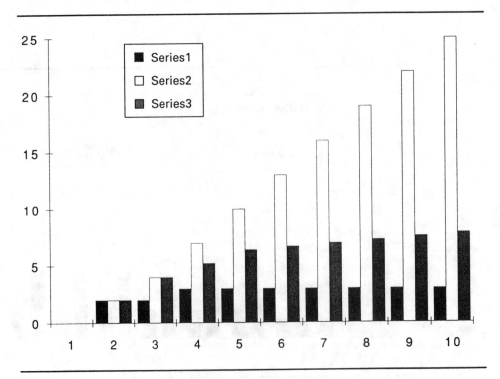

Figure 6.2. History of a different process (series 1 = most recent CPU use, series 2 = cumulative CPU use, series 3 = priority)

usage, it will have a high dynamic priority and thus lower precedence for access to the CPU in the next application of the scheduling algorithm. The process will be temporarily denied access, but will soon be able to use the CPU when the scheduling algorithm makes its computations once again.

It is natural to ask how an ordinary user's process can get more access to the CPU with such a scheduling algorithm. A user has no real control of the computation of the dynamic priority other than in the structure and CPU needs of his or her program, so the most obvious strategy is to lower the base priority. There is a system call to do this: `nice()`.

The `nice()` system call allows a process to change its base priority (in UNIX terminology, the `nice` value). Its syntax is

```
nice(value);
```

The `nice` value can be any integer value from −19 to 20. Obviously, a lower `nice` value is better than a higher one for increasing CPU access. Unfortunately for the ordinary user, however, only the superuser can decrease the `nice` value of a process that is running. Ordinary users don't often use the `nice()` system call, since it actually reduces possibility of their processes getting access to the CPU.

It is often possible to improve the performance of a set of processes that run concurrently. The measure of performance easiest to improve is the average wait time, although other measures could be also improved.

Suppose that we have profiled each process in the set for a number of inputs believed to be similar to the actual behavior of the system in normal operation. We can order the processes by the percentage of time they spend doing disk operations or interactive I/O. Clearly, processes that spend much of their time performing these types of operation are spending relatively little time using of the CPU. This observation is the key to this strategy.

We can raise the `nice` value of disk- or I/O-intensive processes by inserting the statement

```
nice(n);
```

where n is a positive integer. Doing so will increase the dynamically computed priority value of those processes. Since a high value for the dynamically-computed priority means less likelihood of obtaining access to the CPU in the most common scheduling algorithms, this strategy will provide more CPU access for the CPU-intensive processes. Note that the throughput of the disk- or I/O-intensive processes will not be significantly affected.

The performance of the set of processes can be improved further by a judicious choice of the integer n that serves as the argument to `nice()`—

that is, by selecting constant values (in the range 1 . . 20) according to the percentage of disk or I/O use.

One last observation is in order concerning this problem. If we understand each of the processes in the set of processes well enough to determine the portions that are not CPU-intensive, we can place the `nice()` statements at several different places to provide maximum optimization. This may not be worth the trouble, however, since only the superuser can *decrease* the nice value of a process (thereby increasing its chances of getting access to the CPU).

6.6   REAL-TIME SCHEDULING IN UNIX

There is a facility in System V Release 4 for real-time programming. This facility is often missing from earlier versions of System V or other UNIX systems that are not SVR4-based. From a real-time perspective, a major deficiency of the scheduling algorithm described in section 6.5 is that the priority of a process is determined dynamically. That is, there is no mechanism for programmer input to the scheduling algorithm that guarantees that the process will be executed by the CPU before another process gets access.

System V Release 4 is fundamentally different in how processes can be scheduled. There are two schedulers in the system: a default scheduler and a new, real-time scheduler. If no special action is taken, the process becomes an entry into a queue of runnable processes, and the previous discussion of typical UNIX time-sharing schedulers applies.

If the real-time scheduler is invoked by the `setscheduler()` system call, the process is compared by the CPU scheduler against those processes wishing to use the real-time scheduler, and the process with the highest priority is chosen. The clock is interrupted at regular intervals. Only the existence of a higher-priority process in the (real-time) queue can change the process that has the CPU in this case. In the absence of a higher-priority process, the process that has been given the CPU by the real-time scheduler continues to have the CPU until completion.

The key to effective use of the real-time scheduler lies in the programmer determining precisely the real-time constraints of the system; that is, knowing precisely how long the CPU must service one process before any other process can get the CPU. After this information is determined, the programmer can set appropriate parameters for the real-time scheduler using the `setscheduler()` system call.

It is important to note that both the regular and alternate real-time schedulers work only for standard UNIX processes. They do not apply to lightweight processes since these are scheduled within regular UNIX processes by a special scheduler built into the lightweight process library.

6.7 THE READER-WRITER PROBLEM

The design of an operating system to allow multiple processes to execute concurrently requires that the operating system treat problems of the types described earlier. It must provide mechanisms for

- Communicating with processes
- Storing information about processes
- Ensuring that two processes do not have access to a nonshareable resource at the same time

It is easiest to understand these mechanisms in the context of the *reader-writer problem*. This is an abstraction of a fundamental operating system situation in which one process, the "writer," sends data to the other process, the "reader," in a stream. After the data is written to the stream by the writer, it is removed from the stream and processed by the reader. This continues until there is no more data provided by the writer.

The reader-writer problem assumes that there are two processes that may perform at different times and at different rates. If the writer process is faster than the reader process, an error may occur unless we buffer the data.

The reader-writer problem has an elegant solution in UNIX—the pipe, which was introduced in Chapter 1. Pipes can be invoked at the shell level with the pipe symbol (|) as a connection between procedures. Within C programs, they can be invoked with the `pipe()` system call, which we will study in detail in Chapter 7.

One example of a reader-writer problem is the printing of data created by an executing program on a printer. The printer is typically much slower than the executing program, so the writer process (the executing program) and the reader process (the software that controls the printer) must communicate so that no data is lost. Peripherals such as disks also access data at rates different from the CPU rate, so any writing of data by the CPU to or from disk is also an example of a reader-writer problem. Yet another example is the UNIX command `ls | wc -l`, which pipes the output of `ls` to the input of `wc`.

A key to solving the reader-writer problem is recognizing that some type of buffer, or temporary storage, is needed if the reader and writer processes execute at different rates or begin at different times. The writer can send its output to the buffer, where it can wait until the reader process gets the output. If we use the buffer in a FIFO manner, data will be read by the reader in precisely the same order in which it was sent by the writer. This solution is simple and elegant, and requires no special communication or synchronization between the reader and writer processes. However, it has one small disadvantage—it does not work on any actual computers.

The difficulty with using a simple buffer is that we didn't make any assumptions about the size of the buffer. On real computers, storage is limited, which means that a solution to the reader-writer problem using unbounded buffers is not correct.

I learned about the bounded buffer problem the hard way—a program didn't work. The problem being studied was the change in the behavior of the graphs of some surfaces when the values of some parameters were changed. These graphs were needed for a problem in computer-aided design. A program was written to perform the computations and to plot the graphs after the computations were complete. The algorithm was

```
FOR EACH VARIATION OF THE PARAMETERS OF THE SURFACES
     COMPUTE THE SURFACE
     PLOT THE SURFACE
     SEND IMAGE OF THE SCREEN TO A FILE
     SEND THE FILE TO THE PRINTER
```

The image of the screen was sent to the file in a *raster image,* that is, as a collection of pixels or dots.

The workstation I used had 8 MB of memory and 1 million bits (125,000 bytes) on the screen, using 1 bit per pixel since the image was black and white. Thus, 1 million bits were in each raster image of the screen. There were 6 MB in the root file system for use by the print spooler in the directory /tmp.

There were 100 surfaces to evaluate. Because each computation was lengthy, the program began executing on Friday evening. I expected 100 pages of correct output on Monday morning, but only 20 pages were actually printed. What happened?

The boundedness of the buffer showed up in this reader-writer problem. The 100 different screen images took up approximately 12.5 MB of space in the buffer. The computations were so much faster than the printer that the 6 MB of buffer in /tmp filled up. Since the writer process (the computation) didn't block, the data was simply lost.

The above discussion indicates that we need to consider the modified reader-writer problem that looks like this:

Writer process W sends data to buffer B.
Reader process R gets data from buffer B.
Buffer B has a fixed size and can contain at least one item of data.

(This formulation of the reader-writer problem is occasionally called the bounded-buffer problem.)

The essential new feature of assuming a bounded buffer is that there must be some mechanism for temporarily stopping the flow of data from the writer process. If we don't do this, data will be lost. Think about how terrible it would be if data sent to a printer were lost, or if a file sent to a disk were corrupted. We must be able to tell the writer process to suspend processing when the buffer is full and to resume when it has room. We also must tell the reader process to suspend reading if the buffer is empty and to wait for the writer process to produce more data.

Many high-level algorithms will solve the reader-writer problem. Perhaps the simplest is this one:

```
/* Reader and writer are concurrent processes  */
/* that share a single buffer.                  */

while ((more data remains to be written by the
writer) OR (more data remains to be read by the
reader) )
     {
     /* pseudo-code represents a single process */
     while (no more room in buffer)
         {
         block(writer);
         enable(reader);
         }
     /* pseudo-code represents a single process*/
     while (room in buffer)
         {
         block(reader);
         enable(writer);
         }
}
```

There are several difficulties in the implementation of this high-level algorithm. The most obvious is how the state of the buffer can be communicated to either the reader or the writer process. For a kernel process, the buffer might be in the buffer cache, which is a software cache incorporated in the kernel's internal data structures. In this case, we can depend entirely on the UNIX operating system to handle the details.

For user processes that are executing in user mode, the processes must explicitly access some form of interprocess communication. There are some restrictions on the relationships between processes (such as being parent and child and being children of the same parent) that may be enforced before certain methods of interprocess communication are allowed between the processes.

A less obvious problem occurs if an operation to determine the state of the buffer is interrupted by some other process. The determination of the state of the buffer need not be part of either the reader or the writer process; it is much easier to view it as not being part of them. If the state determination operation is interrupted, the reader-writer system is in an inconsistent state and chaos can result. Checking the buffer for overflow could include the C source code

```
if (buffer_count == MAX_BUFFER_SIZE)
    block(writer);
```

This might correspond to several assembly language statements, so that the blocking of the writer process is started even if something else has intervened causing the writer to be blocked unnecessarily.

Thus, such actions need to be atomic; that is, they must not be preemptable. The details of how atomicity is enforced for some system calls and how the state of the buffer is conveyed to the reader and writer processes will be discussed in Chapters 7, 8, and 9, which deal with interprocess communication.

6.8 THE CRITICAL SECTION PROBLEM AND MUTUAL EXCLUSION

Another classic problem in concurrency is the mutual exclusion, or critical section, problem. This problem concerns two or more concurrent processes that access some common resource or data. The processes can each use the common resource or data, but only one can do it at a time, which means the other must wait until the first process using the resource or data is finished. Think of two people accessing the same bank account at the same time using different automatic teller machines.

The best way to understand the critical section problem is to divide the executing code of the individual process into sections. This will show that the only sections that cause problems are those that access the common resource or data. They must be treated to ensure that whenever any process is in its critical section, no other process may begin execution of its critical section until the first process leaves its critical section.

In other words, from the point of view of a correct solution to the critical section problem, the code inside a critical section is an indivisible operation and cannot be forced to give up its essential resources to allow the execution of another process's critical section. This is easy to see if the critical section of a process is something like the incrementation operation in C :

```
x++ ;
```

which can be considered an atomic operation (not subdividable when executed as assembly language instructions) if x is known to be a register variable.

At certain times during its execution life, an instance of the reader-writer problem may be considered a special case of the critical section problem, in that the buffer is a critical resource that cannot be shared when it is full. However, since the buffer is generally neither full (in which case the writer would have to be blocked) nor empty (in which case the reader would have to be blocked), the reader-writer and critical section problems are generally considered different problems, and a different solution must be provided for each.

UNIX provides a solution to the critical section problem that can be implemented with semaphores and the UNIX semaphore data structure. Semaphores can be simulated through the simple concept of a lock file; a lock file can be created by means of the creat() system call. Other methods can be used, although somewhat less easily. We will study these methods in Chapter 8.

We present here a simple high-level algorithm for a solution to the critical section problem when there are only two processes. This algorithm is similar to one in Deitel's operating systems text (see the references at the end of the chapter).

```
/* process one */
while (OK)
    {non_critical_stuff();
    if (process_number == 2)
        ;      /* wait */
    enter_critical_region;
        do_critical_region_stuff();
    leave_critical_region();
    process_number = 2;
    other_non_critical_stuff();
    }
```

```
/* process two */
while (OK)
     {non_critical_stuff();
     if (process_number == 1)
          ;      /* wait */
     enter_critical_region;
          do_critical_region_stuff();
     leave_critical_region();
     process_number = 1;
     other_non_critical_stuff();
     }
```

```
/* main program */
process_number = 1;
fork_and_exec(process_one);
fork_and_exec(process_two);
```

This solution requires the processes to access the CPU in alternating order and is thus highly inefficient. The general operating systems texts provide a more complete discussion of this problem and some common techniques for dealing with it. Details of passing the value of process_number to the processes using the fork() and exec() system calls will be discussed in Chapter 7.

The critical section problem presented here assumes that there are only two processes. The problem is much more complicated if more than two processes wish to access the same critical region. Techniques such as the use of general semaphores are needed for synchronization of ordinary UNIX processes. We will discuss these in Chapter 8.

6.9   MONITORS AND THE CRITICAL SECTION PROBLEM FOR LIGHTWEIGHT PROCESSES

In addition to their low overhead of creation compared with ordinary UNIX processes, lightweight processes have another advantage: They can have a single thread of execution blocked while the other execution threads in the process continue to execute.

This use of lightweight processes is just another degree of concurrency, but without the overhead. As a result, the familiar issues of mutual exclusion and race conditions are as relevant as they were for ordinary processes and interprocess communication.

The advantage of lightweight processes over ordinary, heavyweight UNIX processes is their smoother method of enforcing mutual exclusion than the one employed by the relatively complex UNIX semaphores. Lightweight processes can use several functions in the `lwp` library to act as monitors in a way described in C. A. R. Hoare's original paper on mutual exclusion (see the references).

The relevant functions in Sun's `lwp` library in the Solaris 1.1 standard distribution are

```
mon_create()
mon_destroy()
mon_enter()
mon_exit()
mon_enumerate()
mon_waiters()
mon_cond_enter()
mon_break()
MONITOR
SAMEMON()
```

All of these functions use the `mon_t` data type that is specified by a `typedef` in the header file `<sys/lwp.h>`.

These functions from the `lwp` library illustrate a solution to the critical section problem in a simple example using monitors. Access to its critical section by a lightweight process is granted by the function `mon_enter()`, which blocks the calling thread of execution if the monitor is in use. The first time `mon_enter()` is called, it returns 0. The next time the monitor is entered, `mon_enter()` returns 1.

The exit condition from the critical section is handled by the function `mon_exit()`, which allows the next thread that is blocked by the monitor to resume execution.

The most common solution to the critical section problem for threads uses a variable of type `mon_t` and a monitor to control entrance to the critical section. The controlling variable is given a meaningful name (such as `x_mon` if the controlling condition is based on the value of a variable named `x`):

```
mon_t x_mon;
/* initialize monitor */
    .
    .
```

```
mon_enter(x_mon);
   /* critical section goes here */
mon_exit(x_mon);
```

In theory, monitors can be nested to a considerable depth. However, the reality is that the code in most implementations of the lightweight process library is not as mature as that of the kernel, and the error checking is not up to the standards of the rest of the operating system. It is probably best to keep the level of nesting at one or two, at least at this point in the evolution of the lightweight process library.

An indication of the fragility of the protection provided by the lightweight process library is that I was able to crash a UNIX system by using the value 7,000 for the number of threads in program in example 6.4. (Having a program crash the operating system if there are more processes created than there are slots in the process table is not usual on modern UNIX systems.) The program is simple in concept; it uses threads to compute values in an array. The critical section of the program is the access to the array index. Access to the critical section is controlled by the monitor i_mon and the calls to the functions mon_enter(), mon_create(), and mon_exit(). Many of the other functions for lightweight processes were introduced in Chapter 5.

Example 6.4: One Solution to the Mutual Exclusion Problem Using Monitors

```
/* Example of a solution to a simple mutual-   */
/* exclusion problem for lightweight processes */
/* using monitors.                             */

#include <lwp/lwp.h>
#include <lwp/stackdep.h>
#include <stdio.h>

#define TIME_INTERVAL 16667
#define N_THREADS 4
struct timeval timeval = {0, 20 * TIME_INTERVAL};
static double arr[100];
static int i = 0;
double x = 0.0;
```

```
/* initialize the value of the monitor */
mon_t i_mon = { (caddr_t) 0, 0 };

void thread_func()
{
int temp;

while (1) /* do forever */
   {
   mon_enter(i_mon);
   if ( i < 100)
      {
      temp = i++;
      arr[temp] = temp/(1.0 + (double)temp) +
                 temp/(1 + (double) temp * 4.0);
      }
   else
      {
      mon_exit(i_mon);
      return;
      }
   } /* end while */
mon_exit(i_mon);
}       /* end function */


thread_t threads[N_THREADS];
int clients[N_THREADS];

main()
{
int i, j;

mon_create(&i_mon);
pod_setmaxpri(MINPRIO + 1);

/* block threads until all threads are created */
mon_enter(i_mon);

/* create threads, stacks */
```

```
for(j = 0; j < N_THREADS; j++)
    {
    lwp_create(&threads[j], thread_func, MINPRIO,
            0, (char * ) malloc(1000), 0);

    lwp_fpset(threads[j]);
    }

lwp_setpri(SELF, MINPRIO+1) ;

mon_exit(i_mon);

printf("\nNUMBER OF THREADS IS %d\n",
        lwp_enumerate (( thread_t* ) 0, 0) );

lwp_resched(MINPRIO);
lwp_sleep(&timeval);

/* print results to test correctness */
for (i = 0; i < 100; i++)
    {
    printf(" %f", arr[i]);
    if (( i% 5 ) == 4)
      printf("\n");
    }


/* clean up */
fflush(stdout);
for(j = 0; j < N_THREADS ; j++)
    lwp_destroy(threads[j]);

mon_destroy(i_mon);
lwp_destroy(SELF);
pod_exit(0);
}
```

The symbolic constant SELF stands for the thread itself. Information on the other symbols in the program can be found in the command reference manual for your system. Any tutorial for monitors will provide more information on this use of monitors and the other functions in the lightweight process library. Much of the code that uses lightweight processes and monitors is implementation-specific.

SUMMARY

Most modern UNIX systems use virtual memory, which is usually based on pages. Access to pages is often gained by means of a fixed size fast page array for a limited number of pages and a slower, indirect method for processes that use a larger number of pages. Page information is stored in a page table.

Pages are grouped into regions. There are four types of regions:

- Regions that are not being used
- Regions that contain shareable text
- Regions that have shareable data
- Private regions

Information about regions is stored in a region table.

Much of the essential information about processes is stored in entries in the process table. These entries are accessed by the process-id. Some of the information in the process table is used to schedule processes by an algorithm that attempts to maximize throughput using dynamically computed priorities.

UNIX systems often have two schedulers available to determine CPU use by user processes: the standard scheduler and a real-time scheduler. The scheduler used for a process can be changed by the `setscheduler()` system call.

Concurrency is a fundamental feature of UNIX. Two major problems that occur in concurrent systems are the reader-writer problem and the critical section problem. UNIX has several facilities to help solve these problems.

Many implementations of the lightweight process library include facilities to solve the critical section problem for lightweight processes. They use monitors in the manner described by Hoare (see references that follow).

REFERENCES

There are many references on concurrency. Perhaps the two most important are the original paper by Hoare on monitors and another on a method of writing and reasoning about concurrent processes.

Hoare, C. A. R. *Communicating Sequential Processes*. Englewood Cliffs, N. J.: Prentice-Hall International, 1985.

———. "Monitors: An Operating System Concept." *Communications of the ACM* 17 (October 1974): 549–557.

Little information is available on lightweight processes and monitors in book form.

The standard operating systems texts contain information about fundamental issues in concurrency. For example:

Deitel, H. *Operating Systems*. 2d ed. Reading, Mass.: Addison-Wesley, 1990.
Silberschatz, A., J. Peterson, and P. Galvin. *Operating Systems Concepts*. 3d ed. Reading, Mass.: Addison-Wesley, 1991.

EXERCISES

1. Describe the differences in system throughput produced by the real-time and standard schedulers for the following mix of processes:
   - All processes have intensive numerical computation.
   - All processes have access mainly to files on disk.
   - Most of the processes are computation-intensive, but several require immediate attention to certain external events.

2. Determine the standard scheduling algorithms for several different UNIX implementations. Can you determine why these algorithms differ? What is the relationship between clock speed and the CPU?

3. Design an experiment to determine the effect of the fast frame array on memory access. Implement this experiment and estimate the size of the fast frame array of your system.

4. Which data structures of the UNIX kernel must be protected by a solution to the critical section problem?

5. What is the maximum percentage of CPU usage a user process can have during a 1-minute period? Assume that the kernel will synchronize the buffer cache with the disk every 30 seconds.

6. Consider the high-level solution (given in Deitel) of the common problem in concurrent programming, given below. The four definitions refer to control conditions. Write a solution to this problem using the monitor facility available in your lightweight process library.

```
startread   - entered by reader who wishes to read
endread     - entered by reader who has finished reading
startwrite  - entered by writer who wishes to write
endwrite    - entered by writer who has finished writing

class readers_and_writers: monitor
   begin readercount:integer;
```

```
        busy: Boolean;
        OKtoread, OKtowrite:condition;
    procedure startread;
      begin
        if busy or OKtowrite.queue then OKtoread.wait;
        readercount := readercount + 1;
        OKtoread.signal;
        comment — Once one reader can start, they all can;
      end startread;
    procedure endread;
      begin
        readercount := readercount - 1;
        if readercount = 0 then OKtowrite.signal
      end endread;
    procedure startwrite;
      begin
        if readercount != 0 or busy then OKtowrite.wait
        busy := true
      end startwrite;
    procedure endwrite;
      begin
        busy := false;
        if OKtoread.queue then OKtoread.signal
                          else OKtowrite.signal
      end write;
    readercount := 0;
    busy := false;
end readers_and_writers;
```

7. Can exercise 6 be solved for lightweight processes with just the functions `mon_enter()`, `mon_exit()`, and `mon_create()`? Justify your answer.

8. There is no reason to assume that lightweight processes must live within the same UNIX process. Describe some of the difficulties that might arise when using lightweight processes that were created in different UNIX processes. Read a system manual to find out if this is allowed on your system.

## 7

Introduction to Interprocess Communication

We have already seen how processes are created and initialized in UNIX. This view was adequate for many situations, such as allowing processes of several different users to be executed at the same time. However, it is not adequate for multiple access to online databases, for connecting the output of one process to the input of another, or for many other instances in which information must be shared between processes.

Interprocess communication (ipc) is a means by which two or more processes can communicate either by data exchange or by signals for controlling the execution of certain processes. Such communication is typical of real-time systems. UNIX's standard scheduling algorithm prevents it from being a real-time operating system. Notwithstanding this, it has many ipc features that are appropriate for real-time systems. A real-time scheduling algorithm can enhance the efficiency of programs that use ipc mechanisms.

In this chapter we begin our discussion of ipc by describing in detail two of the mechanisms for allowing two or more UNIX processes to communicate. The discussion in this chapter is limited to ipc based on some form of files or on continuous flow methods such as pipes, FIFOs, and streams. In Chapter 8, we will describe more complex methods such as messages, semaphores, and shared memory. In Chapter 9, we will discuss signals, sockets, remote procedure calls, and process tracing. In Chapter 10, we will present a comparison of the various ipc methods and their relative efficiency. The discussion will be detailed because of the complexity of some of the data structures necessary for interprocess communication.

7.1   INTRODUCTION

In order to understand communication between processes, you must first understand the major features of processes and their scheduling. To ensure that you recall these features, we will repeat some of the information presented in Chapter 5.

A UNIX process can be created in only one way—using the `fork()` system call. The call to `fork()` creates a new process whose executable code is the same as that of the creating process. The executable code of this new process can be changed only by an `exec()` system call from within the thread of execution of the process itself.

Every UNIX process has an entry in a kernel data structure called the process table. The process table is accessed by the process-id, which is a unique integer assigned to the process on its creation. One field in a process table entry is a listing of all open file descriptors. A process gets a copy of all its parent's open file descriptors when it is created.

There is an upper limit to the number of processes that can be active in the system at any one time. This limit can be reset when the operating system is installed or upgraded, but is generally not modifiable during program execution.

The memory allocated to a UNIX process is considered to be broken up into three segments, each with a portion of memory assigned to it. The three segments associated with a process are the text, data, and stack segments.

The purpose of an `exec()` system call is to take a process and overwrite its text and data segments with those of some other executable file. The normal behavior of a data segment is to be modified only by the process that owns it after the data segment has been initialized by the exec that created it.

It would be helpful for you to review the material in Chapter 5 on processes, and the material in Chapter 6 on concurrency, to make sure that you understand them well before beginning the study of interprocess communication. We now turn to the study of ipc.

AT&T System V UNIX provides several ipc mechanisms, such as files, shared file pointers, FIFOs, messages, pipes, semaphores, signals, shared memory, and process tracing. Many of these mechanisms are available on other systems, for example Berkeley 4.3 UNIX, SunOS, Solaris, HP-UX, Ultrix, and Mach. Some changes included in Release 4 of System V UNIX affect the performance of programs that use ipc, including the streams mechanism. These changes are not generally portable. We will discuss process portability in Chapter 10. The ipc methods presented in this chapter are essentially portable.

Typically, ipc methods differ in the type and amount of information communicated between processes, ease of communication, reliability of communication, and efficiency. Each method has some applications for which it is well-suited and others for which it is not. By the end of this book, you will be able to determine an appropriate ipc method for a given application. You will also be able to code the appropriate method, at least in simple applications.

Some ipc methods are implemented more smoothly on other versions of UNIX. For example, Berkeley UNIX version 4.3 has more support for ipc using signals than did the earlier versions of AT&T System V UNIX, and signals in releases 1 and 2 of System V were not guaranteed to be atomic. Under the earlier versions, there was an interval between the time that a signal was sent to a process and the time that the signal-handling routine was entered. During this interval, the arrival of another signal caused a default action to be taken, namely, the termination of the receiving process.

The POSIX standard requires that signals be handled correctly. This solves the problem for System V Release 4, since it is POSIX-compliant, but it does not solve the problem for older systems. The proper method for implementation of certain ipc methods is still a matter of debate, as the papers by Kearns and Hemmendinger on the implementation of general semaphores, and the resulting collection of letters to the editor of the newsletter *Operating Systems Review,* suggest. Berkeley UNIX and System V Release 4 include an implementation of the socket mechanism that allows smooth communication between processes running on the same computer or on different computers on a network.

Portability is a major concern for programs that use ipc. The versions of UNIX based on BSD use sockets, which are more suitable than most of the other ipc methods for communication over a network.

Each of the major sections of this chapter and much of the next two chapters contain a high-level description of a particular ipc method and a sample of code used to implement the method. The ipc methods often require special system calls, which are discussed in detail. We will describe the use of ipc for the special case of two communicating processes. In some ipc methods, the two processes must be related as parent and child processes or as descendants of the same process. Requirements of relationships between communicating processes by ipc methods will be indicated as appropriate.

All ipc methods require the use of header files. In general, at least two header files are needed for each method. The file `ipc.h` is used for all ipc programs with the statement

```
#include <ipc.h>
```

or

```
#include <sys/ipc.h>
```

depending on the version of UNIX.

The contents of this file are octal constants that can be combined in any order using the bitwise OR operation. They refer to keys that are used by the user to determine unique ipc ids, which refer to specific entries in kernel data structures. The constants are interpreted as follows.

- `IPC_ALLOC` determines if an entry is already allocated.
- `IPC_CREAT` creates the entry if a key does not currently exist.
- `IPC_EXCL` indicates failure (return −1) if the key already exists.
- `IPC_NOWAIT` determines if the request must wait.
- `IPC_PRIVATE` specifies the key is to be private and not available to others.
- `IPC_RMID` removes the id.
- `IPC_SET` sets options.
- `IPC_STAT` installs all options.

Other include files that may be needed, depending on the ipc method used, are `sem.h`, `sema.h`, `signal.h`, `shm.h`, and `msg.h`.

One last point is in order. It seems obvious that shared memory will be faster than any other method because it requires no data transfer. As we will see later, shared memory is not easy to implement, and its use is limited on most machines. In Chapter 10, we present the approximate access costs of the various ipc methods relative to one another in terms of time. A software system designer will be able to use the results here as a guideline in the performance analysis of programs. A simpler method than shared memory is often appropriate if the performance can be estimated, if atomic actions are not necessary, and if ease of programming is a major goal.

7.2   FILES

The most common method of interprocess communication available under UNIX is communication by files. One process may write or make changes to a file that is required by another process. The processes do not have to be related to communicate. Unlike some of the other methods of interprocess communication, this one does not require ipc system calls. Thus, it allows portability over different UNIX systems. The only system calls used, other than the `fork()` and `exec()` system calls used to create the processes needed for this ipc method, concern file access and file operations.

However, this method of interprocess communication has disadvantages. Consider the case of one process reading from a single file and another process writing to the same file. Suppose that the file is in the directory /tmp since it was a temporary file. We intended to remove it after termination of the process. This organization constitutes an instance of the reader-writer problem. If one process writes messages to a file for another process to read, the reader process may be faster than the writer process, which may result in an error. Since the file continues to grow until communication is completed, the writer may attempt to write beyond the maximum file size. This will also result in an error.

When we ran an experiment to evaluate the efficiency of various ipc methods, we observed that the second error occurred frequently on an older Sun workstation running SunOS 3.6, because the space in the root file system often was filled by the temporary file created. One way of fixing this problem was to reconfigure the disk, changing the size of the root file system's portion of the disk partition. We followed the simpler approach and allowed the shared file to be in the directory /usr/tmp. The problem disappeared because there was a large amount of room in the /usr file system.

We will need to use the system call lseek(), which we met in Chapter 3. This system call has the syntax

```
long lseek(int fd, long offset,int arg)
```

and is used to adjust the file pointer position. The first argument is a file descriptor indicating the file to be used. The second argument is used in one of three ways, depending on the value of the third argument arg.

- If the value of arg is 0, the second argument is treated as an offset from the first byte of the file, which is considered to be at position 0.
- If the value of arg is 1, the current position of the file pointer is changed to the sum of the current file pointer and the value of the second argument (the value of offset).
- If the value of arg is 2, the current position of the file pointer is changed to the sum of the size of the file and the value of the second argument (the value of offset). The value of the second argument can be negative, as long as the value of the current file pointer remains nonnegative. A value of the current file pointer larger than the current size of the file is allowed, but the new bytes are not automatically initialized to NULL; this is the programmer's responsibility.

In our code given in example 7.1, we have used a value of 0 for arg. This means that the second argument is to be used as an offset from the first byte of the file. In effect, since the value of the second argument increases by a constant amount (the number of bytes specified as a command-line argument) each time, the file pointer is kept so that we write to the file at the end of the file and the size of the file will grow at a constant rate.

The file ipc program has the structure of a main program that forks. The parent process then execs a new process called `writefile`, while the child execs a process called `readfile`. The two processes (parent and child) now execute the writing and reading. They read and write a common file whose full pathname is "`/tmp/sh_file`."

Notice that the code uses the

```
O_RDONLY
```

`flag` argument on the reader process and the

```
O_WRONLY|O_APPEND|O_CREAT
```

as part of the `flag` argument on the writer. This says that the reader process opens the file with permissions to read only, and that the writer process can write only, appending the data to the end of the file, and can create the file if it does not already exist prior to the call to `open()`. The `flag` argument is the bitwise OR of these three constants with the octal value 0666, which indicates that the read and write permissions are set for the owner, the owner's group, and others.

The reader process exits when there is no more data to be read. The writer process waits for a signal from the reader (which was the child process) before terminating. This signaling is done by the `wait()` system call. Note that we did not need to hardcode the name of the file, but could have passed it instead as a command-line argument. We chose not to do so for consistency of user interface with the other ipc programs that follow. Note also that the reader and writer processes could each work correctly without the main program, whose only purpose is to create and initialize the child processes.

The code for file ipc is presented in examples 7.1, 7.2, and 7.3. Since it is our first experiment on ipc that explicitly uses the names of the newly created reader and writer processes, some comments on style are in order. The main program uses two command-line arguments that represent the number of bytes per communication and the number of repetitions. Therefore, we can experiment on the use of two variables when evaluating the performance of an ipc method. We can change the number of times the two processes are to communicate with one another and keep constant the number of bytes of information communicated each time. Alternatively, we can fix the number of times that information is conveyed between processes and vary the number of bytes communicated each time.

The command-line arguments are read in as text and are converted to integer by the C function `atoi()`. A check is made for the correct number of command-line arguments, and if there are not at least three, the program exits. Excess command-line arguments are ignored. Note the use of error messages if a system call fails. We have not bothered to use the variable errno and the function perror( ), since the causes of error are obvious here.

Example 7.1: Main Program for File ipc

```
/*  Program communicates from parent process to its */
/*  child through the use of files.                  */

#include <stdio.h>
main( int argc, char *argv[])
{
    if (argc < 3)
        {
        fputs("Usage: file_ipc num_messages, bytes", stderr);
        exit(1);
        }

    /* create processes and begin communication */
    switch ( fork() )
        {
        case -1: fputs("Error in fork", stderr);
            exit(1);
        case 0:
            if(execl("readfile","readfile", argv[1],argv[2],
                        NULL) ==-1)
                fputs("Error in exec in child", stderr);
            exit(1); /* only get here if exec fails */
        default
            if(execl("writefile","writefile",argv[1],argv[2],
                    NULL) ==-1)
                fputs("Error in exec in parent", stderr);
            exit(1); /* only get here if exec fails */
        } /* end switch */
}
```

Example 7.2: Reader Process for File ipc

```
/**********************************************/
/* Reader process for reading of shared file */
```

```c
#include <stdio.h>
#include <fcntl.h>
#define MAXBYTES 4096
main( int argc, char *argv[])
{
    int fd;
    long i;
    char message[MAXBYTES];
    int nbytes, number_of_messages;
    int j;

    number_of_messages = atoi(argv[1]);
    nbytes = atoi(argv[2]);
    /* Check for maximum byte size */
    if (nbytes > MAXBYTES)
        {
        fputs("Max bytes/message is 4096", stderr);
        exit(1);
        }


    /* Read messages from shared file */
    for (i=0; i<number_of_messages; i++)
        {
        /* Open and read next data from shared file */
        while ((fd= open("/usr/tmp/sh_file",O_RDONLY)) == -1)
                ;
        lseek(fd,i*nbytes*1L,0);
        while ((read(fd,message,nbytes)) == 0)
          ;
        close(fd);
        }      /* end for loop */
    exit(0);
}
```

Example 7.3: Writer Process for File ipc

```c
/***************************************************/
/* Writer process for communication via a shared file */
#include <stdio.h>
#include <fcntl.h>
#define MAXBYTES 4096
```

```
main( int argc, char *argv[]}
{
int fd;
int i, j, status, message_num;
int number_of_messages, nbytes;
char message[MAXBYTES];
number_of_messages = atoi(argv[1]);
nbytes = atoi(argv[2]);
/* Check for maximum byte size */
if (nbytes > MAXBYTES)
        {
        fputs("Number of bytes too large",stderr);
        exit(1);
        }
    /* Write messages to shared file */
    for (i=1; i<=number_of_messages; i++)
        {
        /* Create message with nbytes */
        message_num = itoa(i,message);
        for (j = message_num; j < nbytes; j++)
            message[j] = 'd';
        /* Open and write to shared file */
        while ((fd = open("/usr/tmp/sh_file",
                    O_WRONLY|O_APPEND|O_CREAT,0666)) ==-1)
            fputs ("Can't open for writing",stderr);
        write(fd, message, nbytes);
        close(fd);
        }

    wait(&status);
    system("rm /usr/tmp/d_shared_file");
}
```

As indicated before, this program uses the wait() system call, which we met in Chapter 5 and will discuss in detail in Chapter 9. For now, just note that this system call stops the parent process from proceeding until it gets the information that the child process has terminated.

7.3   SHARED FILE POINTERS

Another method of interprocess communication involves the use of shared file pointers. This method of ipc is implemented by one process positioning a file pointer to a location in a file, and a second process reading or writing to or from the same file at that communicated position. The major problem with this form of ipc is the synchronization of the reading and writing. For example, if the reader reads before the writer writes, the program will terminate with an error.

There is another problem with the general use of shared file pointers: Only related processes can share file pointers. For this reason, communication using shared file pointers is rarely used if speed is essential and any other methods are available.

It is important to understand this limitation on the processes that can share a common file pointer. They must be related, and the common file pointer must be available to each. If the two processes are parent and child, the shared file pointer must refer to a file that is opened in the parent process before the child process is created. This way, the child can share the parent's file pointer, since a child process always inherits the parent's open file descriptors. If the child is created before the parent process opens the file, the two processes can access the same file only by using different file pointers.

This method of shared file pointers differs from the file method presented in the previous section in that the file pointer was always at the end of the file so that the data was appended to the file; this was the result of setting the O_APPEND flag in the writer process. Again, the name of the file was hardcoded instead of being passed as a command-line argument. It could also have been passed as a file descriptor if the two processes had been related. The shared file pointer was changed using the fseek() function.

This ipc method was extremely slow because of the need to move the shared file pointer and to synchronize the file operations. Some of the code to synchronize the two processes is based on the simulation of semaphores using the creat() system call. This synchronization code is similar to the code in the section on file descriptors in Chapter 3.

The code for ipc using shared file pointers is given in examples 7.4, 7.5, 7.6, and 7.7.

Example 7.4: Main Program for Shared File ipc

```
/*                                                      */
/* This is the main program for shared file ipc.        */
/* Communication uses shared file pointers.             */
/*                                                      */

#include <stdio.h>
#include <fcntl.h>
#define MAXBYTES 4096
```

```c
/* function prototype for simulation of semaphore action */
void semaphore_simulate(void);


main( int argc, char *argv[])
{
    FILE *fp;
    char message[MAXBYTES];
    long i;
    int message_num, nbytes, j, number_of_messages;
    int sid;
    int status;

    if (argc < 3)
        {
        fputs("Bad arg count",stderr);
        fputs("Usage:num_messages num_bytes", stderr);
        exit(1);
        }
    number_of_messages = atoi(argv[1]);
    nbytes = atoi(argv[2]);
    /* Check for maximum byte size */
    if (nbytes > MAXBYTES)
        {
        fputs("Number of bytes exceeds maximum",stderr);
        exit(1);
        }
    /* Open file before creating second process. This is
    necessary */
    /* for the two processes to share a common file
        pointer */
    else if ((fp = fopen("/usr/tmp/d_shared_file","w+")) ==
    NULL)
        {
        fputs("Can't open for writing", stderr);
        exit(1);
        }
    /* create processes and begin communication */
    switch ( fork() )
        case -1:
                fputs("Error in fork", stderr);
                exit(1);
```

```
    case 0:
        sleep(2);
        if (execl("readfile","readfile",argv[1],
                        argv[2], NULL) ==-1)
            fputs("Error in exec in child", stderr);
        exit(1); /* only get here if exec fails */
    default:
        if (execl("writefile","writefile",argv[1],
                        argv[2], NULL) ==-1)
        fputs("Error in exec in parent", stderr);
        exit(1); /* only get here if exec fails */
    }  /* end switch */
}    /* end main */
/*****************************************/
```

Example 7.5: Semaphore Simulation for Shared File ipc

```
/*****************************************/
#include <stdio.h>
void semaphore_simulation(void)
{
if (creat("creation",0444) == -1)
{
   fputs("Error in create",stderr);
   system("rm creation");
   }
else
   fputs("No error in creation",stderr);
}
/*****************************************/
```

Example 7.6: Reader Process for Shared File ipc

```
/**********************************************/
/**********************************************/
/* reader process */
#include <stdio.h>
#include <fcntl.h>
#define MAXBYTES 4096

/* function prototype for simulation of semaphore action */
void semaphore_simulate(void);
```

```
main( int argc, char *argv[])
{
    FILE *fp;
    char message[MAXBYTES];
    long i;
    int message_num, nbytes, j, number_of_messages;
    int sid;
    int status;

    /* Read messages from the shared file */
    for (i=0; i<number_of_messages; i++)
       {
       semaphore_simulation();
       fseek(fp,i*nbytes*1L,0);
       while ((fgets(message,nbytes+1,fp)) == NULL);
          fseek(fp,i*nbytes*1L,0);
       semaphore_simulation();
       }
    exit(0);
}
```

Example 7.7: Writer Process for Shared File ipc

```
/*****************************************************/
/*****************************************************/
/* writer process */
/* Communicate using shared file pointers */
#include <stdio.h>
#include <fcntl.h>
#define MAXBYTES 4096

/* function prototype for simulation of semaphore action */
void semaphore_simulate(void);

main( int argc, char *argv[])
{
    FILE *fp;
    char message[MAXBYTES];
    long i;
    int message_num, nbytes, j, number_of_messages;
    int sid;
```

```
    int status;

    /* Write messages to file */
    for (i=0; i<=number_of_messages; i++)
      {
      /* Create message with specified number of bytes */
      message_num = itoa(i+1,message);
      for(j=message_num; j<nbytes;j++)
      message[j] = 'd';
      /* Use semaphore to control synchronization */
      /* Write to end of file */
      semaphore_simulation();
      fseek(fp,0L,2);
      while ((fputs(message,fp))==-1)
          fputs("Can't write message", stderr);
      fseek(fp,0L,2);
      semaphore_simulation();
      }
    wait(&status);

    /* remove file used for semaphore simulation      */
    /* and shared data file after end of communication */
    unlink("creation");
    unlink("/usr/tmp/sh_file");
    fclose(fp);
}
```

The code in examples 7.4, 7.5, 7.6, and 7.7 has a few new features. We have created a new function called semaphore_simulation() in order to illustrate the action of a semaphore function. Such a function would prevent any processing from taking place until the file "creation" was removed by the other process. In a program to use shared file pointers, we would not simulate this action because of the added time it would take and because we would certainly use the more efficient method of semaphores we will meet in Chapter 8.

(Source code for this use of semaphores is included in the optional disk available from the publisher in the directory named SH_FP_SE of the code for Chapter 7.)

We also used the system call sleep(), which takes an integer argument and delays the process for a time that is at least as long as the number of seconds indicated in the argument. (It may delay longer since the process cannot predict what time the CPU scheduling algorithm will select for this process to access the CPU.) The purpose of this system call was to prevent the child process from accessing a file that may not have been created when the child wanted access. On several occasions, some data was lost when the code was run without this system call.

The difficulty here is that the parent's request for file creation may not have been carried out before the child's request. We placed the request to create the file in the parent's code before the child was created to have all the parent's open file descriptors available to the child. Yet it seems that there might be some difficulty. How is this possible?

The answer is that placing a data file on a disk is not an instantaneous operation. A write request normally sends the request from the data segment of a user's process to the buffer cache in the kernel. If there is no file created on disk when the kernel's request to write to the file is executed, data will be lost. The purpose of the `sleep()` call is to eliminate the possibility of data loss at the beginning of the program.

This data loss can occur because there may be a process switch between the statement to open the file for reading and the statement to move the file pointer to the end of the file so that data can be appended. The pair of statements does not form an atomic operation. Thus, the exact state of the data in the output file can vary in unpredictable ways with certain relationships between the execution of these two statements and the kernel's process scheduling algorithm, if some other process accesses the same output file.

You may not observe this data loss when you run this program, because the timing or scheduling algorithm is different on your system and there are only two processes accessing the same file. However, defensive programming is always a good idea.

There is another solution to this problem of possible data loss if the child's request for a read is executed before the parent's creation of the file. It involves the use of the flag O_SYNC as part of the argument to the call to `open()` in the child, or reader, process. The O_SYNC flag ensures that the file is not created until the first attempt at a physical write.

7.4   PIPES

We now continue our discussion of interprocess communication. The methods that we use here follow the model of the reader-writer problem in the sense that there is a process that sends a flow of information and a process that receives information. There may be one or more intermediate steps within the information flow.

Pipes are the simplest, most elegant UNIX solution to the reader-writer problem. The idea is that the output of one process (the writer) is sent directly to the input of the other process (the reader). If the reader is ready for data but the writer is not ready to supply any, the reader is suspended until the writer provides data. If the writer wishes to send data to its output, but either the reader is not ready or the buffer used to aid synchronization of the processes is temporarily full, then the writer is suspended until the situation improves. Compare this strategy with the high-level algorithm that was presented in Chapter 6 for the solution of the reader-writer problem.

Both the buffer and the code to handle the blocking of the reader process when the buffer is empty, or the blocking of the writer process when the buffer is full, are provided naturally with pipes. The size of the buffer is no less than 4 KB, which is at least twice the size of a typical page for many computer virtual memory organizations.

Pipes can be handled easily at the shell level. The two processes are simply connected by the pipe (|) symbol, as in the simple example

```
ls | wc
```

which sends the output of the ls command directly to the input of the wc command. The shell automatically pairs up file descriptor 1 of the ls process (standard output) to file descriptor 0 of the wc process (standard input). Since the shell has forked a copy of itself and is aware of the process-ids of its children, matching the file descriptors is easy.

Programming pipes for communicating information between processes other than at the shell level is not especially difficult. However, it does require that the two processes be able to communicate their file descriptors. The only easy way of doing this is to use processes that are related, such as parent and child or siblings of a common parent.

Pipes are a solution to the synchronization problem that occurred when we used files and shared file pointers. They allow the use of the file system for temporary data storage. A pipe is not a file, although it has an i-node. Using pipes for interprocess communication restricts implementation to related processes, since file descriptors for pipes are inherited from the parent process in which the pipe is created. The pipe() system call creates a file descriptor that permits reads only after a write has been performed.

The syntax of the pipe() system call is

```
int pipe(int fd);
```

where the argument fd is the file descriptor that is to be passed to the process using the fork. Note that the file descriptor is opened in the parent process before the child is created. We can be sure that the parent and child share the same file descriptor, since a child always inherits all open file descriptors from its parent.

As mentioned earlier, the processes must be related, which may be too constraining for some applications. In fact, a pipe cannot be set up between two arbitrary processes after the processes have been created. Instead, it must be created in one process, and the other process must be a child process so that it inherits the pipe's file descriptors from the parent.

On many computer systems running derivatives of Berkeley 4.3 UNIX or SVR4, pipes are implemented using sockets.

There is one final observation about pipes. The reads and writes are not guaranteed to be atomic operations if there is more than a single byte of data. It is possible that we might have read or write interrupted. This is not a problem with a single reader process and single writer process, since the data is in the output buffer of the writer process until read by the reader process.

This prohibits the use of pipes when there are multiple readers and writers. A solution to a many-reader, one-or-more-writer problem, with multiple processes wishing to read from one or more writers, will not work with the UNIX pipe mechanism because of the lack of atomicity. Note that this lack of atomicity of pipes is an example of a failure of a solution to the critical section problem in the instance of a multiple-reader, single-writer problem.

The code for a solution to the reader-writer problem using pipes is presented in examples 7.8 and 7.9. Note that the reader and writer processes use the `read()` and `write()` system calls in the same way they are used in writing to and reading from files. Since pipes are not files but are assigned i-nodes temporarily, the use of file descriptors in this program makes sense.

To emphasize the requirement that the two processes at the ends of a `pipe()` system call be related, we will give the code for this pipe example (examples 7.8 and 7.9) in the form of a parent process that writes the data to a child process that reads it at the end of the pipe.

Example 7.8: Main Program Using Pipes

```
/*************************************************************/
/*        Purpose:   This program implements communication
 *                   using pipes.  This is the parent
 *                   process which can send a variable
 *                   number of messages of different bytes
 *        Input:     The program takes the following arguments:
```

```
*                     1). number of messages
*                     2). number of bytes in messages
*********************************************************/

#include <stdio.h>
main( int argc, char *argv[])
{
    int pfd[2], nread, i;
    char fdstr[10];        /* character string for file
    descriptor */
    char strg1[500];       /* storage for message */
    int loop;              /* number of messages */
    int bytes;             /* number of messages */


    loop = atoi(argv[1]);  /* convert argument to number */
    bytes = atoi(argv[2]); /* convert argument to number */
    if (pipe(pfd) == -1)    /* create pipe */
        fputs("pipe".stderr);

    switch (fork()) /* create child process */
    {
    case -1:
        fputs("Error in fork",stderr);
        exit(1);
    case 0:
        if (close(pfd[1] == -1 ))
            fputs("Error in close",stderr);

        /* convert number to character */
        sprintf(fdstr, "%d", pfd[0]);
        if (execlp("./childp","childp", fdstr, argv[1], NULL)
                        == -1)
            fputs("Error in exec",stderr);
        break ;
    default:
        /* creating message */
        for (i=0; i <= bytes; i++)
            strg1[i] = 'a';
        /* sending message */
```

```
        for (i=0; i < loop; i++)
            if (write(pfd[1], strg1, sizeof(strg1)) == -1)
                fputs("Error in write",stderr);


        } /* end switch */
} /* end main */
```

Example 7.9: Child Process Receiving Data from Pipe

```
/****************************************************/
/* Purpose: This is the child process executed      */
/* as the receiver of the communication test        */
/* using pipes.                                      */
/*                                                   */
/****************************************************/
#include <stdio.h>
main( int argc, char *argv[])
{
    int fd, nread, i;
    int loop;
    char s[500];

    fd = atoi(argv[1]);    /* convert file desc to an int */
    loop = atoi(argv[2]); /* convert num_loops to an int */
for (i=0; i < loop; i++)
    {
    switch(nread = read(fd, s, sizeof(s)))
    {
    case -1:
        fputs("Error in read".stderr);
        exit(1);
    default:
        printf("read %d bytes: %s n", nread, s);
    } /* end switch */
    } /* end for loop */
}   /* end main */
```

Note the use of the character string `fdstr` to hold the information about the open file descriptor. We used `sprintf()` because command-line arguments must be in the form of character strings.

7.5   **FIFOs/NAMED PIPES**

In the previous section, we learned about pipes as an ipc method. Pipes are relatively simple to code and are even available directly from the shell. As an ipc method, pipes have two failings: They require the reader and writer to be related, and they are not atomic, making them unsuitable as an ipc method with more than two processes. The related ipc method of FIFOs, or named pipes, was developed to address these deficiencies.

A FIFO (or named pipe) exists as a special file, and thus any process with appropriate permissions can open it for reading and writing. That is, FIFOs may be used to create pipes between unrelated processes. Processes use the `open()` system call for named pipes, whereas the `pipe()` system call is used to create an unnamed pipe.

Unlike regular pipes, atomicity is guaranteed for FIFOs. The guarantee of atomicity means that either rollbacks to the beginning of the reading of data chunks, or blocking of processes until the affected read or write can be completed, are likely to take place frequently when reading large amounts of data from FIFOs. Hence, the time for ipc should be slower for FIFOs than for regular pipes. Note that the bytes that are written or read via a single system call are always contiguous, allowing both multiple readers and writers. Otherwise, communication using FIFOs is the same as that when pipes are used.

The code for ipc using FIFOs is given in examples 7.10 and 7.11. Note that the FIFO is created with the system call `mknod()`, which sets up an i-node for the process. Any process can now have access to the FIFO by means of its name, assuming the permissions allow it. The name is created via the C function `strcpy()`, which you can use as a template for creation of unique FIFO names. You may also wish to use the UNIX utility function `makekey()`. Note also the use of `read()` and `write()`.

The system call `mknod()` is used with three arguments. The first argument is the name that is attached to the i-node. The next argument is computed as the logical OR of the two constants `S_FIFO` and `0666`. The first constant, `S_FIFO`, indicates that the type of the i-node is a FIFO and that this is to be treated as a special file. (These constants can be found in the header file `fcntl.h`.) The permissions are given in the third argument, `0666`, which means that the permissions on this file are read and write by anyone. The third argument is a device number. It should be 0 except for a block or character special file.

Example 7.10: Parent Process for FIFO ipc

```
/* Parent process for FIFO ipc. The FIFO is set    */
/* up here.                                         */
```

```c
#include <stdio.h>
#include <fcntl.h>
#include <ctype.h>
#include <sys/types.h>
#include <sys/errno.h>
#include <sys/stat.h>
#define MAXBYTES 20

main( int argc, char *argv[])
{
    int fd, nread, i;
    char fifo[20];
    char strg1[500];
    int loop;
    int bytes;
    int pid, status;
    extern int errno;

    if (argc != 3)
      {
      fprintf(stderr,"USAGE: fifoparent number bytes\n");
      exit(1);
      }

    strcpy(fifo, "/usr/tmp/fifo1");
    loop = atoi(argv[1]);
    bytes = atoi(argv[2]);

    /* Make sure that no file exists with the name fifo.*/
    unlink(fifo);

    if (mknod(fifo, S_FIFO | 0666, 0) == -1 )
      {
      perror("mknod");
      exit(1);
      }

    if((pid = fork()) == 0)
      {
      if (execlp("fiforec","fiforec",argv[1],argv[2],0)
         == -1)
          {
```

```
                perror("execlp");
                exit(1);
                }
            }
        if ((fd = open(fifo, O_WRONLY )) == -1)
          {
          perror("open");
          exit(1);
          }

        for(i=0; i < bytes; i++)
            strg1[i] = 'a';
        strg1[bytes] = ' ';
        for (i=0; i < loop; i++)
            {
            if (write(fd, strg1, sizeof(strg1)) == -1)
                {
                perror("execlp");
                exit(1);
                }
            }
        wait(&status);

        /* clean up */
        if (unlink(fifo) < 0)
          perror("unlink");
}
```

Example 7.11: Child Process for FIFO ipc

```
/* Child process for FIFO ipc.                          */

#include <stdio.h>
#include <fcntl.h>
#include <ctype.h>
#include <sys/types.h>
#include <sys/errno.h>
#include <sys/stat.h>


main(int argc, char *argv[])
{
```

```
int fd, nread, i;
char fifo[30];
char strg1[500];
int loop;
int bytes;
extern int errno;

strcpy(fifo, "/usr/tmp/fifo1");
loop = atoi(argv[1]);
if ((mknod(fifo, S_FIFO | 0666, 0) == -1) && (errno !=
EEXIST) )
    {
    fputs("Error in making fifo",stderr);
    exit(1);
    }
if ((fd = open(fifo, O_RDONLY| O_NDELAY)) == -1)
    {
    fputs("Error in receive FIFO",stderr);
    exit(1);
    }
for (i=0; i < loop; i++)
    while (read(fd, strg1, sizeof(strg1)) > 0)
        ;
} /* end main */
```

7.6   STREAMS

There are some changes in interprocess communication in System V Release 4 and the related, newer operating systems such as Solaris. The STREAMS package has been extended and can apply to single-CPU or networked systems. We have looked briefly at some UNIX device drivers. The STREAMS mechanism provides a two-directional communications path between two processes or between processes and devices. It allows the insertion or deletion of some of the kernel's modules within a data path set up by a user process, without rebuilding the kernel.

STREAMS are essentially a faster implementation of pipes and FIFOs. They generally use the pipe() system call in the case of an unnamed or anonymous pipe, or the mknod() system call in the case of a FIFO or named pipe, for the creation of these objects.

A STREAM is a path between a so-called "STREAMS driver" in kernel space and a user process in user space. In a STREAM, a user process requests kernel services, including:

- A STREAM HEAD
- Zero or more optional STREAMS modules
- A STREAMS driver
- An external interface to a device or a "pseudo-device" (See the configuration file on your system for information on pseudo-devices.)

A STREAMS driver converts data from a STREAM to and from data structures used by the device.

A STREAMS module is a set of kernel routines and data structures used to process data, status, and control information. A module can add or delete header and packet information if a network is used, or convert the information to another format (for any system). Every STREAMS module interacts only with those modules directly connected to it.

In SVR3, pipes and the `tty` subsystem did not use the STREAMS interface, but most other device drivers did. In SVR4, all character-based I/O uses STREAMS.

There are several system calls for SVR4 programs that use STREAMS. Many of them are familiar.

- `open()` creates a STREAM between user a data space and a device driver.
- `pipe()` creates a STREAM pipe for ipc.
- `mknod()` creates a named STREAM pipe for ipc.
- `ioctl()` controls a stack of STREAMS modules, including file descriptor passing.
- `poll()` detects events on a STREAM.
- `write()` writes data to a STREAM.
- `read()` reads data from a STREAM.
- `putmsg()` sends data and control messages down a STREAM.
- `getmsg()` receives data and control messages from a STREAM.
- `mount()` attaches a STREAM pipe to a file system point.
- `close()` closes a STREAM.

The use of STREAMS in SVR4 leads to several improvements in the perfomance and ease of use of some ipc methods. For example:

- It avoids blocking on `read()` or `write()`, using the `poll()` system call to detect data arrival or CLEAR_TO_SEND.
- It can detect data arriving on the pipe by having the kernel, not the user process, generate a signal when data arrives.
- It can push and pop STREAMS modules to and from a stack to enhance user formatting of data.

- Using ioctl(), it can send an open file descriptor from one process to another along the pipe.
- It can send normal or control data using putmsg() and getmsg(). It also indicates ranges of good data and sends "out-of-band" data.
- It can attach a STREAM to one end of a pipe.

The advantage of polling is the following. Suppose that we have two processes using a pipe to communicate. Considered by themselves, the writer process produces data, and the writer process reads the data, with blocking of the writer if the pipe is full and blocking of the reader if the pipe is empty. There is a performance problem if, for example, the writer process has more time left on its CPU time slice but is blocked because the pipe is full. The writer process is entitled to the CPU for the remainder of its time slice, but no processing can take place. A similar performance problem can occur for the reader process.

The unavailability of the pipe to the writer because it is full, or the unavailability of the pipe to the reader because it is empty, is significant. If we allow the writer process to communicate an event to indicate that the pipe is blocked, then we can allow the more efficient scheduling of CPU time.

Since STREAMS modules are in the kernel, they can use other kernel resources, and lower-level processes can dynamically control kernel processes.

SUMMARY

The simplest methods of interprocess communication (ipc) involve the use of files or pipes. Interprocess communication between files can be carried out either with separate file pointers for the files or with a single shared file pointer for each process.

Pipes are a simple method of ipc that uses an automatically controlled buffer. They allow the reading process to block if no data is ready to be read, and the writer process to be blocked if the buffer is full. Pipes require that the reader and writer process be related so that they can share a file descriptor.

FIFOs are similar to pipes in their use of buffers. They can be referred to by name so that unrelated processes can use the same FIFO. Writing of data to FIFOs is an atomic operation, as is reading data from them; thus, FIFOs are safer than pipes for multiple readers or writers.

STREAMS are a feature of SVR4 that improves the performance of several pipe and FIFO operations.

REFERENCES

Hemmendinger, D. "A Correct Implementation of General Semaphores." *Operating Systems Review* 22 (1988): 46–48.

Ritchie, D. M. "A Stream Input-Output System." *Bell Laboratory Systems Technical Journal* 63 (October 1984): 1897–1910.

Peacock, J. "Gently Down the STREAMS." *UNIX Review* 9 (September 1992): 33–38.

EXERCISES

1. Describe the differences between shared and nonshared file pointers in interprocess communication.

2. Would there have been a need for the `sleep()` system call if we had placed the code of the writer process in the body of the parent process instead of execing this code in the parent in example 7.4? Explain.

3. Encode the desired synchronization operations that were simulated in the function `semaphore_simulation()`. Write the code for two functions: one to get a semaphore and keep it until the process that created the file wishes to release it, and another to release a semaphore so that another process can use it. (This exercise will be easier to do later in this book.)

4. Can file descriptors be used in the file ipc examples without the use of file pointers? Explain your answer.

5. What effect should the STREAMS implementation have upon the performance of pipes? Design and implement an experiment to determine the correctness of your answer.

6. Before the ready availability of computer networks, terminals attached to a remote mainframe usually shared a common line from the mainframe to a multiplexer, or terminal concentrator, which separated the data from the mainframe into a large number of separate channels from the multiplexer to the individual terminals. Describe an appropriate use of the `poll()` feature of STREAMS in this situation.

7. A feature of SVR4 is record locking, which provides some degree of protection for data shared by several processes. Devise and implement an experiment to determine the overhead of incorporating record locking in an ipc program.

8. Rewrite the file ipc experiment code for both separate and shared file pointers to have more than two reader processes and a single writer

process. Test your code carefully and determine if there are any "race conditions."

9. Rewrite the file ipc experiment code for both separate and shared file pointers to have more than two writer processes and a single reader process. Test your code carefully and determine if there are any "race conditions."

## 8

The System V IPC Package

In this chapter we consider three methods of interprocess communication that are often grouped together in what is known as the System V IPC Package. These methods are: messages, semaphores, and shared memory. This package is a standard feature of UNIX systems based on some release of System V, and it is often available on other UNIX systems as a special option to be included in the UNIX kernel.

8.1   INTRODUCTION

Each of the three methods of ipc that make up the System V IPC package we describe in this chapter requires the use of special kernel resources. The kernel resources needed for the System V IPC package are message queues, semaphore data structures, and shared memory regions.

The three methods follow the same paradigm:

- Get the resource.
- Operate on the resource.
- Control the resource.

It is easy to determine if the System V IPC package is installed as part of the UNIX kernel on your system. The `ipcs` utility shows the current usage of the appropriate kernel resources. The user can remove unused kernel resources for these ipc facilities with the related utility `ipcrm`.

Messages, semaphores, and shared memory are not immediately available in systems based on Berkeley UNIX. For example, in many of the earlier versions of SunOS, the UNIX kernel had to be reconfigured to accept the options `IPCMESSAGE`, `IPCSEMAPHORE`, and `IPCSHMEM` before several of the ipc programs would work. Later versions of this system allow the easier incorporation of all the System V IPC package.[*]

Each of the ipc methods studied in this chapter is persistent in the sense that the resource used by the method will remain as a kernel data structure even after the process that created the resource terminates. Thus, errors in programming with the methods can take up available slots in the kernel and make it impossible for other processes to use any of these limited resources. The `ipcrm` utility can help to clean up the unused resources if there are not too many. It is better to make sure that the programs always clean up after they complete execution.

The ipc methods in the System V IPC package are complex, and they have interesting interfaces between kernel data structures and user programs. We will describe each of these methods in detail and provide code using these methods for a software solution of the reader-writer problem discussed in Chapter 6.

8.2   MESSAGES

The System V IPC package includes message queues. Messages allow processes to send formatted data streams to arbitrary processes. They can be of different types, and any process with appropriate permissions can receive messages from a queue. The paradigm for message operations is the standard one for the System V IPC package: Get the resource, control it, and operate on it. Messages can be formatted in their structure rather than in an application process that uses them. Note also that pipes and FIFOs send streams of data between processes, with no other organization.

Messages are the ipc method of choice for many applications and environments, including several parallel computers. They are well-suited to many transaction-based applications. The Intel hypercubes, for example, use a message-based system for communicating information between processes. Messages as long as .5 MB can be sent from one processor to another in this system. The syntax is similar to that of System V messages, with additional fields for specifying processors as well as processes.

The concept of using messages for ipc is thus quite general. However,

---

[*]Many applications use the System V IPC package. Use of the `ipcs` utility is explained in the installation instructions for the ADS software for processing image data, which is available from NASA. The installer must run the command `ipcs -m` to determine the availability of shared memory on his or her system.

having a portable *concept* does not necessarily mean that its implementation is portable. Even if the system has the ipc facility for sending messages, programs using System V message queues are generally not portable because of differences in the message data structure. Fortunately, the changes needed to port programs that use messages for ipc are generally straightforward.

There are four system calls for messages:

- `msgget()` returns (and possibly creates) a message descriptor that designates a message queue for use in other system calls.
- `msgctl()` has options to set and return parameters associated with a message descriptor and an option to remove descriptors.
- `msgsnd()` sends a message via a message queue.
- `msgrcv()` receives a message via a message queue.

8.2.1   The `msgget()` System Call

The purpose of the `msgget()` system call is to take its primary argument, the `key`, and its second argument, a `flag`, to return an integer called a `queue_id`. The `queue_id` returned by a successful call to `msgget()` is an index into the kernel's message queue data structure table. The system call returns –1 if there is an error.

The system call `msgget()`, whose syntax is

```
int msgget(key_t key, int flag);
```

gets the resource (a message queue).

The type `key_t` of the first argument is defined in the include file `sys/types.h` as being of type long; the definition is made using a C language `typedef` construction, which is consistent with much of the older code using messages in which the type of `key_t` is declared as long.

The second argument comprises allowable flags, such as

- `MSG_R`   The process has read permission on the message queue.
- `MSG_W`   The process has write permission on the message queue.
- `MSG_RWAIT`   A reader is waiting to read a message from the message queue.
- `MSG_WWAIT`   A writer is waiting to place a message on the message queue.
- `MSG_LOCKED`   The message queue is locked.
- `MSG_LOCKWAIT`   The message queue is waiting for a lock.

and the flags `IPC_EXCL` and `IPC_NOWAIT`, which we described in Chapter 7. Several of these options may be combined into the same flag by using the bitwise OR operation.

The proper determination of the key argument can be a tricky business. It is important to have the reader and writer of a message queue use the same message queue so that they each know the same `queue_id`. The key can be kept relatively private by using the `makekey()` function, which is commonly used for data encryption as the key argument. For simple programs, it is probably sufficient to use the process-id of the creator process (assuming that the other processes wishing to access the message queue know this number) or even to hardcode the key argument as a particular constant.

An internal algorithm of the kernel attempts to translate the key into a `queue_id`. It does this in several stages. If the key is not currently used in a message queue data structure in the kernel, and the flag argument includes the bits of both the appropriate permissions and either `IPC_CREAT` or `IPC_EXCL`, then a new entry in the kernel's message queue data structure table is made by the `msgget()` system call. If the key is already in use in the kernel's message queue data structure table, an error occurs unless the `IPC_CREAT` bits are set.

The access permissions for the ipc methods in the System V ipc package are stored in the ipc permissions structure, which is a simple table.

Entries in the kernel's message queue data structure table are C structures with several fields, including permissions, size of the queue, and some additional information about the messages in the queue.

```
/* MESSAGE QUEUE DATA STRUCTURE */
struct msqid_ds
    {
    struct ipc_perm msg_perm;    /* Permission struct. */
    struct msg      *msg_first;  /* Pointer to first
                                    message.*/
    struct msg      *msg_last;   /* Pointer to last
                                    message. */
    ushort          msg_cbytes;  /* Number of bytes on
                                    queue */
    ushort          msg_qnum;    /* Number of messages on
                                    queue. */
    ushort          msg_qbytes;  /* Max number of bytes on
                                    queue. */
    ushort          msg_lspid;   /* pid of last msgsnd */
    ushort          msg_lrpid;   /* pid of last msgrcv */
    time_t          msg_stime;   /* last msgsnd time */
    time_t          msg_rtime;   /* last msgrcv time */
    time_t          msg_ctime;   /* last change time */
    };
```

There is one message structure for each message that may be in the system. The data structure for System V messages is this:

```
/* SYSTEM V MESSAGE STRUCTURE */
struct msg {
    struct msg *msg_next;    /* ptr to next message */
    long     msg_type;       /* message type */
    ushort   msg_ts;         /* message text size */
    ushort   msg_spot;       /* Internal address*/
};
```

Many processes can send a message to the same message queue. The type portion of the message can be used to determine which of several different processes is the originator of any message received by another process; this can be done by hardcoding a particular number into the type or simply using the process-id of the sender as the msg_type.

Perhaps the term "message queue" is misleading. "Queue" suggests a first-in-first-out organization. Message queues allow a more complicated access in the sense that they are "multiplexed." That is, the receiving process can take off the first message of a particular type, leaving other messages of different types and later arriving messages of the same type still on the queue. Regardless, the term "queue" is entrenched in the literature.

8.2.2   The msgctl() System Call

The system call msgctl() is used to perform three basic actions. The most obvious one is to remove the message queue data structure from the kernel. The second action allows a user to examine the contents of a message queue data structure by copying them from the kernel into a buffer in the user's data space. The third action allows a user to set the contents of a message queue data structure in the kernel by copying them from a buffer in the user's data space.

This system call has the syntax

```
int msgctl(int queue_id,
           int command,
           struct msqid_ds *ptr);
```

and controls the resource (a message queue).

The msgctl system call has three arguments, the first of which is a queue_id. It is assumed that the queue_id exists before the call to msgctl(); otherwise the system is in an error state. Note that if the two system calls msgget() and msgctl() are called by different processes, then there is a potential for a "race condition"—that is, the result of the program depends on the execution timing of the system calls. To avoid a race condition, a concurrent software system design using these two system calls should include both in the same process.

The second argument, command, is an integer constant that must be one of the following constants defined in the header file sys/msg.h.

- IPC_STAT places the contents of the kernel structure indexed by the first argument, queue_id, into the data structure pointed to by the third argument, ptr. This enables the user to examine and change the contents of a copy of the kernel's data structure, since this copy is in user space.
- IPC_SET places the contents of the data structure pointed to by the third argument, ptr, in user space, in the kernel's data structure indexed by the first argument queue_id. This enables the user to change the contents of the kernel's data structure, copying the data from a structure in the user's space. The only fields that can be set by an ordinary user are msg_perm.uid, msg_perm.gid, msg_perm.mode (only the lowest nine bits), and msg_qbytes. (The first three fields can be found in the ipc_perm data structure that is described in sys/ipc.h.)
- IPC_RMID removes the kernel data structure entry indexed by the first argument queue_id.

8.2.3   The msgsnd() and msgrcv() System Calls

The system call msgsnd() has the following syntax:

```
int msgsnd(int queue_id,
     struct msgbuf * msg_ptr,
     int message_size,
     int flag);
```

The syntax of system call msgrcv() is

```
int msgrcv( int queue_id,
     struct msgbuf * msg_ptr,
     int message_size,
     long msgtype,
     int flag);
```

Both operate on the resource (a message queue) by sending and receiving messages, respectively.

The first three arguments to each of these two system calls are the same: a queue_id, a pointer to the simple message buffer structure, and an integer representing the message size.

```
/* MESSAGE BUFFER STRUCTURE */
struct msgbuf {
  long    mtype;                /* message type */
  char    mtext[1];            /* message text */
};
```

The flag specifies the actions to be taken if the queue is full or if the total number of messages on all message queues exceeds a prespecified limit. If the flag is set to IPC_NOWAIT, no message is sent and the calling process returns without any error action. If the flag is set to 0, which means that IPC_NOWAIT is not set, the calling process suspends execution until one of two events occur.

The first event is that either some message is removed from this or from another queue so that a message can be sent from this queue, and therefore we are able to send the message.

The second event is that the queue is removed by another process. If the message data structure indexed by queue_id is removed when the flag argument is 0, an error occurs and the system call msgsnd() returns −1.

The fourth argument to msgrcv() is a long integer representing the message type. Recall that messages on a queue may be accessed according to type. The type argument is used as follows.

- If the value of this argument is 0, the first message on the queue is received.
- If the value of this argument is positive, the queue is scanned until the first message of this type is received. The pointer is then set to the first element of the queue (which might have been changed).
- If the value of this argument is negative, the message queue is scanned to find the first message with a type whose value is less than or equal to the absolute value of this argument (which might have been changed).

The fifth argument to msgrcv(), flag, is treated essentially in the same manner as in the msgsnd() system call. This argument is used when there is no message of the indicated message_type on the message queue.

It differs from msgsnd() in that the blocking in the event of IPC_NOWAIT is stopped by a message being placed on the queue.

The successful execution of either msgsnd() or msgrcv() always updates the appropriate entries in the msqid_ds data structure.

8.2.4   The Message Code

The code for the ipc program using messages is given in examples 8.1, 8.2, and 8.3. It follows our usual pattern of getting command-line arguments. The main program has two forks, each of which execs a child process. The child process execs two processes called messerver and mesrec for the send and receive processes, respectively. This pattern emphasizes that there is no need for processes using messages to have the parent-child relationship that is necessary for communication using pipes. For simplicity, we have hardcoded the value of key as 100.

Example 8.1: Main Message-Passing Program

```
/* main message passing program */
main( int argc, char *argv[])
{
    int status;
    int pid, pid1;

    if((pid = fork()) == 0)
        execlp("./messerver","messerver",argv[1],argv[2],0);
    if((pid1 = fork()) == 0)
        execlp("./mesrec", "mesrec", argv[1],0);
    wait(&status);/* wait for some child to terminate */
    wait(&status);/* wait for other child to terminate */
}
```

Example 8.2: Message Server

```
/* Purpose:  This program is a server of two processes    */
/*           communicating a message using System V IPC    */
/*           message queues.                               */
/* Arguments: Two required.                                */
/*    1).  The number of messages to be sent               */
/*    2).  The number of bytes per message                 */
```

```
#include <sys/types.h>
#include <sys/ipc.h>
#include <sys/msg.h>

key_t MSGKEY = 100 ;
struct msgformat{
    long mtype;
    int mpid;
    char mtext[256];
    } msg;
int msgid;

main(int argc, char *argv[])
{
    int i, pid, *pint;
    int loop, bytes;
    extern cleanup();

    loop = atoi(argv[1]);
    bytes = atoi(argv[2]);
    for (i=0; i <= bytes; i++)
        msg.mtext[i] = 'a';


    msgid = msgget(MSGKEY, 0660|IPC_CREAT);
    msg.mtype = 1;
    msg.mpid = getpid();
    /* send number of messages specified by user argument */
    for (i=0;  i < loop; i++)
        msgsnd(msgid, &msg, bytes, 0);
    /* cleaning up maximum number queues(32) */
    for(i=0; i < 32; i++)
        signal(i, cleanup);
}

/* signal handler - note the presence of mscgtl */
cleanup()
{
  msgctl(msgid, IPC_RMID, 0);
  exit(0);
}
```

Example 8.3: Message Receiver

```
/* Purpose:  This program is the receiver process.  */
/* communicating a message using System V IPC       */
/* message queues.                                   */

#include <sys/types.h>
#include <sys/ipc.h>
#include <sys/msg.h>


key_t MSGKEY = 100;
struct msgformat{
   long mtype;
   int mpid;
   char mtext[256];
} msg;


main( int argc, char *argv[])
{
   int i, pid, *pint;
   int msgid, loop;

   msgid = msgget(MSGKEY, 0777);
   loop = atoi(argv[1]);     /* convert arg to int */
   for (i=0; i < loop; i++)
      msgrcv(msgid, &msg, 256, 2, 0);
}
```

The code in the message ipc examples just presented used a message of a particular type, which was to be sent to the message receiver process from the message writer process. If there are multiple writer processes, a single reader process must have code in it something like

```
if (message_type == 1)
    {
    search message queue for message of type 1
    process next message of type 1
    }
if (message_type == 2)
    {
```

```
      search message queue for message of type 2
      process next message of type 2
      }
      .
      .
      .
if (message_type == N)
      {
      search message queue for message of type N
      process next message of type N
      }
```

The timing of any code based on this construction depends on the distribution of the messages of different types in the message queue.

The number and size of the message queues available is limited by some constants that can be set when the System V IPC package is installed. The values of these constants are kept in the msginfo data structure. Listed here are the values of these constants on a Sun SPARC 2, with the appropriate data structure.

```
MSGPOOL  8
MSGMNB   2048
MSGMNI   50
MSGTQL   50
MSGMAP   100
MSGMAX   (MSGPOOL * 1024)
MSGSSZ   8
MSGSEG   ((MSGPOOL * 1024) / MSGSSZ)


/* MESSAGE QUEUE INFORMATION STRUCTURE */
struct msginfo { int
    msgmap, /* # of entries in msg map */
    msgmax, /* max message size */
    msgmnb, /* max # bytes on queue */
    msgmni, /* # of message queue identifiers */
    msgssz, /* msg segment size */
    msgtql; /* # of system message headers */
    ushort msgseg; /* # of msg segments */
    };
```

8.3   SEMAPHORES

A semaphore is a flag that signals a process that it cannot use a resource until another process using that resource releases it. Semaphores are one of nine methods for interprocess communication available in UNIX. Each methods is complex and requires considerable familiarity with the details of the operating system for its implementation. For this reason, many programs use the simpler method of testing the value returned by the system call `creat()` as a semaphore.

The idea is simple. All processes attempting to use a critical resource agree in advance on the name of a particular file whose existence or nonexistence is to serve as a semaphore. Any process wishing to use the critical resource then checks the existence of the file by applying `creat()` to it with the file's name as the first argument. If `creat()` returns a positive integer, there is no problem and the process may proceed. If it returns –1, the file already exists and the process must wait until the file no longer exists, thereby indicating that the resource is available. A file used for this purpose is often called a *lock file*.

This method was used on an Ada compiler designed for a small UNIX-based computer. The memory was somewhat limited on this machine, and hence only one user could use the compiler at one time. The existence of a file named, say, `ada.lk` was the key to compiler access. A user wishing to use the Ada compiler checked the lock file's existence using the system call `creat()`. If the value returned by

```
creat("ada.lk", 0444)
```

was 0, the user could continue compilation, but if the value returned was –1, the user waited. Obviously, this slows down the work of the waiting user. However, a slowing or delay in computation would be better than an error in the compilation caused by a lack of room in the compiler's internal data structures.

Note that what we have really done is use an event, namely, the prior existence or nonexistence of a file, to signal information back to a program. Note also that this event is external to the program and thus can be used by many different programs at the same time. This approach allows us to implement semaphores for communicating between processes.

The approach has some deficiencies. If a user logs out in the middle of a compilation (accidentally or intentionally), the lock file, `ada.lk`, might still exist and so the compilation system will be unavailable to any user until the system manager removes the file manually. A less permanent, more flexible solution is clearly necessary.

8.3.1   Binary and General Semaphores

Many operating systems provide semaphores, which serve as flags to indicate the availability of a process. Many non-UNIX systems provide binary semaphores, which can only take the values 0 or 1.

The problem is that a single flag does not provide enough information. The only information that can be conveyed by a binary semaphore is if a resource is in use, which is insufficient if several processes wish to determine efficiently the resource's availability. A single flag cannot indicate the number of waiting processes.

As an example of the limitation of binary semaphores, consider the efficient scheduling of a solution to the multiple readers and single writers problem. We can avoid data corruption in several ways: Two of the more obvious are blocking the writer when a single reader wishes access to data and blocking all readers if the writer wishes to write. A single binary semaphore tells if either a reader or writer wishes to access the data. However, if we had additional information about the number of processes wishing to read the common data, we could know about the improvement in throughput obtained by using a scheduling system that favors blocking the writer. Note that a scheduling algorithm based on the recent amount of CPU time used by each process is inadequate, since the reader processes themselves may be blocked.

The alert reader might ask about the possibility of using several binary semaphores to solve the problem. We could use binary semaphore number 1 to provide information about critical data for the first reader process and the writer process, binary semaphore 2 to provide information about critical data for the second reader process and the writer process, and so on up to binary semaphore number N to provide information about critical data for the last reader process and the writer process. This works well if the processes alternate their efforts to read the critical data. However, what about the processes that do not alternate but behave in an unpredictable manner?

Consider the case of two reader processes and one writer process. The first reader process has the corresponding value of its binary semaphore set to 1, which means that it is allowed to read and so the writer process is blocked. The second reader process has the corresponding value of its binary semaphore set to 1, which means that it, too, is allowed to read and the writer process is blocked. What happens if the writer is allowed to write by the second binary semaphore being set to 0? The second reader process is blocked by the second binary semaphore value being set to 0, and thus the writer process is enabled. However, the value of the first binary semaphore is still 1, and thus the writer process is still blocked. Since the value of the first binary semaphore is 1, the first reader can read. However, when the first reader process exhausts all data provided to it by the writer, it will eventually be prevented from reading any new data, since the writer's blockage will prevent it from producing any more. Thus, all processes can become deadlocked and no new processing can occur.

The problem is that changes can occur to one binary semaphore without the other binary semaphores being changed as necessary. This is always possible, since the changing of one binary semaphore does not affect the others.

The proper use of semaphores in this setting is to use a general semaphore that can take on several values. We could, for example, use a semaphore whose values were 0, 1, or 2 in the previous discussion to determine if the writer process should be blocked. The values of the semaphore could be used to represent the number of processes waiting for the resource—that is, the number of processes that are waiting for a particular semaphore value.

Programs that use UNIX semaphores can be extremely complex. The major problem is that the semaphore facilities have been enhanced over the years to include general semaphores and sets of semaphores.

8.3.2   Semaphore System Calls

This method of interprocess communication is used to prevent processes from accessing a shared resource simultaneously. In UNIX System V, the semaphore system calls include `semget()`, which gains access to a set of semaphores; `semop()`, which allows processes to manipulate the semaphores; and `semctl()`, which performs other operations, including removal, on the semaphores. These system calls use an implementation of Dijkstra's P and V operations to control synchronization. (In their simplest form, the P operation indicates that a resource has been acquired, and the V operation indicates that a resource has been released.) The system requirements for semaphores include data structures for semaphore ids, semaphore information, and several others.

One of the most important fields of a semaphore data structure is `sem_op`, which controls the "value" of the semaphore. If the value of the field `sem_op` during the execution of the `semop()` system call is –1, the process gains access to the shared resource, if accessible, and blocks other processes' access. If the resource is unavailable, the process sleeps until the resource becomes available once again. If the value of the field `sem_op` is 1 during the execution of the `semop()` system call, the resource is released and all processes waiting for the resource are awakened. Since the operations are atomic, only one P or V operation may occur at a time. We now describe the structure and use of semaphores in more detail.

8.3.3   **Semaphore Organization**

The semaphores in UNIX can be found in the header file `sem.h` as a collection of structures following the basic organization given here.

- Semaphores are grouped into sets.
- Each set of semaphores in the system has its own semaphore data structure. This includes permissions for the semaphores, a pointer to the first semaphore in the set, the number of semaphores in the set, the time of the last semaphore operation, and the time of the last change to any semaphore in the set. These are incorporated into a structured data type called `sem_ds`.
- Each semaphore in the system has its own semaphore structure, which is defined in a data structure called `sem`. The semaphore structure includes the semaphore value called `semval`; the process-id of the last process that operated on the semaphore; a variable named `semncnt` to count the number of processes waiting for the value `semval` to be greater than some determined value called `cval`; and a variable named `semzcnt` to count the number of processes waiting for the value `semval` to become 0.
- Each semaphore has a set of allowable operations. These operations are performed by the `semop()` system call and follow the pattern described in the `sembuf` data structure.

We will describe each of the three data structures needed for proper use of semaphores in conjunction with the system calls that use them.

The three semaphore system calls follow the paradigm of the System V IPC package

- Get the ipc mechanism.
- Operate on the ipc mechanism.
- Control the ipc mechanism.

You will see the similarity of some of the details of the semaphore implementation to some of the system calls and data structures used for message queues.

8.3.4   **The `semget()` System Call**

The first system call that we use with semaphores is `semget()`, whose syntax is

```
int semget( key_t key,
            int num_sems,
            int flags);
```

This system call returns a unique semaphore id. The first parameter to semget() is key, which is essentially a long int. It is used in a global table in the kernel's data space to provide common access for different processes to the same semaphore id that is returned by the call to semget(). The treatment of the key and the production of the sem_id as the return value are the same as in message queues.

A successful call to semget() returns an index to a semaphore id data structure, whose form is

```
/* SEMAPHORE ID DATA STRUCTURE */
struct semid_ds {
    struct ipc_perm sem_perm;
        /* operation permission struct */
    struct sem *sem_base;
        /* ptr to first semaphore in set */
    ushort sem_nsems;
        /* # of semaphores in set */
    time_t sem_otime;       /* last semop time */
    time_t sem_ctime;       /* last change time */
};
```

The semaphore id data structure that is accessed by the index sem_id, which is returned by semget(), contains a pointer to a new structure called the semaphore structure. The semaphore structure is described by the data structure, whose form is

```
/* SEMAPHORE STRUCTURE */
struct sem {
    ushort semval;
        /* semaphore text map address */
    short sempid;    /* pid of last operation */
    ushort semncnt; /* # awaiting semval > cval */
    ushort semzcnt; /* # awaiting semval = 0 */
};
```

The first parameter, key, is used in the same way as the msgget() system call.

The second parameter determines the number of semaphores in the set of semaphores being created by a successful call to semget().

The third parameter determines the appropriate flags for the semaphore. The purpose of these flags is to incorporate the appropriate permissions for reading, writing, and executing (with the same interpretation as for access permissions on files) in each of the semaphores in the semaphore set. The possible flags are obtained by taking the bitwise OR of the three octal digits representing read, write, and execute permissions with one of four flags: ·

```
0
IPC_NOWAIT
SEM_UNDO
IPC_NOWAIT | SEM_UNDO
```

SEM_UNDO is an unusual flag—it is intended to release kernel resources if a process terminates incorrectly. If this flag is set, a new structure called a semaphore undo structure is set up in the kernel to detect adjustments to semaphore values by processes. The existence of an undo structure for a process means that if that process terminates, the values of the semaphore are set to those that would have occurred if the terminated process did not exist. In essence, such a structure means that the software system and the kernel can recover resources blocked by an erroneous semaphore value set by a defunct process. Unfortunately, only a small number of undo structures are allowed at one time.

8.3.5 The `semop()` System Call

The second semaphore system call is `semop()`. Its syntax is

```
int semop(int semid, struct sembuf * sem_op, int num_ops);
```

This system call returns 0 if it generates no errors and returns –1 if unsuccessful. It has three parameters: `semid`, `sem_op`, and `num_ops`. The first parameter is the id of the semaphore we are operating on. If there is no semaphore with that id in the kernel's data space, the system call returns –1.

The second parameter provides an encoding of either the incrementation or the decrementation operation. It is always a pointer to a variable of type `sembuf`. There are three fields to each such semaphore data structure:

`sem_num,`

an unsigned integer (usually also a short integer);

`sem_op,`

a short integer; and

`sem_flg,`

which is also a short integer that is similar to the flags used with `semget()`.

The second field, sem_op, of the structure is of type short integer and is interpreted as an operation on the existing semaphore value. The simplest case requires the kernel to:

increment the semaphore by x

if the parameter is a positive int x, and

decrement the semaphore by y

if the parameter is a negative int y, and the result of the decrementation still has the value of the semaphore nonnegative.

Generally speaking, if the result of a negative value of sem_op is to make the value of the semaphore less than 0 after performing the operation, then the process requesting the semop() sleeps and waits for the value of the semaphore to increase. If the value were equal to 0, then all processes that are sleeping and waiting for the value of the semaphore to be 0 are awakened. Since many processes are involved, the kernel is involved. We now describe some of the details.

If the semaphore operation would make the value of the semaphore negative and the IPC_NOWAIT flag is set, then semop() returns immediately. If the IPC_NOWAIT flag is not set, then the value of semncnt is incremented by one and the caller is blocked until one of three things happens:

- Some process increments the value of semval so that the desired semaphore operation can occur, after which the calling process is unblocked.
- The calling process receives a signal. (We will discuss signals in Chapter 9.)
- The semaphore id data structure is removed from the system. In this case the system call returns with the value –1, indicating an error.

The existence of an undo structure for the semaphore in question also requires action. A successful incrementation or decrementation action modifies the value of the semaphore's semadj value. An unsuccessful decrementation operation resets the semadj value after the calling process is unblocked, but need not reset it otherwise, although the point is moot if the semid_ds indexed by sem_id is removed from the system.

The situation is also complex if the semaphore operation is 0. There are two cases to consider depending on whether the current semaphore value is already 0. If the current semaphore value is 0, then the other operations in the sem_buf array are performed. Otherwise, the number of processes that are sleeping and waiting for the semaphore to become 0 is incremented. Since many processes are involved, the kernel is involved.

The data structure associated with the `semop()` system call is the `sembuf` structure.

```
/* SEMBUF DATA STRUCTURE */
struct sembuf
   {
   short    sem_num;   /* semaphore # */
   short    sem_op;    /* semaphore operation */
   short    sem_flg;   /* operation flags */
};
```

The `sembuf` structure that is pointed to by the second argument is in the user data space and is copied to the kernel's data space by the `sem_op` instruction. The other two fields are the number of the semaphore (in the field `sem_num`) and the flags (in the field `sem_flgs`). The flags are restricted to one of the four options:

```
0
IPC_NOWAIT
SEM_UNDO
IPC_NOWAIT | SEM_UNDO
```

The bitwise OR operator, not the logical OR, should be applied to the flags in this system call.

The third parameter to the system call `semop()` is an int representing the number of semaphore operations to be performed on the set of semaphores.

8.3.6   The `semctl()` System Call

The third system call used with semaphores is `semctl()`. Its syntax is somewhat complex because of the presence of a union as the type of the fourth argument. For clarity, we will use the notation of the older Kernighan and Ritchie version of C for the function header.

```
int semctl(semid,semnum,sem_action,value)
    int semid;
    int semnum;
    int sem_action;
    union semun
        {
        int val;
        struct semid_ds *buf;
```

```
    ushort *arr;
    } value ;
```

Here the arguments represent the semaphore id, the number of the semaphore, an action to be taken with the semaphore, and the value of the operation. The possible options for the third argument, `sem_action`, and their
meanings are as follows.

- Values of sem_action that affect a single semaphore:
  - GETVAL gets the value of the semaphore selected by the first two
    arguments.
  - SETVAL sets the value of the semaphore selected by the first two
    arguments.
  - GETPID gets the process-id.
  - GETNCNT gets the number of processes waiting for the semaphore
    to be greater than a specific value.
  - GETZCNT gets the number of processes waiting for the value of the
    semaphore to become 0.
- Values of sem_action that affect all the semaphores in the list indi-
  cated by the field `arr` of the union in the third argument:
  - GETALL gets values of all semaphores in the array that is part of
    the union.
  - SETALL sets values of all semaphores in the array that is part of
    the union.
- Values of sem_action that affect the `semaphore_id` data structure
  pointed to by the field `buf` of the union in the third argument:
  - IPC_STAT places the contents of the `semid_ds` into the user's
    space in `buf`.
  - IPC_SET sets the values of the members of the `semid_ds` to the
    corresponding values in the structure pointed to by `buf`.

```
    sem_perm.uid
    sem_perm.gid
    sem_perm.mode
```

  - IPC_RMID removes the `semid_ds` indexed by `sem_id` from the kernel.

Note that there is a possible problem with the two system calls
`semget()` and `semctl()`, in that the semaphore may be controlled before
the initialization is complete. This race condition is similar to the one we
saw with messages, and is most easily prevented by having all calls to
`semctl()` in the same process that created the semaphore. Be certain that
the `semget()` call is executed before a `semctl()` on the same semaphore.

8.3.7   General Semaphores, Binary Semaphores, and Semaphore Sets

A general semaphore is one that can take on a range of integer values. In this it is unlike a binary semaphore, which can only take on the values 0 or 1. A binary semaphore is useful when we simply need to identify use or non-use of some resources. This is fully adequate for the case of two processes wishing to access a single instance of a nonshareable resource. It is not generally adequate for many processes wishing to share a resource, since we cannot determine the number of processes wishing to access the resource in a way that is atomic—that is, in a way that this information cannot be corrupted by an unexpected context switch. A general semaphore can be used to contain information in a single place about the number of processes wishing to access some resource.

A semaphore set contains information about a number of resources. If there were three semaphores in a set, the first could be used to determine the number of processes wishing to use a disk, the second could be used to determine the number of processes wishing to use a kernel data structure, and the third might be used to identify the number of processes wishing to use a data bus. The advantage of a set of semaphores over multiple semaphores is that the changing of values in an entire set of semaphores can be handled by the operating system as an atomic action.

8.3.8   The P and V Operations

The important operations on a semaphore are the P and V operations introduced by Dijkstra for the incrementing and decreasing of values. The P operation, the incrementation, is implemented as a function that provides an interface to the system call semop():

```
void P(int sid)      /* acquire semaphore */
{struct sembuf sb;

    sb.sem_num = 0;
    sb.sem_op = -1;
    sb.sem_flg = SEM_UNDO;
    if ((semop(sid,&sb,1)) == -1)
     puts("semop error");
}
```

The V operation, the decrementation, is also implemented as a function providing an interface to semop():

```
void V(int sid)        /* release semaphore */
{
struct sembuf sb;
  sb.sem_num = 0;
  sb.sem_op = 1;
  sb.sem_flg = SEM_UNDO;

  if ((semop(sid,&sb,1)) == -1)
    puts("semop error");
}
```

Semaphores have their disadvantages. If two or more are used, deadlock may occur. Also, they require ipc system calls, limiting portability from one UNIX system to another. The semaphore data structure is quite complex to begin with, and its complexity was increased when Release 2.0 of System V was replaced by Release 3.0. On the Sun 3/60, the option IPCSEMAPHORE had to be incorporated into the system kernel before this ipc method would work correctly.

8.3.9   The Semaphore Code

The ipc code presented in examples 8.4 and 8.5 is written as a main program that forks. Both the parent and child alternate a number of P and V operations on the same semaphore. The semaphore is created by the semget() system call, and the number of repetitions is given as a command-line argument. An important feature of the code is the cleanup operation. A cleanup function should be placed in the most reliable (least likely to crash) process to ensure that the semaphore structure will be removed from the kernel when the process terminates.

The number of semaphores available in any system is limited by the system parameters described earlier. The semaphore set used for this program is removed by the cleanup() function. You should check this by using the ipcs command in any program you write using semaphores. The SEM_UNDO flag is also set to allow backtracking if either process terminates unexpectedly.

Example 8.4: Main Semaphore Program

```
/* Interprocess Communication using Semaphores */
#include <stdio.h>
#include <sys/types.h>
```

```c
#include <sys/ipc.h>
#include <sys/sem.h>
int sid;
main( int argc, char *argv[])
{

  int i, j, status, number_of_communications;

  if (argc < 2)
     {
     fputs("Bad arg count",stderr);
     printf("Usage:%s number_of_communications",
        argv[0]);
     exit(1);
     }

  /* remove semaphore if an interrupt occurs */
  for (i=0; i<32; i++)
     signal(i,cleanup);
  number_of_communications = atoi(argv[1]);

  /* get semaphore id */
  sid = semget(100, 1, 0660 | IPC_CREAT);
  V(sid);

  /* Create child process */
  if (fork() == 0)
    {
    for(i=0; i<number_of_communications; i++)
       {
       /* Race to execute critical section */
       P(sid);
       for(j=0; j<20; j++)
          printf("In child's critical section\n");
       V(sid);
       }
    exit(0);
    }

  for(i=0; i<number_of_communications; i++)
     {
```

```
        P(sid);
        V(sid);
        }
    wait(&status);
    /* remove semaphore */
    semctl(sid,0,IPC_RMID,0);
}

cleanup()
{
    semctl(sid,1,IPC_RMID,0);
    exit(1);
}
```

Example 8.5:   Semaphore Tools

```
/* semaphore tools */

#include <sys/types.h>
#include <sys/ipc.h>
#include <sys/sem.h>
void P(int sid)        /* acquire semaphore */
{
    struct sembuf sb;

    sb.sem_num = 0;
    sb.sem_op = -1;
    sb.sem_flg = SEM_UNDO;

    if ((semop(sid,&sb,1)) == -1)
        puts("semop error");
}

void V(int sid)        /* release semaphore */
{
    struct sembuf sb;

    sb.sem_num = 0;
    sb.sem_op = 1;
    sb.sem_flg = SEM_UNDO;
```

```
    if ((semop(sid,&sb,1)) == -1)
        puts("semop error");
}
```

8.3.10   Semaphore Constants

The number and size of semaphores are limited. Some of the constants they require are tunable by the operating system. In System V UNIX, these constants are found in the include files sem.h and sema.h. The constants and their default values on one system are

```
SEMMAP  = 10
SEMMNI  = 10
SEMMNS  = 60
SEMMNU  = 30
SEMMSL  = 25
SEMOPM  = 10
SEMUME  = 10
SEMVMX  = 32767
SEMAEM  = 16384
```

The most important of these constants are SEMMNI, which is the maximum number of semaphore ids, and thus the number of semaphore sets, that can exist at any one time; SEMMNS, which is the total number of all semaphores in all data sets on the entire system; SEMMNU, which is the maximum number of semaphore undo data operations that can be involved at any one time; SEMMSL, which is the maximum number of semaphores in any semaphore data set; and SEMVMX, which is the maximum value a semaphore can have. These system-wide constants are stored in the seminfo data structure that follows.

```
struct seminfo
{
int semmap, /* # of entries in semaphore map */
semmni,     /* # of semaphore identifiers */
semmns,     /* # of semaphores in system */
semmnu,     /* # of undo structures in system */
semmsl,     /* max # of semaphores per id */
semopm,     /* max # of operations per semop call */
semume,     /* max # of undo entries per process */
};
```

SHARED MEMORY

The main idea behind shared memory is that two processes can share the same data space. Before we discuss this notion, we will review what happens to the various segments of processes during the `fork()` and `exec()` system calls.

A process has three segments: the text segment, which contains the executable code of the process; the data segment, which contains the data used by the process; and the stack segment, which contains system data information. When a process forks, it creates a new process called the child process. The child process has pointers to the same text and data segments the parent process has, but it has a different stack segment. At this point, the parent and child share the same memory for the text and data segments (Figure 8.1).

The call to exec in either the parent process or the child process means that a new region is associated with the execing process and that pointers are set from the process to its new text and data segments, which are now overwritten by the text and data segments of the newly initialized process. The parent and child no longer share the same text and data segments, and the situation looks like Figure 8.2.

Shared memory is the mechanism that allows these two processes to share some portion of common data segments. It is more general than we might think from the previous discussion. It allows any number of processes, whether related or not, to have access to the same data segment as part of the virtual address space of each process.

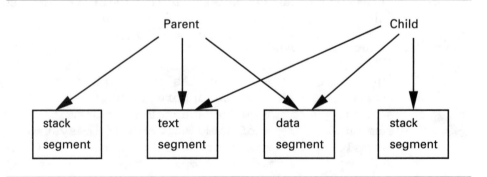

Figure 8.1.   Parent and Child Processes before exec

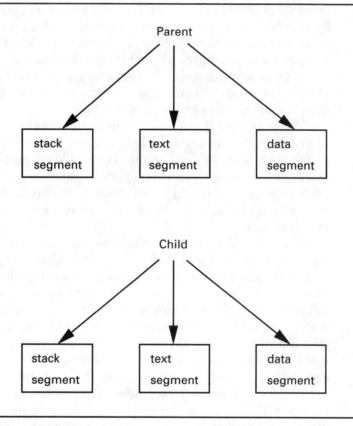

Figure 8.2.   Parent and Child Processes after exec

There are restrictions on the type of memory that can be shared between several processes. The shared memory must be part of the data segments of the processes and not part of the text or stack segments. A parent
and a child process share the same text and data segments after the creation of the child by a fork; their stack segments are similar but not identical. After an exec system call, the segments are generally different, since
the exec reinitializes the text, data, and stack segments. With a few exceptions, after the exec system call, the parent and child processes do not ordinarily share any information in their text or data segments.

As we learned in Chapter 5, several processes can share the same text
segment. Sharing usually takes place when different system or standard
application processes are intended to be used by different processes. A good

example of this is the vi editor, which allows its executable code to be used by several users who are simultaneously editing different files. The information about the shareability of the entire text segment is obtained in the header of the executable file and is stored in the value of the magic number. Many processes can share the text segment of a process, and no special use of the kernel's data structures is made except for the page tables used to map virtual memory to physical memory.

The sharing of the data segment is different from the sharing of the text segment, in that a considerable amount of preliminary work has to be done by the operating system. The number of shared memory regions that can be active in the system at any one time is limited, as is the number of shared memory regions that can be attached to any single process. There are also size restrictions on shared memory regions, which we will discuss in detail in this section.

Like all other segments that are associated with a process, the data segment is made up of different regions that form the process's virtual address space. These regions are ordinarily controlled by actions within the process. The data segment is initialized by the exec() system call, and the information in the segment is changed as the process runs. To visualize what happens to the data segment, think of the process as being a program that initializes and modifies an array. The normal behavior of a data segment is to be modified only by the process owning the segment after the data segment has been initialized by the exec that created it.

Thinking of the data segment of a process as an array will help you understand the way memory is shared between processes. The kernel provides a mechanism for two processes to read the same data in the shared memory region. The reading of information from the shared memory region follows the same principles as the reading of information from files. The operating system assumes that the information is accessed as a collection of bytes and provides no other organization. The interpretation of the information as some other format such as integers, floating point numbers, double precision numbers, or some structured data type is left to the applications program. Thus, from the point of view of the operating system, a shared memory region, like any other memory, is an array of bytes.

The use of shared memory follows the standard high-level paradigm that is common to all ipc methods in the System V IPC package:

- Get the resource.
- Operate on the resource.
- Control the resource.

This paradigm, for shared memory, comprises six steps:

1. Create a shared memory mechanism in the kernel for use by the processes that will use it.
2. Determine a safe place in each process to attach the shared memory region.
3. Attach the shared memory region to a safe place in each of the processes that need it.
4. Use the shared memory region in a consistent manner in all processes that need it.
5. Detach the shared memory region from all processes to which it is attached.
6. Remove all the information about the shared memory from the kernel.

We will explain how to perform these six steps in detail.

Programs using shared memory must have the include files `shm.h` and `ipc.h`.

The first step in shared memory use is the creation of the appropriate kernel data using the `shmget()` system call. The syntax of this system call is

```
int shmget( key_t key, int size, int flag);
```

The `key` parameter to `shmget()` is a long integer. It is usually declared internally as

```
key_t key;
```

where `key_t` is an alias for a long int that is defined in `sys/types.h` using the typedef construction. If the key is set to `IPC_PRIVATE`, the system call always creates a shared memory region.

The second parameter is the size of the shared memory region in bytes.

The third parameter is a combination of the usual file access permissions of read, write, and execute for the owner, group, and world with the following ipc constants.

```
0
IPC_CREAT
IPC_EXCL
IPC_CREAT| IPC_EXCL
```

The first nonzero choice, `IPC_CREAT`, creates a `key` in a structure for interprocess communication if the key does not already exist. The contents of the ipc structure can be viewed by the `ipcs` command. The second nonzero choice, `IPC_EXCL`, indicates that a failure (with a system call return value of –1) will occur if the key already exists. The third nonzero choice is the bitwise OR of both these choices.

A successful call to shmget() will result in the creation of a shared memory id data structure called shmid_ds.

```
/*SHARED MEMORY ID DATA STRUCTURE */
struct shmid_ds
{
struct ipc_perm shm_perm;
int shm_segsz;          /* size of segment in bytes */
struct region *shm_reg; /* ptr to region struct */
char pad[4];            /* for swap compatibility */
ushort shm_lpid;        /* pid of last shmop */
ushort shm_cpid;        /* pid of creator */
ushort shm_nattch;      /* used only for shminfo */
ushort shm_cnattch;     /* used only for shminfo */
time_t shm_atime;       /* last shmat time */
time_t shm_dtime;       /* last shmdt time */
time_t shm_ctime;       /* last change time */
};
```

We have now completed the first step and have created the appropriate kernel data structure. The next step is to determine safe places to attach shared memory to processes.

It is slightly complicated to find a safe place for a shared memory region in a process. By a safe place we mean a portion of shared memory that cannot be corrupted by another process using the same memory. Of course, the whole point of shared memory is that two or more processes can share the same data and read and write this data when necessary. We want the organization of the data to be interpreted the same way by all processes sharing it. Since the operating system only provides methods for reading from memory in bytes, this protection by processes of the higher-level organization of data is essential.

There is some disagreement on this point. Most of the manuals suggest that the kernel be given the responsibility of finding a safe place, which corresponds to the second argument being 0 in the system call shmat() that we will meet later in this section. Stevens (see the references) also recommends this, but notes that there can be difficulties if there is a substantial amount of dynamic memory allocation in the process's data segment.

We illustrate the point by two examples:

```
main()
{
  int i;
  float f;
  int j;
/* more code here */
}

main()
{
  int i;
  int j;
  float f;
  /* more code here */
}
```

Assume that in each system, an integer takes four bytes, a floating point number takes eight bytes, and the shared memory region must stop on a double word boundary (a multiple of eight bytes). In each example, there are a total of sixteen bytes in the data segment.

In the first example, a shared memory region of eight bytes cannot be placed, since its boundaries would fall in the middle of the storage of the floating point number. Any other process writing to such an area would corrupt the organization of the data. In the second example, a shared memory region can start at the beginning location, byte 0, or after the second integer in byte 8. Any other place would allow the possibility of data corruption.

There is another possibility for sharing memory between processes—taking an unused portion of memory. We can find the upper limit of the data segment, and anything added after this place would appear to be safe. This upper limit is called the *break value*. The upper boundary of the data segment can be found via the sbrk() system call, such as in

```
break_val = sbrk(0);
```

There is a problem, however. If the program uses any dynamic storage allocation, the original size of the data segment, and hence the break value, may be modified as the process runs. Thus, any use of dynamic storage allocation, whether explicitly by the user's calling of the storage allocator malloc() or by pointers, character strings, or structured data types, requires making sure that the area chosen for shared memory is the proper one.

Clearly, the decision about where to attach a shared memory region requires extensive knowledge of the organization of the process's data segment. All this information gathering must be done by the user, not the kernel. The next step is the attachment of the shared memory region to the processes in the safe places. This requires the use of the shmat() system call. The return value is not ordinarily used except for testing success (a nonnegative value) or failure (–1). Since the only use of the return value is to test for error, we need only cast the return type as an int to check for failure (return value = –1).

The system call shmat() has the syntax

```
char *shmat(int shmid,
            char *shmaddr,
            int shmflg);
```

The second argument should be set to 0, as in (char *) 0, if the kernel is to determine the place for attachment. Otherwise, user should select the place, as discussed above.

The system call shmat() uses either 0 or three possible nonzero flags for its third argument. These nonzero flags are SHM_RND, SHM_RDONLY, and the combination SHM_RND | SHM_RDONLY. The SHM_RDONLY flag is the easiest to understand. If set, it indicates if the shared memory region is to be read-only; if not set, the default value is to have the shared memory both readable and writable. The flag SHM_RND requires the shared memory system call to force the byte address of the shared memory region to coincide with a double word boundary by rounding. As before, the third possibility is the bitwise OR of the first two.

The fourth step is the reading and effective use of the shared memory region. The user must write code to ensure locking of the region when a reader and a writer process wish to use it. The blocking of a process wishing to change the contents of a shared memory region when a reader process wishes to read them is performed by a synchronization method such as semaphores in most versions of UNIX. This is an excellent example of the mutual exclusion problem. We will attend to this topic in our code example.

After a process has finished using a shared memory region, the region can be detached from the process with the system call shmdt(). This system call decrements the number of processes wishing to access the region. It allows the simplification of programs, in that a process's execution code may be made smaller and simpler if there is no longer any need for another process to access its memory. All information about the number of processes attached to the same shared memory region is kept in the kernel's data space, but can be accessed by a user process through appropriate use of the `shmctl()` system call.

The system call `shmdt()` has a single argument, which is the address of the shared memory region, expressed as an integer. It returns a value that is not ordinarily used except for testing success (a nonnegative value) or failure (–1).

The last step is the cleanup of the kernel's data space, using the system call `shmctl()`. This system call takes three parameters: a shared memory id, a set of flags, and a buffer that contains a large amount of information about the shared memory region that can be copied to and from the kernel's data space.

A considerable amount of information can be found in the data structure pointed to by the third parameter to `shmctl()`. A call to `shmctl()` with the `command` parameter set to `IPC_STAT` gives access to following information about the shared memory segment:

- User's id
- User's group-id
- Creator's id
- Creator's group-id
- Operation permissions
- Key
- Segment size
- Process-id of the last shared memory operation
- Process-id of the creator
- Current number of segments attached
- Current number of attached segments in memory
- Last time of attachment
- Last time of detachment
- Last time of change

In using this ipc method, we have observed differences in shared memory in different UNIX versions. The description here is specific to Solaris (Version 1.1), which is based on System V Release 4. The behavior on other systems will be similar but not identical.

The data structures the kernel uses for shared memory are accessed by an integer known as the *shared memory id*, or `shmid`. The `shmid` is used in conjunction with four system calls: `shmget()`, `shmat()`, `shmdt()`, and `shmctl()`.

8.4.1   **The shmget() System Call**

The first of the four system calls, shmget(), has the syntax

```
int shmget(key_t key,
           int region_size,
           int flags);
```

and it has three parameters: the key (which is a user-defined integer), the size in bytes of the region to be attached, and a flag that usually turns on some of the bits in IPC_CREAT.

The shmget() system call does one of two things depending on whether there is an entry in the kernel's shared memory table corresponding to the value of the key when the system call is made. If an entry was already present in the table, shmget() returns an integer indicating the position of the entry. If no entry existed before the system call, a region of the given size is created and an entry is made in the kernel's shared memory table. It is important to note that no process has access to a shared memory region newly created by shmget().

Here are the specific details of shmget(). The key is either a unique integer or 0. Perhaps the best way to obtain a unique integer is to use one of the functions makekey() or stdipc() to get a unique key. The special value of 0 is the value of the constant IPC_PRIVATE and is used to limit access to the shared memory whose id is being returned by shmget(). If the value of the key is the same as the value of an existing shared memory id, then we have access to the shared memory accessed by this id.

The size of the shared memory is specified by the user, but must satisfy certain system constraints. On some systems, the constraints are found in the directory /etc/master.d and refer to certain tunable parameters that affect performance. The file shm in the directory /etc/master.d contains values of the following constants in one version of UNIX:

```
SHMMAX  = 131072
SHMMIN  = 1
SHMMNI  = 100
SHMSEG  = 6
SHMALL  = 512
```

The values of these constants will be different on different systems. They can be found in the shared memory info data structure.

```
/* SHARED MEMORY INFORMATION STRUCTURE */
struct  shminfo
```

```
{
  int
  shmmax,   /* max shared memory segment size */
  shmmin,   /* min shared memory segment size */
  shmmni,   /* # of shared memory identifiers */
  shmseg,   /* max attached segments per process */
  shmall;   /* max total shared memory system */
};
```

SHMMAX is the maximum size of any shared memory region that can be used in any situation; SHMMIN is the minimum size. SHMMNI is the number of unique shared memory ids that can be on the system at any one time, which effectively limits the total number of shared memory segments that can be available to processes. SHMSEG is the maximum number of shared memory segments that can be available for attachment to any one process. Finally, SHMALL is the total number of assigned physical pages designated as shared memory pages that can be in physical memory at any one time. The size parameter to shmget() must meet all of these limitations, or the system call will return an error.

The third parameter to shmget(), flags, is an integer that provides information about the access permissions for ownership and execution plus control commands. It uses some of the constants in the include file shm.h in the manner described in the following paragraphs.

The last three octal digits of flags are a set of access permissions, with the last three defined as

```
400   read by user
200   write by user
040   read by group
020   write by group
004   read by others
002   write by others
```

The first two of these access permissions are often referred to by the names given in the include file shm.h, namely, SHM_R for read-only permission by the user and SHM_W for write permission by the user. No names are commonly used for access permissions by the user's group or by others.

The command modes of the command are used by selecting one or more of the constants IPC_CREAT or IPC_EXCL as defined in the include file ipc.h. These constants have the same meaning as before. All of these permissions and commands can be incorporated into the same flag by the bitwise OR operation available in C. For example, to allow reading and writing by the user (owner), reading but not writing by the user's group, and no access by others, and to create the shared memory, we would use the value

```
SHM_R | SHM_W | 0040 | IPC_CREAT
```

as a flag to a call to shmget().

There are many possible combinations of parameters that can cause failure of a shmget() system call because of the interaction between parameters and the system constants—far too many to be listed here.

8.4.2   The shmat() System Call

We now describe the shmat() system call. Its syntax is

```
char *shmat(int shmid,
            char *address,
            int flags);
```

This system call also has three arguments. It has a return value that is a pointer to the shared memory being attached. It is used to attach a shared memory region to a process after the shared memory has been created. Thus, a call to shmat() must always be preceded by a call to shmget().

The first argument is the shared memory id that was returned by a previous call to shmget(). The shmid parameter is an integer.

The second argument is a valid memory address that specifies where in the virtual address space of the attaching process the shared memory is to be attached. It is possible to attach the region anywhere in the user's virtual address space. For some applications, however, we might want to attach the region only at the boundary of a virtual memory page for the sake of efficiency. This can be done either by knowing the actual address or by using a flag. As indicated earlier, we can let the compiler decide where to attach the shared memory region by giving a second argument of (char *) 0, if we simply want to add a shared memory region to the process at the end of the data segment.

The flags argument is used primarily to communicate the permissions restriction SHM_RDONLY, which allows the process to which the shared memory is being attached only to read the data in this shared memory. Another, less common use is rounding off to the nearest page boundary by use of SHM_RND. Of course, we can combine the two by using the bitwise OR operation and setting the flags to be

```
SHM_RDONLY | SHM_RND
```

In the case of the SHM_RND bits being set, the value returned by shmat() might be different from the value passed to it in the parameter address.

8.4.3 The shmdt() System Call

The next system call for shared memory is shmdt(), whose syntax is

```
int shmdt(char *address) ;
```

This system call detaches a shared memory region from the address space of a process. It must follow a call to shmat() with the same base address returned by shmat(). Note that since many processes may be using the same shared memory region, a call to shmdt() does not remove the region from the kernel's shared memory table. This system call has only a single parameter—the starting address of the process in the user's address space. Thus, processes that attach several regions to the same base address may cause some problems. It is the responsibility of the user to know where the regions were attached. Since the system call shmdt() does not have any way of entering the size of the shared memory region, attaching shared memory regions of different size to the same place won't work.

8.4.4 The shmctl() System Call

We now turn to the study of the system call shmctl(), whose syntax is

```
int shmctl(int shmid,
           int command,
           struct shm_ds *buf_ptr) ;
```

This is the final system call that applies to shared memory. It is used to change ownership and permissions of the shared memory region; it is also used to completely remove shared memory from both the kernel's shared memory data structure and all processes' user memory space. Proper use of shmctl() is after a shmget(), and its most common use is only after a call to shmat().

The first argument is the shared memory id that was returned by a previous call to shmget(). It is an integer.

There are five possible commands that can be included in the command argument, which is the second parameter to shmctl(). The first of these is IPC_STAT, which returns the status of the associated data structure for the shared memory from the kernel, and stores information about the shared memory area in question in a data structure pointed to by a variable called buf_ptr. This command allows the user to access this information, since it gets moved from the kernel's data space to the user's. IPC_SET can be used to set permissions. IPC_RMID can be used to remove the shared memory id and all of the shared memory information, including its data structures. The last two commands, SHM_LOCK and SHM_UNLOCK, are used to lock and unlock the segment in core memory; they can only be used by the superuser of the system.

The third argument is a pointer to a data structure that is used to hold either the values returned by a call that used the flag IPC_STAT or the values placed in the data structure by setting the bits in the IPC_SET flag in a shmctl() call. The data structure pointed to by buf_ptr is in the user's address space and can be directly manipulated by the user while the process executes in user mode. Its purpose is to allow the user access to a copy of the data for shared memory that is usually stored in the kernel. The system call shmctl() is an atomic operation that permits the user to change data in the kernel.

When a region (shared memory or otherwise) is attached to a process, it must be removed from a list of free regions and placed in a list of active regions. Following its placement there, the region must be incorporated into a region table. There is a region table for each process. Detachment of a region from a process follows the reverse order. Of course, there is a considerable amount of error checking at each stage for valid virtual memory addresses, number of processes the region is attached to, size of region, related i-nodes, and so forth. The error checking is done by the kernel. We will not consider this type of error checking in any detail, but will continue with the same error checking techniques for system call failure that we have used elsewhere in this book.

8.4.5   The Shared Memory Code

Consider the simplest case of a single process using a single shared memory region. Of course, the code is silly since there is no other process to connect the shared memory to. However, it is informative. We must first create the shared memory region using the shmget() system call, and then this new memory can be attached to the process with the shmat() system call. The process uses the shared memory, and after it is finished, the shared memory is removed from both the kernel's and user process's data spaces with the shmctl() system call. (The shmdt() system call would remove the shared memory from the memory space of the user's process, but would not affect the shared memory data structure of the kernel.) The code is presented in example 8.6.

Example 8.6: A Simple Shared Memory Example

```
/* This example illustrates the order in which system */
/* calls for shared memory are used.                   */

#include <ipc.h>
#include <shm.h>

main()
{
  int arr[1000];
  key_t key;
  struct shmid_ds buffer;

  shmget(key, 1000* sizeof(int), IPC_CREAT|IPC_EXCL));
  shmat(key, F0 ,SHM_RDONLY|SHM_RND);
  shmdt(F0);
  shmctl(key,IPC_RMID,0);
}
```

This code attaches a shared memory region that can hold an array of 1,000 integers to a memory address of F0 (hexadecimal), which is 240 in decimal. The shared memory is rounded, if necessary, to match double word boundaries.

We now show a more realistic use of shared memory as an ipc mechanism. The organization of this code is the same as before: Two processes will communicate a fixed number of data bytes and will repeat this a fixed number of times. The amount of data communicated each time and the number of repetitions of communications will be read in as command-line arguments.

This code makes use of the C library function memcpy(), which is used in a manner somewhat similar to the use of the standard C library function strcpy(). The syntax of this library function is

```
char *memcpy( char *s1, char *s2; int n);
```

This copies from the memory area pointed to by the second argument into the memory area pointed to by the first argument. The copying stops whenever the count of bytes specified by the third argument is exceeded.

There are several related functions:

```
char *memccpy( char *s1,
               char *s2,
               int c,
               int n);
```

```
char *memchr( char *s,
              int c,
              int n);

int memcmp ( char *s1,
             char *s2,
             int n);

char *memset ( char *s,
               int c,
               int n);
```

Their meanings are similar to that of string functions with similar names. The major difference is that the copying of memory by functions such as memccpy() is terminated by either copying the number of bytes specified in the fourth argument or if the special character given as the third argument is detected.

We must use some form of locking mechanism to preserve data integrity in our shared memory. This is the critical section problem we have seen several times before. The solution is a method that we have already seen: using semaphores to control which process gets access to the shared memory region.

The code in examples 8.7, 8.8, and 8.9 borrows heavily from Rochkind (see references). It is clearly more complex than that for shared memory without semaphores or for semaphores without shared memory. It is also likely to be slower than either of those simpler codes.

Example 8.7: Shared Memory—Main Program

```
/* Interprocess Communication Using Shared Memory */
#include <stdio.h>
#include <string.h>
#include <sys/types.h>
#include <sys/ipc.h>
#include <sys/sem.h>
#include <sys/shm.h>

#define MAXBYTES 4096 /* Maximum bytes per shared segment */

main(argc,argv)
int argc;
char *argv[];
```

```
{
  char message[MAXBYTES];
  int i, message_num, j, number_of_messages, nbytes;
  int key = getpid();
  int semid;
  int segid;
  char *addr;

  if (argc != 3)
      {
      printf("Usage: %s num_messages");
      printf(" num_of_bytes\n", argv[0]);
      exit(1);
      }
  else
      {
      number_of_messages = atoi(argv[1]);
      nbytes = atoi(argv[2]);
      if (nbytes > MAXBYTES)
      nbytes = MAXBYTES;
      if ((semid=semget((key_t)key, 1,0666|IPC_CREAT))
          == -1)
          {
          printf("semget error\n");
          exit(1);
          }

  /* initialize the semaphore value to 1 */
  V(semid);
  if ((segid = shmget((key_t) key,MAXBYTES,
                  0666| IPC_CREAT)) == -1)
      {
      printf("shmget error\n");
      exit(1);
      }

  if ((addr = shmat(segid,0,0)) == (char * ) -1 )
      {
      printf("shmat error\n");
      exit(1);
      }
```

```
switch (fork())
    {
    case -1:
        printf("Error in fork\n");
        exit(1);
    case 0:
        /* Child process, receives messages */
        for (i = 0; i<number_of_messages; i++)
        if (receive(semid, message, sizeof(message)))
            ;
        exit(0);
    default:
        /* Parent process, sends messages */
        for (i = 0; i < number_of_messages; i++)
            {
            /* Create message of give byte size */
            message_num = itoa(i+1, message);
            for(j = message_num; j < nbytes; j++)
                message[j] = 'd';
            if (!send(semid, message, sizeof(message)))
                printf("Cannot send message\n");
            } /* end for loop */

    cleanup(semid, segid, addr);
        } /* end switch */
    } /* end else */
}
```

Example 8.8: Synchronization Tools

```
/* semaphore tools */
#include <sys/types.h>
#include <sys/ipc.h>
#include <sys/sem.h>

void P(int sid)      /* acquire semaphore */
{
    struct sembuf *sb;

    sb = (struct sembuf *) malloc (sizeof(struct sembuf *));
    sb->sem_num = 0;
```

```
    sb->sem_op = -1;
    sb->sem_flg = SEM_UNDO;

    if ((semop(sid, sb, 1)) == -1)
      printf("semop error\n");
}


void V(int sid) /* release semaphore */
{
    struct sembuf sb;

    sb = (struct sembuf *) malloc (sizeof(struct sembuf *));
    sb->sem_num = 0;
    sb->sem_op = 1;
    sb->sem_flg = SEM_UNDO;

    if ((semop(sid, sb, 1)) == -1)
        printf("semop error\n");
}
```

Example 8.9: Shared Memory send and receive

```
/* Shared memory send and receive. */
#include <sys/types.h>
#include <sys/ipc.h>
#include <sys/sem.h>
#include <sys/shm.h>

/* Send "message" from addr to buf. */
send(semid, addr, buf, nbytes)
int semid;
char *addr;
char *buf;
int nbytes;
{
    P(semid);
    memcpy(addr,buf,nbytes);
    V(semid);
}
```

```
/* Receive "message" from buf to addr. */
receive(semid, buf, addr, nbytes)
int semid;
char *buf;
char *addr;
int nbytes;
{
  P(semid);
  memcpy(buf,addr,nbytes);
  V(semid);
}


/* Remove semaphores and segments. */
cleanup(semid, segid, addr)
int semid;
int segid;
char *addr;
{
  int status;

  /* Wait for the child process to die before */
  /* removing semaphores. */
  wait(&status);

  semctl(semid, 0, IPC_RMID, 0);
  shmdt(addr);
  shmctl(segid, 0, IPC_RMID, 0);
}
```

We used semaphores in these examples, in that the two processes could not read and write the same shared memory region. The data in this region could easily be corrupted if it is read during a period when a write occurs or vice versa. The only way to ensure that the reading and writing do not conflict is to use a synchronization mechanism. In the exercises, you will be asked to use messages for the synchronization. This is another example of a critical section problem requiring mutual exclusion.

Note the use of the call to V() in the main program to ensure that the value of the semaphore was 1 before the first call to the function send(). This was done to prevent deadlock. You should also note that we could have used the system call `semctl()` to initialize the value of the semaphore instead of using the initial call to `V()`.

SUMMARY

In this chapter, we studied three methods of interprocess communication. These methods are commonly bundled together in what is often known as the System V IPC package. They are messages, semaphores, and shared memory, and they follow the same paradigm:

- Get the resource.
- Operate on the resource.
- Control the resource.

Messages use the system calls `msgget()`, `msgctl()`, `msgsnd()`, and `msgrcv()` for implementation of the standard paradigm. Processes wishing to communicate by messages must use a message queue whose message queue id is known to them. A receiving process can choose to select the first message on the queue, or it can wait for a message of a specified type.

Messages are also becoming the standard method of communication between different processors on distributed memory parallel computers.

Semaphores are a complex ipc mechanism. UNIX semaphores are general semaphores. That is, they are not restricted to taking binary values, which allows considerable generality but makes their use tricky. Semaphores can be created in sets, and each semaphore has a semaphore data structure.

System calls for semaphores are `semget()`, `semctl()`, and `semop()`.

Shared memory is the fastest ipc mechanism because there is no data transfer. It requires four system calls: `shmget()`, `shmctl()`, `shmdt()`, and `shmdt()`.

Proper use of shared memory requires the determination of a safe place in memory to which the shared memory region is to be attached. The use of the `sbrk()` system call to determine the size of the data segment is essential. However, calls to a dynamic storage allocator such as `malloc()` may affect the size of the data segment and thus the size of any shared memory segment that can be attached safely.

REFERENCES

Perhaps the most useful reference for this material is a combination of your system manual and a local expert on the System V IPC package.

Other detailed references on this material are

Rochkind, M. *Advanced UNIX Programming.* Englewood Cliffs, N. J.: Prentice-Hall, 1985.

Stevens, W. R. *Advanced Programming in the UNIX Environment.* Reading, Mass.: Addison-Wesley, 1992.

EXERCISES

1. The purpose of this exercise is to determine which of the System V IPC methods is the most "primitive," in the sense that the other methods can be implemented using it. (Of course, there might be a substantial loss of efficiency and atomicity when doing this.)

   a. Rewrite the code for shared memory, of examples 8.7, 8.8, and 8.9, assuming that the only facility for doing this is messages.

   b. Rewrite the code for semaphores, of examples 8.4 and 8.5, assuming that the only facility for doing this is messages.

2. The code in the shared memory example in section 8.4 used semaphores to synchronize access to the shared memory region. Rewrite the code to use the sending and receiving of messages instead of semaphores for synchronization.

3. Explain in detail how deadlock could occur in the programs given in section 8.4 to demonstrate shared memory synchronization with semaphores if there was no initial call to V() in the main program.

4. Which of the system calls in the System V IPC package are atomic? Does your answer depend upon the size of buffers? Explain.

5. Explain how the improper use of the two system calls msgget() and msgctl() can lead to a race condition in which the state of the system cannot be determined. Can deadlock occur in this situation?

6. Repeat exercise 5 for the two system calls semget() and semctl().

7. Repeat exercise 5 for the two system calls shmget() and shmctl().

8. Devise and perform an experiment to determine the break value for several small programs. Determine where the compiler places a shared memory segment of size 4 bytes, 256 bytes, 512 bytes, and 1,024 bytes if no address is specified. Try to discover the compiler's algorithm for finding a place to attach a shared memory region of different sizes.

9. Implement a function, pipe_m(), that emulates the pipe() system call but uses messages instead of pipes.

Signals, Sockets, and RPC

In this chapter, we consider some additional methods of ipc. The first section describes signals, which are used to inform processes of special events. The second section discusses sockets and their use. The third and fourth sections describe remote procedure call (RPC) and the use of the `rpcgen` utility and RPC language to allow programs to run procedures on other computers on a network. In the fifth section of this chapter, we briefly describe process tracing.

9.1 SIGNALS

Signals are a conceptually simple method of communication between processes. There are a fixed number of UNIX signals, and each has a unique nonnegative integer associated with it. Two or more processes can communicate by one process sending a signal and the other one receiving it. The receiving process frequently acts upon the received signal, the action is usually described in a piece of code called a *signal handler*. The term *signal catcher* is often used instead of signal handler. The signal handler is a function within a process and is written to have a specific action: detecting the signal and taking an action that is appropriate to the signal.

Before we discuss the specifics of signals, we will give an example of a typical application.

9.1.1   Two Signal Examples

A common workstation programming environment involves a window system, such as X Windows, running with the UNIX operating system. In such an environment, the user may have access to many different windows, with a different process running in each. The windows may be placed anywhere on the display monitor, and their size may be adjusted by the user. The user typically uses a device such as a mouse to move a cursor around the display monitor and to select options by pressing one or more mouse buttons. Movement of the mouse is tracked and interpreted as a cursor position by a dedicated process.

The user may also enter text and data with the keyboard. Imagine that one or more processes are used to control the creation and movement of the windows, and that they are considered to be separate from the processes that are running in the windows. Information about which window is selected by the mouse or which window is getting input from the keyboard arrives in an asynchronous, unpredictable manner. Generally, only one window can receive keyboard input at any one time.

It is essential that none of the processes running in different windows require any specific information about the window in which they are running. Not allowing a process to depend on information about the associated window means that the process cannot know enough to communicate with the process that controls the window.

How can these processes communicate? Consider the various possibilities for interprocess communication. It is unlikely that an ipc message such as semaphores could be used, since this method requires that the processes share some information about either a semaphore id or a semaphore key. The use of a small shared memory region is difficult because of the need for processes to know the shared memory id. Methods such as messages and pipes require the processes to know something about one another, such as file descriptors or process-ids. Both of the file-based methods seem awkward in this environment, since only a small amount of information needs to be communicated.

A method such as FIFOs or named pipes eliminates the need for the process that is tracking the mouse's cursor position to know anything special about the process-id of the process controlling a window or a process running in a window. However, requests for interpretation of a mouse movement or for the pressing of a mouse button need not be done in a first in-first out manner if several processes are waiting for a particular window. Since a window can be opened, closed, or destroyed frequently, a system with many processes that uses the FIFO ipc method can easily use up a large number of i-nodes.

Clearly all these ipc methods leave something to be desired in a work-station environment. What is necessary is an ipc method with the following characteristics:

- The amount of information communicated can be small.
- The processes do not need to share any common kernel data structures.
- The communication can be asynchronous.
- Different actions can be specified depending on the information communicated by the ipc method.

These are precisely the features that are available with UNIX signals. Signals permit processes to communicate easily without their knowing much about each other.

Here is another, simpler application. A signal can be sent to a process from its parent shell process. Consider a program that prints the integers 1,2,3, . . . in succession. Suppose that we compile the program into an executable program called a.out and run it. The process runs forever unless we stop it by sending a kill signal; this is frequently done by pressing the delete key.

To see the use of signals more clearly, run the a.out process in the background using the shell command

```
a.out &
```

The shell responds by printing the process-id of this process. Since this process is running in the background, we have access to the shell via the keyboard. The shell command kill, whose syntax is one of

```
kill process_id
```

or

```
kill -kill_signal_level process_id
```

will terminate the process because it sends a special signal, SIGKILL, to the process whose id is given. The background process receives the signal (since the SIGKILL signal cannot be ignored by any process) and takes the only appropriate action—termination. The level of killing action is specified in the argument *kill_signal_level*; the highest level of killing action is 9.

This discussion of background processes points out another feature of signals. A process can choose to mask one or more signals so that it can ignore them. When the shell executes a process in the background, the process is allowed to mask the signal SIGINT, which would ordinarily react to a press of a key such as delete or termination. SIGINT is the signal that an interrupt has occurred. This is why keyboard actions do not affect background processes.

9.1.2   The `signal()` System Call

The most important system call needed for signals is `signal()`, the syntax of which is

```
signal(signal_number, sig_action);
```

The first argument is an integer denoting an allowable signal. The second argument is one of three options:

- `SIG_DFL`, which is used to set default actions for the signal. It cannot be used for the signal `SIG_CLD`, which signifies the death of a child process.
- `SIG_IGN`, which is used to ignore the signal. (Recall that the signal `SIGKILL` cannot be ignored.)
- A pointer to a function that is used as a signal handler.

A signal is usually sent to a process by the kernel. It can also be sent to a process by another process.

There is a fundamental problem with the use of signals in some versions of UNIX. The status of system calls interrupted by signals cannot be easily determined. It is possible that some of the kernel data structures may be corrupted if a signal is acted upon in the middle of the execution of a system call. This lack of synchronization of kernel data structures is one of the reasons for the existence of the "semaphore undo structure" that is available with System V semaphores.

9.1.3   The `wait()` System Call

The `wait()` system call is related to signals, in the sense that it sends a single piece of information to a process. The use of this system call is for a parent process to issue a call to `wait()` in order for the parent to resume its computation after the child process terminates. The syntax is

```
wait(& status);
```

where `status` is an integer. The information in the rightmost two bytes of the integer `status` is used as follows (see Figure 9.1).

- If the rightmost byte is 0, the next-to-rightmost byte is the child's argument to `exit()`.

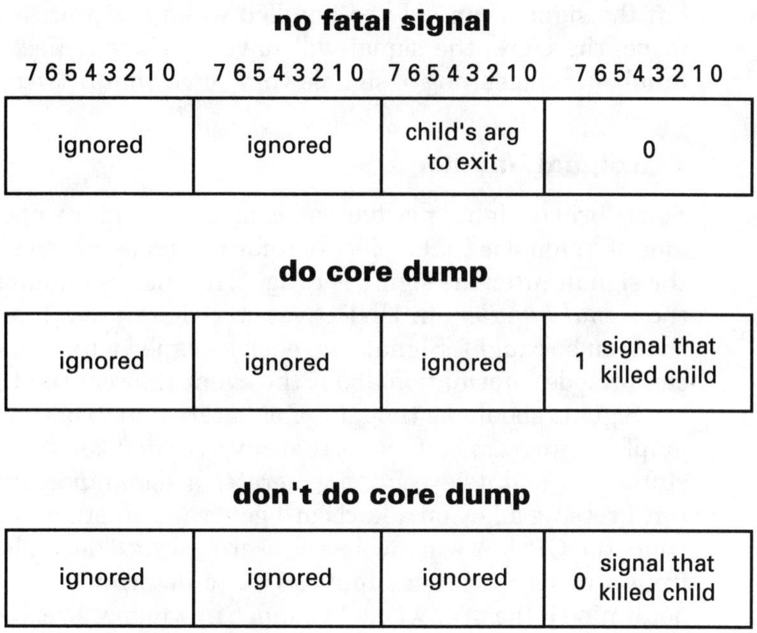

no fatal signal

7 6 5 4 3 2 1 0	7 6 5 4 3 2 1 0	7 6 5 4 3 2 1 0	7 6 5 4 3 2 1 0
ignored	ignored	child's arg to exit	0

do core dump

7 6 5 4 3 2 1 0	7 6 5 4 3 2 1 0	7 6 5 4 3 2 1 0	7 6 5 4 3 2 1 0
ignored	ignored	ignored	1 signal that killed child

don't do core dump

7 6 5 4 3 2 1 0	7 6 5 4 3 2 1 0	7 6 5 4 3 2 1 0	7 6 5 4 3 2 1 0
ignored	ignored	ignored	0 signal that killed child

Figure 9.1.   Details of `wait()`

- If the rightmost byte is not 0, the rightmost seven bits represent the number of the signal that killed the child, and the leftmost bit of the rightmost byte indicates a core dump if it is set to 1. In either case, the next-to-rightmost byte is ignored if the rightmost byte is not 0.

9.1.4   Signal Drawbacks

Signals are sent from one process another to inform the second process of a condition. They are not used to send messages. The signal method of interprocess communication is the simplest to employ, but it has many drawbacks in certain systems. For one, a second signal may arrive before the process executes the system call in System V Release 4 UNIX, forcing a default action to be taken even if a signal handler is present. Signals are treated differently in Berkeley 4.2 and 4.3 UNIX, where a caught signal is blocked within a signal handler even if a previous signal is being handled. The mode of the process changes from user mode to kernel mode when a signal arrives, but the signals can only be handled when the process returns from kernel mode; therefore, the signal will have a delayed effect on the process. The number and meaning of signals vary somewhat between UNIX systems.

9.1.5   The Signal Handler

Some form of signal mechanism is present in many operating systems. The idea of a signal is that a piece of information is sent to a process that catches the signal. After the signal is caught, it must be handled, which is the job of the *signal handler*. In UNIX systems, there are a fixed number of signals that can be caught. Signals are each assigned a unique number so that they can provide information about the event that caused them.

Signals should be thought of as interrupts to normal processing. For example, a program statement that involves division by zero is an exceptional statement, and its execution generates a signal indicating an arithmetic error. Pressing a key on a keyboard generates another signal that often interrupts the CPU. A window-based user interface depends on signals obtained from a mouse or other input device to determine the active window or to determine if the user wishes a change in window size, position, and so on. An especially important signal is `kill`, which terminates a process.

Signals are used for asynchronous events, and in general they cannot be queued. They are caught and handled differently in System V and BSD versions of UNIX. We first discuss System V UNIX.

In System V UNIX, a process catches a signal, passes it to a signal handler, and then is ready for the next signal to arrive. This works perfectly if no new signal arrives during the time the original signal is being handled. However, signals in System V Release 3 cannot be queued up by a signal catcher because of the design of this mechanism. Thus, it is quite likely that if many signals are sent to a process, some of them will be ignored; that is, they will not be caught by a signal handler.

In BSD UNIX, a caught signal is blocked within a signal handler even if a previous signal is being handled. You may already have encountered this problem any time you tried to kill a running program with the kill key and had to press it several times before you got a response. You were sending signals that were ignored (not caught) and therefore not handled.

9.1.6   Signals Available in UNIX

There are many signals available in UNIX. In System V Release 3, for example, there are 19. Typical signal numbers and their meanings are given in Table 9.1.

Table 9.1.   System V Release 2 and Release 3 signals

SIGHUP	1	hangup
SIGINT	2	interrupt
SIGQUIT	3	quit
SIGILL	4	illegal instruction (not reset when caught)
SIGTRAP	5	trace trap (not reset when caught)
SIGIOT	6	IOT instruction
SIGABRT	6	used by abort (replace SIGIOT in the future)
SIGEMT	7	EMT instruction
SIGFPE	8	floating point exception
SIGKILL	9	kill (cannot be caught or ignored)
SIGBUS	10	bus error
SIGSEGV	11	segmentation violation
SIGSYS	12	bad argument to system call
SIGPIPE	13	write on a pipe with no one to read it
SIGALRM	14	alarm clock
SIGTERM	15	software termination signal from kill
SIGUSR1	16	user-defined signal 1
SIGUSR2	17	user-defined signal 2
SIGCLD	18	death of a child
SIGPWR	19	power-fail restart

There are additional signals in BSD and SVR4 UNIX. The typical signal numbers and their meanings are given in Table 9.2.

Note the minor differences in dialect between the two systems. The names SIGCHLD and SIGCLD are particularly strong evidence of the concurrent development of these two versions of UNIX.

There are often other signals that are relevant to particular hardware systems. They concern such issues as the possible problems concerned in a page fault or memory access, even if the memory request is to an address within the address space of the process. The mnemonic names associated with these nonstandard UNIX signals and their meanings can be found in the include file signal.h, in which all signals are defined. This file also contains definitions of the data structures that are used to control the information pushed on the stack when a signal is delivered. The kernel uses this information to restore the proper state following execution of the signal handler.

Table 9.2.   BSD and SVR4 signals

SIGHUP	1	hangup
SIGINT	2	interrupt
SIGQUIT	3	quit
SIGILL	4	illegal instruction (not reset when caught)
SIGTRAP	5	trace trap (not reset when caught)
SIGIOT	6	I/O trap instruction
SIGEMT	7	EMT instruction
SIGFPE	8	floating point exception
SIGKILL	9	kill (cannot be caught or ignored)
SIGBUS	10	bus error
SIGSEGV	11	segmentation violation
SIGSYS	12	bad argument to system call
SIGPIPE	13	write on a pipe with no one to read it
SIGALRM	14	alarm clock
SIGTERM	15	software termination signal from kill
SIGURG	16	urgent condition on I/O channel
SIGSTOP	17	sendable stop signal not from tty
SIGTSTP	18	stop signal from tty
SIGCONT	19	continue a stopped process
SIGCHLD	20	to parent on child stop or exit
SIGCLD	20	System V name for SIGCHLD
SIGTTIN	21	to readers pgrp upon background tty read
SIGTTOU	22	like TTIN for output
SIGIO	23	input/output possible signal
SIGPOLL	SIGIO	System V R4 name for SIGIO
SIGXCPU	24	exceeded CPU time limit
SIGXFSZ	25	exceeded file size limit
SIGVTALRM	26	virtual time alarm
SIGPROF	27	profiling time alarm
SIGWINCH	28	window changed
SIGLOST	29	resource lost
SIGUSR1	30	user-defined signal 1
SIGUSR2	31	user-defined signal 2

9.1.7   The Signal Code

The code in example 9.1 has a somewhat unusual organization. It uses command-line arguments to show the number of repetitions of communication. (The number of bytes communicated is ignored in signals, but we indicate it for consistency of interface with the other ipc codes, and include it in our source code.) Since we wanted the code to be relatively portable across UNIX systems, we used a mechanism that requires the receiver to catch the signals and not just send them to another process.

In example 9.1, a child process sends signals to the parent process until a given number of signals are acknowledged by the parent process. The use of the system call `pause()` is necessary to ensure that all the signals are received when the code is run on a machine running System V Release 3 UNIX. It might not be necessary to use `pause()` if the experiment is run on other UNIX systems; we have not noticed this problem on other systems.

The code consists of a main program that forks a child process. The code for the child process to execute is made as simple as possible. Note the assumption of the process-id of the child being exactly one more than the process-id of the parent. This might not be true on a system with many users. In any event, the syntax of the `kill()` system call shows how to send a signal to a process simply by knowing its process-id; no other relationship is necessary.

Example 9.1: Use of Signals

```
/*  Test of efficiency of UNIX ipc */
/*  Communication using signals     */
#include <stdio.h>
#include <signal.h>

sigcatcher()
{
signal(SIGALRM,sigcatcher);
}

main(argc,argv)
int argc;
char *argv[];
{int ppid, i, number_of_signals_sent;

if( argc < 2)
```

```
        {
        puts("Bad arg count");
        printf("Usage: %s num_signals\n",argv[0]);
        exit(1);
        }

number_of_signals_sent = atoi(argv[1]);
signal(SIGALRM,sigcatcher);
if (fork() == 0)
        { /* Get process id of parent */
        ppid = getppid();
        for (;;)
            if (kill(ppid,SIGALRM) == -1)
                {
                puts("Dead");
                exit(1);
                }
        } /* end child */

puts("Parent");
/* Wait for signals from child process */
for (i=0; i< number_of_signals_sent; i++)
        pause();
kill(getpid()+1,SIGINT);
}
```

9.2   SOCKETS

We have discussed eight different ipc methods so far, all of which were originally designed to allow communication between processes running on the same CPU. However, this discussion does not exhaust the possible ipc methods available under UNIX. The increase in networking has encouraged the development of methods that allow communication between processes running on different computers.

The methods presented in the previous two chapters and in the first section of this chapter are all portable to some extent, especially in System V UNIX or versions of BSD UNIX with the System V IPC package installed. Unfortunately, the socket method described in this section is not always portable.

The socket mechanism was originally developed and implemented as part of BSD UNIX. The idea is that two processes wishing to communicate set up a pair of "sockets" to create a communication channel between them. This by itself is nothing new; we have seen many versions of this idea before in other ipc methods. What is new is that the socket mechanism allows communication between processes that are running on the same computer or on different computers on a network.

The socket mechanism is therefore the most powerful ipc method, at least in its generality. It allows communication between processes on the same or on different computers by means of mechanism similar to messages. (Clearly, a mechanism based on shared memory would produce nonsense if applied to processes running on different computers.)

A complete discussion of sockets would move us too far afield from the main topics of this book. However, detailed information can be found in many books on data communications and network programming, including the references listed at the end of this chapter. We will be content with a quick overview of sockets in this section and an equally brief discussion in the next section of remote procedure call (RPC), which is based upon sockets.

9.2.1   Client-Server Model

Use of a socket for communication often follows the client-server model. One method of communication between server and client processes is to design the server following these steps:

- Create the socket.
- Assign a name to the socket.
- Attach a connection to the socket.
- Transfer data via the socket.
- Clean up the socket after use.

The connection to a socket also uses a socket. The connecting socket used for a client follows a similar paradigm, except that the assignment of a name is not always necessary.

Programs following the client-server model can be grouped broadly into two classes: connection-oriented servers and connectionless servers. A connection-oriented server means that a reliable path has been set up for the delivery of data, that uses what is known as a *virtual circuit*. This virtual circuit is set up before any data transmission is attempted.

In a connectionless server, no predetermined virtual circuit exists for the transmission of data, and so each amount of data being transmitted must contain its own addressing information. Connectionless servers are subdivided further into datagram and reliable datagram servers. We will not consider connectionless servers in any detail in this book.

The easiest way to understand the use of sockets is to reason by analogy with the way that pipes and FIFOs are treated by the `pipe()` and `mkfifo()` system calls. The result of a successful call to the system call `socket()` behaves like a file descriptor in the `pipe()` system call. The use of names for sockets is similar to the way that FIFOs are treated. The analogy to pipes is reinforced by the fact that pipes are often implemented as sockets.

Reading and writing on sockets is by means of the `read()` and `write()` system calls or by the newer `send()` and `recv()` system calls. The relative efficiency of these two pairs of system calls with sockets is discussed in the exercises. A socket can be closed with either the `close()` or `shutdown()` system calls.

Recall that the `socket()` system call is likely to be present only on systems using BSD, SVR4, or similar variants of UNIX such as Solaris or HP-UX. Obviously, both computers communicating on a network must have the socket facility for this method to work. Just being able to communicate via electronic mail is not sufficient to ensure the availability of sockets.

9.2.2   The `socketpair()` System Call

Example 9.2 illustrates nonportability in a program using sockets. The program's goal is to implement a pipe using sockets instead of the `pipe()` system call. The shortcut used here involves the `socketpair()` system call available under Solaris 1.1 (SunOS 4.1.3) on a Sun SPARC 2. The shortcut sets up communication links at both ends of the socket at once (the action is assumed to be atomic). To our knowledge, the `socketpair()` system call is not commonly available on systems other than those running Solaris. The program does more than replace the `pipe()` system call; the connection it sets up is bidirectional.

Example 9.2: Use of `socketpair()` under Solaris

```
/* Program to demonstrate use of socketpair()  */
/* It creates a pair of socket descriptors in   */
/* the array fd[2] for use by the main (parent)*/
/* process and the child process that is        */
/* created by a fork().                          */


#include <sys/types.h>
#include <sys/socket.h>
#include <stdio.h>
```

```
main()
{
  int fd[2], length;
  char *str = "THIS IS A TEST";

  if (socketpair( AF_UNIX, SOCK_STREAM, 0, fd) < 0)
        {
        fputs("ERROR IN SOCKET CONNECTION",stderr);
        exit(1);
        }

  switch (fork())
        {
        case -1:
          fputs("ERROR IN FORK", stderr);
          exit(1);
        case 0 :          /* child process */
          if (read(fd[0], str, length) < 0 )
            {
            fputs("ERROR IN READ", stderr);
            exit(1);
            }

        default:          /* parent process */
          length = strlen(str);
          if (write(fd[1], str, length) != length)
            {
            fputs("ERROR IN WRITE", stderr);
            exit(1);
            }
        }
  close(fd[0]);
  close(fd[1]);
}
```

Two of the arguments to socketpair() require discussion. The first argument, AF_UNIX, is a symbolic constant that indicates that the entire communications system set up by this call is in the "UNIX domain." That is, both the sender and receiver of data reside on the same computer, which is running a version of UNIX.

The second argument, SOCK_STREAM, is a symbolic constant indicating that the data is reliably delivered in a stream format instead of in packets.

Both these arguments will be discussed in more detail later, in our description of the `socket()` system call.

It would be easy to modify this example to have a stream of data, instead of a single test string, passed along the socket, and to have both the number of bytes communicated and the number of communications between processes set up as command-line arguments. You will be asked to do this in the exercises.

9.2.3   Other Socket System Calls

We have another way to create a pipe that uses the `socket()` system call in place of the `pipe()` system call. This approach (illustrated in example 9.3) will not use `socketpair()` and thus will be much more portable. The overall design of the approach is familiar. The difference between it and previous ones is that the socket descriptors must be explicitly sent from the process in which the socket is created to the other process.

We will need to use five new system calls: `socket()`, `bind()`, `connect()`, `listen()`, and `accept()`. We will discuss each of these calls before we present our solution.

Creation of a socket is done by the `socket()` system call, whose syntax is

```
int socket(int domain,
           int type,
           int protocol);
```

Its arguments are as follows.

- The first argument, `domain`, is an integer that is defined in the header file `socket.h` and is often one of the values `AF_INET` or `AF_UNIX`, denoting either the Internet or UNIX domains. Other domains are possible.
- The second argument, `type`, is also an integer that is defined in the file `socket.h`. The most common types of sockets are `SOCK_STREAM` (for a stream socket used for pipes), `SOCK_DGRAM` (for a "datagram"), `SOCK_RAW` (for a raw or nonbuffered device), `SOCK_RDM` (for a reliably delivered message), and `SOCK_SEQPACKET` (for a stream of packets that are to be delivered in sequence).
- The third argument, `protocol`, is an integer that represents the type of protocol to be used with the socket. (The need for a protocol is clear if we consider that sockets can be used to connect different machines.) A commonly used value for the `protocol` argument is 0,

indicating that the operating system is to look up the correct protocol from the header file.

The value returned by a successful call to socket() is an int known as a socket descriptor. An unsuccessful call returns the value −1.

The assignment of a name to a socket is by the bind() system call. Its syntax is

```
int bind(int socket_id,
    struct sockaddr * sockaddr,
    int length) ;
```

The meaning of the first argument to bind() is obvious.

The second argument to bind() is a pointer to a structured data type with two fields. The first field of the structured data type, called sockaddr, is always a symbolic constant that represents what is known as the *application family*. For server and client processes that reside on the same computer, the value of this constant is AF_UNIX, which is defined in the header file sys/socket.h. Its type is either an int or a short int, depending on the operating system version.

The second field of the structured type sockaddr is an array of characters, which for portability reasons, is allowed to be 108 bytes long. This field contains the name that is bound to the socket. Programs may not assume that the character array is terminated in a null byte. Instead, the programmer must explicitly control the number of bytes in the name of the socket. The two fields are generally called sun_family and sun_path.

The details of the interpretation of the second parameter are often machine-specific and can be found in your system manual. A more detailed discussion of sockets can be found in any current text on data communications, such as Stevens on network programming (see the references).

The third argument to bind() is the size of the significant bytes of the structured type specified in the second argument. The best way to use this argument is to add the two expressions

```
sizeof(AF_UNIX)
```

```
strlen(sun_path)
```

Here we have explicitly placed a null byte at the end of the filled-in bytes in the field sun_path. This will be made clear in example 9.3.

The value returned by a successful call to bind() is an int; an unsuccessful call returns the value −1.

As indicated earlier, the use of sockets follows the client-server model. The connection of a socket to a server is by the connect() system call, whose syntax is

```
int connect(int socket_id,
            int socket_id,
            struct sockaddr *address,
            int length);
```

The third argument for the connect() system call depends on the computer on which the processes are run. On the Sun SPARC 2 running Solaris 1.1, it represents the length of the name of the second argument, which is of type

```
struct sockaddr *sockaddr;
```

On other systems, it might be

```
struct sockaddr_un *sockaddr;
```

These types may be equivalent, depending on the contents of the header file socket.h.

The server process listens for data from clients using the listen() system call:

```
listen(int socket_id, int MAX__ATTEMPTS);
```

The maximum value of MAX_ATTEMPTS is currently 5 on UNIX systems. It represents the number of times the socket will try to receive a request for connection before failure. The reason for a limit is that the process attempting to communicate may have terminated unexpectedly and a graceful exit may be needed from the listener process.

The accept() system call provides the means of transmission between the server and the client. It has the syntax

```
int accept(int sock_fd,
           struct sockaddr * client_addr,
           int length);
```

In the most common usage of this system call, the first argument, sock_fd, is specified as the same in a previously executed socket() system call. The other two arguments are not initialized and receive their values as a side effect of accept(). This call returns the value −1 if unsuccessful; otherwise, it returns a positive int.

We now provide examples of the use of some of these system calls. Example 9.3 illustrates a server program that uses the hardcoded name SERVER to be bound to the socket. The name is used extensively in the initialization of the fields of the object pointed to by the sockaddr argument to the bind() system call. The server design for this example is:

- Create a socket with socket().
- Initialize a pointer and the contents of the sockaddr structure.
- Bind a name to the socket using bind().
- Use listen() to tell the kernel that we are a server process.
- Use an infinite loop to take requests using the accept() system call and new, temporary socket ids.
- Provide cleanup after completion.

This server design uses an infinite for-loop to receive data. The data is provided in the short string THIS IS A TEST, specified in the example. Because the amount of data transmitted is so small, there is no need to read the data in a while-loop. In general, the action performed by the server would be much more complex than the single calls to read() and write(), and a realistic server would not exit after servicing one data transmission. However, the example is sufficient to illustrate the concepts.

Note the use of the system call perror(). This provides helpful information, since many things can go wrong. We have provided several print statements so that execution of the program can be traced easily.

Example 9.3: A Server Connection

```
/* SERVER PROGRAM                                      */
/* This program demonstrates the use of the system    */
/* calls socket(), bind(), listen(), and accept() to   */
/* create a server for a pipe.                         */
/* It creates a single socket descriptor in the       */
/* value fd for use by the main (server) process.      */
/* The socket descriptor in the value temp_id is used  */
/* for the connection to the client process using      */
/* the accept() system call.                           */

#include <sys/types.h>
#include <sys/socket.h>
#include <sys/un.h>
#include <sys/errno.h>

#include <stdio.h>
```

```
main()
{
    int fd, temp_id, length, i;
    char *str = "THIS IS A TEST\n";
    char *name = "SERVER";
    struct sockaddr_un *sockaddr;
    struct sockaddr_un *client_addr;

    extern int errno;

    unlink(name);
    printf("\nLENGTH OF NAME IS %d\n", strlen(name));

    if ((fd = socket(AF_UNIX, SOCK_STREAM, 0) ) < 0 )
        {
        close(fd);
        exit(1);
        }

    printf("The socket descriptor is %d\n", fd);

    sockaddr = (struct sockaddr_un *)
                malloc( sizeof (struct sockaddr_un ));

    /* initialize contents of *sockaddr */
    sockaddr->sun_family = (u_short ) AF_UNIX;
    for (i = 0; i < 108; i++)
       sockaddr->sun_path[i] = '\0';
    strcpy(sockaddr->sun_path,name);

    length = sizeof(sockaddr->sun_family) +
                strlen(sockaddr->sun_path);

    printf("\nLENGTH = %d\n", length);
    printf("sun_family = %d\n", sockaddr->sun_family);
    printf("sun_path = %s\n", sockaddr->sun_path);

    if (bind(fd, (struct sockaddr *) sockaddr, length ) < 0)
        {
```

```c
    perror("SERVER BIND");
    if (unlink(name) < 0)
       perror("UNLINK IN SERVER");
    close(fd);
    exit(1);
    }

if (listen(fd, 5 ) < 0)
   {
   perror("listen IN SERVER");
   exit(1);
   }

/* infinite loop to get requests from client */
for( ; ; )
      {
      if (( temp_id = accept(fd, (struct sockaddr *)
                       client_addr, length ) ) < 0)
        {
        perror("ACCEPT IN SERVER");
        exit(1);
        }

      printf("The new socket descriptor is %d\n",
           temp_id);

      if (read(temp_id, str, length) < 0)
        {
        fputs("SERVER PROCESS; ERROR IN READ\n",
            stderr);
        if (unlink(name) < 0)
           perror("UNLINK IN SERVER");
        exit(5); /* abnormal exit from child */
        }

      close(temp_id);

      /* echo the string to stdout */
      if (write(1, str, strlen(name) ) < 0 )
        {
```

```
                    fputs("ERROR IN WRITE IN SERVER\n", stderr);
                    exit(5);
                    }
               close(temp_id);
               exit(0);
               } /* end for loop */
}
```

The design of the client program in example 9.4 is similar to that of the server in example 9.3. The fundamental differences are that there is no call to `bind()` and the essential system calls and initializations are in the following order:

- Create a socket with `socket()`.
- Initialize a pointer and the contents of the `sockaddr` structure.
- Use a new, temporary socket id to make a request using the `connect()` system call.

Example 9.4: A Client Connection

```
/* CLIENT PROGRAM                                      */
/* This program demonstrates the use of the system    */
/* socket() and connect() to create a pipe.           */
/* It creates a single socket descriptor in the       */
/* value fd for use by the main (server) process.     */

#include <sys/types.h>
#include <sys/socket.h>
#include <sys/un.h>
#include <sys/errno.h>

#include <stdio.h>

main()
{
   int fd, temp_id, length, i;
   char *str = "TEST\n";
   char *name = "SERVER";
   struct sockaddr_un *sockaddr;

   extern int errno;
```

```
        printf("\nLENGTH OF NAME IS %d\n", strlen(name));

        sockaddr = (struct sockaddr_un *)
                        malloc( sizeof (struct sockaddr_un ));

        /* initialize contents of *sockaddr */
        sockaddr->sun_family = (u_short ) AF_UNIX;
        for (i = 0; i < 108; i++)
            sockaddr->sun_path[i] = '\0';
        strcpy(sockaddr->sun_path,name);

        length = sizeof(sockaddr->sun_family) +
                            strlen(sockaddr->sun_path);

        printf("\nCLIENT LENGTH = %d\n", length);
        printf("CLIENT sun_family = %d\n", sockaddr->sun_family);
        printf("CLIENT sun_path = %s\n\n", sockaddr->sun_path);

        if ((fd = socket(AF_UNIX, SOCK_STREAM, 0) ) < 0 )
                {
                perror("ERROR IN CLIENT SOCKET");
                close(fd);
                exit(1);
                }

        printf("The CLIENT socket descriptor is %d\n", fd);

        if ((temp_id = connect(fd, (struct sockaddr *)
                            sockaddr, length)) < 0 )
            {
            perror("CLIENT CONNECT");
            if (unlink(name) < 0)
              perror("UNLINK IN CLIENT");
            fputs("EXITING CLIENT\n", stderr);
            exit(1);
            }

            if (write(temp_id, str, strlen(name) ) < 0 )
                {
                fputs("ERROR IN WRITE IN CLIENT\n", stderr);
```

```
        exit(1);
        }

    if (unlink(name) < 0)
        perror("UNLINK IN CLIENT");
    exit(0);
}
```

Our program's design is very simple. We send a single character string, TEST, from the client process to the server process, so there is only one transmission of data. A more realistic program might have multiple transmissions, and the call to exit() in the last line of the server program would be eliminated.

Our program follows the design of a *sequential server*. If there were multiple requests, the server program would treat the service requests in the order they were received. A different design, a *concurrent server*, would allow the forking of a new process to treat each service request as it arrived. Both designs are *connection-oriented servers*.

Other server and client designs are possible, including ones that use the SOCK_DGRAM type of argument to socket() but do not use bind(). These are called *connectionless servers*. A connectionless server is illustrated in example 9.5.

Example 9.5: A Connectionless Server Using "Datagrams"

```
/* This program demonstrates the use of sockets for   */
/* communication without the use of socketpair().     */
/* It creates a pair of socket descriptors in the     */
/* array socket_id[2]] for use by the main process    */
/* and the child process that is created by a fork().  */
/* The message sent is a "datagram."                  */
/* The name of the socket is precisely 14 characters. */

#include <sys/types.h>
#include <sys/socket.h>
#include <stdio.h>

main()
{
  int length;
  int fd[2];
```

```
char *str = "THIS IS A TEST";
struct sockaddr addr;

if (fd[0] =socket("AF_UNIX", SOCK_DGRAM, 0) < 0 )
    {
    fputs("ERROR IN SOCKET", stderr);
    exit(1);
    }

length = sizeof("MY_DGRAM_SOCKET_") +
         sizeof("AF_UNIX");

switch (fork())
    {
    case -1:
      fputs("ERROR IN FORK", stderr);
      exit(1);
      case 0 : /* child process */
      if (bind(fd, "MY_DGRAM_SOCKET_",
               strlen("MY_DGRAM_SOCKET_")) < 0 );
        perror("ERROR IN CHILD BIND");
      if (read(fd[0], str, length) < 0 )
        {
        fputs("ERROR IN READ", stderr);
        exit(1);
        }

      default: /* parent process -- server */
        if (bind(fd, "MY_DGRAM_SOCKET_",
                 strlen("MY_DGRAM_SOCKET_")) < 0 );
          perror("ERROR IN PARENT BIND");

        length = strlen(str);
        if (write(fd[0], str, length) != length)
          {
          fputs("ERROR IN WRITE", stderr);
          exit(1);
          }
    }
close(fd[0]);
```

```
        close(fd[1]);
}
```

For more information on these program models, see the references.

9.3   **REMOTE PROCEDURE CALL**

The socket mechanism allows multiple processes running on either the same or different computers to communicate with one another. The idea underlying the most common usage of sockets is the client-server model, in which a server process can provide information to a client process. This improves the performance of many programs by allowing portions of the programs to run concurrently and communicate essential information. This is why sockets are considered to be an ipc method. The client-server model also avoids duplication of resources by having essential software reside on the appropriate host computer.

This method is fairly coarse-grained, in the sense that a distributed computation using this model is divided into concurrently executing processes. A more finely grained computation would allow a process to have other processes run procedures on its behalf, rather than complete processes. The calling process would block waiting for the return of execution from the called procedure. This blocking is identical to the blocking of a process from a procedure or function that is called within the process in ordinary sequential program execution.

We can use remote procedure call (RPC) to allow a process to use either the same or different computers on a network to run procedures for itself. RPC allows a client process to request information from a server process. The server process calls a procedure to perform the computation and then sends back the result of the procedure or function. (The term "procedure" is confusing in this context. Except for a few scattered instances in which there are bindings to other languages, UNIX RPC is generally implemented commercially only for C programs, and there is no concept of a separate entity called *procedures* in C. C functions that do not return values are still called functions.) For simplicity, we will use the term "procedure" to mean "function" in this section.

More specifically, the server process follows these steps:

- Receive a request for a computation.
- Determine the arguments for the procedure.
- Invoke the procedure.
- Send back results.
- Wait for the next message.

The client process follows these steps:

- Send information to the server about the procedure to be called and the arguments.
- Block execution and wait for the request to be serviced and the data to be sent back.
- Continue execution.

How does this RPC method differ from the much more common call of an ordinary procedure from within a program? The main differences are the following:

- Parameters are passed by value, since there is no way to convert addresses on one machine to addresses on another.
- The environment in which a procedure is running is not passed. Therefore, global variables in the caller process are not available to the remote procedure.
- The return to the caller process will not occur if the remote procedure never terminates. The remote procedure call can also fail if there is a network transmission problem.

RPC is somewhat more general than ipc because there can be multiple types of data returned by different "procedures," instead of a socket or other ipc mechanism being used to convey a stream of data of the same type.

There is a fair amount of work necessary for the initiation of programs that use RPC.

Implementations of RPC are slightly different on different versions of UNIX, although they are similar to the RPC version first developed by Sun based on BSD UNIX. For example, Solaris 1.1 includes a total of 76 library routines that can be used with programs that use RPC, while HP-UX version 7.0 has 60 such routines. Many of the most important routines are common to each. Regardless of the version of RPC used, programs that use RPC generally follow the client-server model.

9.3.1 RPC Layers

Most RPC implementations provide several layers of RPC action. We will present an overview of each of these layers and then proceed to a somewhat more detailed discussion of each.

Some standard utility functions are available to C programs, and thus their use is transparent to the user, in the sense that they appear to be ordinary library functions. The user need not know anything about the client-server model to use this layer of RPC. This is the highest layer of RPC use and is available in most implementations. In general, the highest layer includes library functions for monitoring network usage. Unfortunately, few functions are available for computations at this level.

Intermediate layers of RPC usage include functions such as `registerrpc()` and `callrpc()`. These routines are available in both the Sun Solaris and HP-UX implementations of RPC. The user of programs in this layer must be aware of issues of where the remote procedure is executing and how data is to be transferred between client and server.

Passing of arguments at this and the lower level must allow some form of transformation of data, since different computers may store integers, floating point numbers, or arrays differently. There is a standard conversion of many different data formats based on what is known as XDR, or external data representation.

Note: On some SVR4-based systems, the two RPC calls `callrpc()` and `registerrpc()` are named `rpc_call()` and `rpc_reg()`, respectively. For simplicity, we will use the names `callrpc()` and `registerrpc()` exclusively. The syntax of the equivalent calls is similar.

The lowest layer commonly used employs lower-level routines in a manner similar to the use of sockets in the previous section. It provides more control over security and allows the use of particular protocols and values of constants that override the default values.

Perhaps the best way to use RPC is to determine if your problem can be solved by facilities available at the highest layer. If not, use the intermediate layer, and use explicit sockets only if the facilities at the higher layers are not available or do not have sufficiently fast performance.

We will discuss each of these three RPC layers in turn. Only a few of the library routines will be mentioned.

9.3.2 The Highest RPC Layer

The highest layer of RPC is only as useful as the set of standard library functions provided with it. In general, there are procedures available for monitoring network usage. Example 9.6 shows the use of one such library function, `rnusers()`. This function prints the number of users logged onto a node that is accessible from the node on which the process is executing.

Example 9.6: Highest-Level Use of RPC

```
#include <stdio.h>

main(argc, argv)
int argc;
char * argv[];
```

```
{
    if (argc != 2)
      {
      printf("Use: num_users hostname\n");
      exit(1);
      }
    printf("There are %ld users on %s\n",
             rnusers( argv[1]),
             argv[1]);
}
```

It remains to link the object code for this function with the appropriate library. This library is called lrpcsvc on both Solaris and HP-UX.

Example 9.6 is clearly no different in concept from an ordinary C program running on a single machine. The details of the client-server relationship are hidden from us. Essentially, the computer on which we are running the program is a client. The server is the (probably remote) host on which we wish to determine the number of users. The server receives the request for execution of the procedure to compute the number of users and returns this number as its return value. The calling program on the client then resumes execution after determining the result returned by this remote procedure call.

Included in the lrpcsvc library are the functions rnusers() (for the number of remote users), rusers() (for information about the names of remote users), rstat() (to obtain performance information about a node), and rwall() (to write to all remote users). Other facilities available include a routine for determining the availability of local disks and routines for managing remote password files. The libraries are different on different systems.

You may have noticed that we can perform some of the actions available in the lrpcsvc library by using the remote shell facility rsh (known as remsh on older versions of System V). This is a different interface to the same routines. Thus, much of the output of the shell command

```
rsh sysname who
```

is equivalent to the call

```
rusers sysname
```

9.3.3 The Intermediate RPC Layer

We now discuss the intermediate layer of RPC facilities. Recall that use of this layer of RPC requires us to know where procedures are executing and to be able to transfer data between different computers.

The first step when using the intermediate layer of RPC is to register the name and "version" of the remote procedure. The reason for "registering" the remote procedure is to prevent accidental use of different procedures with the same name by other users of the network.

There are two ways of registering procedure names. The safest way is to use the `registerrpc()` library function (`rpc_reg()` on some systems) to automatically assign the program number to a procedure name. This library function takes six arguments and returns 0 if the attempt to register the name succeeds. A negative return value indicates failure. This call is used with the following syntax.

```
registerrpc(int PROG,
            int VERSION,
            int PROC_NUM,
            char *proc_name,
            arg_type *arg,
            return_type *return_value);
```

The values of the first three arguments of the call to the function `registerrpc()` are generally set by the user as constants in a separate header file. The first argument, PROG, is set according to a standard convention described later in this section. The second argument is an integer denoting which version of the procedure is to be used. (This is useful if we are updating procedures in the server and don't wish to make major changes to client programs.) By convention, the number 1 is usually used for the value of the version number, unless a newer version of a procedure will be replacing an older one. The third argument, PROC_NUM, indicates which procedure in the code is to be executed. Also by convention, the NULL procedure is given version number 0, so that the value of the third argument is 1 for the first procedure used.

The fourth argument, `proc_name`, is the name of the procedure that is to be registered as the first argument. The last two arguments, `arg` and `return_value`, refer to the nature of the arguments and the return value of the procedure named in the argument `proc_name`. In order to execute a procedure such as that of Example 9.5, the value of `proc_name` might be something like "remote_users"; the type of the argument `arg` would be `xdr_bytes` (to be defined later), since this argument is a string; and the return type would be `xdr_long` (also to be defined later), since the library function `nrusers()` returns a long int. (Technically `xdr_bytes` and `xdr_long` are Boolean functions performing conversions to these types.)

You may have noticed that there was only a single argument for passing an actual parameter that was given to `registerrpc()`. (The other arguments indicate that there is a single value returned, with no side effects.) This is not an error. The convention is that RPC procedures called have only one argument and one return value, with no other variables being affected by side effects. The way to have multiple arguments or multiple side effects is to incorporate the desired variables into a single structure and pass that structure. For simplicity, we will consider only procedures with simple arguments and refer the reader to the references for more information on the more complex cases.

It also appears that we are passing arguments by reference because of the use of pointers. This is not completely correct, since the remotely called procedure cannot understand addresses from the caller process. The addresses are only used by registerrpc() and not by the remotely called procedure.

Each program can set its number directly without the use of the registerrpc() library call. In order to do this, the following convention must be observed.

Range of Numbers	Usage
0 - 1fffffff	Reserved by Sun
20000000-3fffffff	User-defined
40000000-5fffffff	Temporary use
60000000-7fffffff	User-defined, reserved
80000000-9fffffff	User-defined, reserved
a0000000-bfffffff	User-defined, reserved
c0000000-dfffffff	User-defined, reserved
e0000000-ffffffff	User-defined, reserved

Use of the first group is reserved by Sun for general applications, in much the same way that Internet addresses are assigned. The second group is the most common one for new programs during debugging. This is why many published examples in the popular networking literature use the fixed number 20000000 for a procedure number, avoiding the use of the function registerrpc(). There is clear danger in programs that avoid use of registerrpc() if the network is heavily used.

We now consider data transmission. The client-server model becomes much more powerful if it allows the different computers to have different operating systems or even different architectures. This forces us to have a set of routines for translating between different forms of data representation on different computers. Most operating systems now contain a set of standard library routines to handle external data representation, or XDR. Routines are available both for encoding local data into the XDR format and for decoding data from the XDR format into the format of local data. The set of library routines is extensive and includes facilities for the following:

- Detection of the end of a logical record (example: xdrrec_ endofrecord) and the end of a file (example: xdrrec_eof).
- Translation of standard data types (examples: xdr_char, xdr_ double, xdr_long, xdr_bytes, and xdr_boolean).
- Translation of user-defined data types, such as strings (example: xdr_string), pointers (example: xdr_pointer), and unions (example: xdr_union).
- Manipulation of the "xdr stream" (examples: xdrstdio_create and xdr_destroy).

The most essential library function for programs using the intermediate layer of RPC is callrpc() (or rpc_call()). This function is used after a successful registering of the name either by use of registerrpc() or by hand. The function callrpc() returns the value 0 if it is successful and returns a negative value otherwise.

This function takes eight arguments. Its syntax is

```
callrpc(char *node_name,
        int program_number,
        int version_number,
        int procedure_number,
        char *arg_type,
        arg_type arg,
        char *return_type,
        return_type return_value);
```

The first argument is a null-terminated character string indicating the name of the node on which the procedure is to be run. The next three arguments are the program, version, and procedure numbers, as in registerrpc().

The next two arguments to callrpc() indicate the type of the arguments to the remote procedure specified in the first argument. The type xdr_void is used for the fifth argument to callrpc() if there are no arguments to the remote procedure. A similar statement holds for the last two arguments to callrpc(), since this is where the information about the return type of the remote procedure is stored.

We now describe the use of the RPC intermediate layer. We will need to include the header file rpc/rpc.h in each program that uses this layer of RPC. This header file contains the names of other header files for most lower-level RPC functions, so that its inclusion allows access to all standard RPC library functions.

At the intermediate levels of RPC, a server program has the form

```
create_RPC_support();
registerrpc(...);
svc_run();
if (error)
  exit();
```

Here the function `create_RPC_support()` is pseudo-code for the techni-cal details of making a program usable by persons other than its creator. The call `svc_run()` is an actual RPC function that takes no arguments and returns no values. It goes into an infinite loop, waits for requests, and serv-ices them. In normal operation, the server program would never execute any statements after the call to `svc_run()`. We simulated the action of `svc_run()` previously.

In order to simplify the explanation of examples 9.8 and 9.9, which illustrate the intermediate layer of RPC, we omit the details of the imple-mentation of the actual code that is used to replace the pseudo-code for the function `create_RPC_support()`. Example 9.7 shows the user-defined header file named `my.h` that is used for this illustration.

Example 9.7: Intermediate Level of RPC—Header File `my.h`

```
#define PROG            0x20000000
#define VERSION         1
#define PROC_NUM        1
```

Example 9.8: Intermediate Level of RPC—Server Program

```
#include <stdio.h>
#include "my.h"

main(argc, argv)
int argc;
char * argv[];
{
  /* define arg and return type here */

  if (registerrpc(PROG,VERSION, PROC_NUM,
              proc_name, arg,return_value) <0)
    {
    fprintf(stderr,"Error in registerrpc\n");
    exit(1);
    }
```

```
    svc_run();
    /* Can only get here if a major error occurs. */
    fprintf(stderr,"Error in registerrpc\n);
    exit(1);
}
```

Example 9.9: Intermediate Level of RPC—Client Program

```
#include <stdio.h>
#include "my.h"

main(argc, argv)
int argc;
char * argv[];
{
  if (callrpc(argv[1], PROG,VERSION, PROC_NUM,
        f, NULL, 0) <0)
      {
      fprintf(stderr,"Error in registerrpc\n);
      exit(1);
      }
}
```

You should recognize that, because of oversimplification of the initialization of the server, the code presented here is far from being satisfactory as a model for a general intermediate-level RPC program. See the references on network programming by Rago or Stevens for more detailed information about the process of creating server programs that we have denoted by the pseudo-code `create_RPC_support()`.

RPC programs at the intermediate level can be made somewhat more portable through the technique of conditional compilation that we saw in Chapter 2. We can allow the program to use one of several similar versions of RPC functions. The program can have several alternatives for compilation of code, depending on the local environment.

We illustrate this technique with an example. Suppose that we want an RPC client program that calls a remote function called `f()`. We want the client program to compile and execute correctly on both a Sun computer running Solaris and an HP computer running HP-UX.

An outline of code for a client program that uses this technique might look something like the following fragment.

```
      .
#ifdef _HPUX_SOURCE
```

```
        -----
        -----
callrpc(argv[1],PROG,VERSION, PROC_NUM, f, NULL, 0);
#endif
#ifdef Sun_SOURCE
        -----
        -----
rpc_call(argv[1],PROG,VERSION, PROC_NUM,f, NULL, 0);
#endif
```

This technique will work on programs that use RPC directly. It will not work with programs that use the rpcgen utility described in the next section; fortunately, rpcgen generates the needed interfaces. Note that there is a potential penalty in program readability when this technique is used.

9.3.4   The Lowest RPC Layer

We now provide a brief discussion of the lowest level of RPC. As expected, the lower-level routines provide the programmer with more control of some of the default values set by the higher-level routines. This is done at the expense of program clarity and portability.

An example of Burke's, available in the popular UNIX literature, provided the impetus for our inclusion of a low-level RPC example in this book. The example we present here involves the use of a remote procedure to compute the values of a function for many different input values. Computation of the values of a function for many input values is a common situation in computer graphics and numerical analysis. Burke's example makes excellent use of a network by having each function evaluation performed by a remote procedure. For computationally intensive functions, his method can produce considerable speedups, at least theoretically.

Our example differs from Burke's, in that we do not use lightweight processes in the main program. We use a single additional computer and compute the values in a single remote procedure. Thus, the maximum theoretical speedup possible in our program is less than 2. Actual speedups in his example and ours are considerably less than the theoretical limits because of the limits in the network's speed of data transmission. A final difference between the two programs is that we have used the simplest form of data organization possible for the arguments to the remote function and its return value.

The header file for this program is called my_new.h. We gave a different number for the value of PROG in case the previous one was still active.

The lowest level of RPC requires us to use several RPC functions that we have not seen before. We describe the functions used on a Sun SPARC 2 running Solaris 1.1. For the server side of the system, the new functions are:

- `pmap_unset()`
- `svctcp_create()`
- `svc_register()`
- `svc_getargs()`
- `svc_decode()`
- `svc_sendreply()`

On the client side, there are three new functions:

- `clnt_create()`
- `clnt_call()`
- `clnt_perror()`

We describe each of these functions briefly.

The function `pmap_unset()` is used to remove any previous mapping of the program and version numbers. It expects two arguments of type int.

The function `svctcp_create()` is an initialization of the service. It uses any available socket, and the last two arguments are 0, which indicates the use of default values.

The function `svc_register()` provides a registration service similar to that performed by the intermediate-level function `registerrpc()`. It provides slightly more control because it allows the particular protocol to be indicated. In this case, the protocol is TCP/IP.

The function registered by the function `svc_register()` is called `calcprog_1` in our example. The `server` argument is of type SVCXPRT.

The function `svc_getargs()` is used to decode the arguments to the appropriate function in the server. It takes three arguments. The first argument is the `server`, the second is a Boolean function that represents the type of the argument to the server function called, and the third is the address of this argument. This portion of the function call can be very complicated.

We have used the built-in `xdr` function `xdr_double()` to indicate that the argument is to be changed from the xdr_double format data sent by the client to the double format required by the local function. This built-in function returns TRUE if the decoding of the data works and FALSE otherwise. This is easier than using a structured data type and writing our own decoding routine for each field of the structured type. The `rpcgen` example in the next section shows one way to do this.

The function `svc_decode()` is used when an error occurs in the decoding process using `svc_getargs()`.

The computation performed by the necessary function in the server is then performed. The value is returned to the client by the function svc_sendreply(), *not* by a return of the function.

The function svc_sendreply() has three arguments: the server, the Boolean function used to decode the arguments from xdr format (in this case xdr_double()), and the address of the value being returned to the client (in this case called temp). Note that the same Boolean function, in this case xdr_double(), is used to decode data from the client to the server, and to encode data from the server to the client. This happens automatically with the xdr routines.

The new client routines for the lowest level of RPC are somewhat simpler to understand than the server routines.

The first client function is clnt_create(). It is similar to the svc_register() function, in that it includes the protocol used. The protocol used in our example is TCP, which is represented by the string "tcp."

The function to perform the remote procedure calls is clnt_call(). This function uses the obvious argument of the client, so that the server knows which client should be sent the return value, if any. The arguments are as follows:

- The client, which uses the client structure.
- The number of the procedure called in the server.
- The Boolean conversion function mentioned earlier that converts the arguments into xdr format.
- The address of the argument. This is often a pointer to a structure, but we did not need to use anything more complex than a pointer to double in our example.
- A Boolean conversion function to transform the xdr format of the result.
- The address into which the result will be placed.
- The maximum time to wait for a response from the server.

The return value of clnt_call() is of type clnt_stat, which is an enumerated type representing various error conditions. The return value is used with the final new function clnt_perror().

Example 9.10: Lowest Level of RPC—Header File **my_new.h**

```
#define PROG            0x20000001
#define VERSION         1
#define PROC_NUM        1
```

Example 9.11: Lowest Level of RPC—Server Program

```
/* This file is the server process for a low-  */
/* level RPC programming example.  It uses      */
```

```
/* the TCP/IP protocol.  All computation     */
/* is done in the function calcprog_1().      */
/* Some debugging code is left in the example */
/* to illustrate the action of the system.    */

#include <stdio.h>
#include <rpc/rpc.h>
#include "my_new.h"

void *calcprog_1();
main()
{
   SVCXPRT *server;

   printf ("SERVER START\n");
/* clean up any existing RPC versions */
(void) pmap_unset (CALCPROG, CALCVERS);

   if ((server = svctcp_create (RPC_ANYSOCK, 0,))
              == NULL)
      {
      fprintf(stderr, "Cannot create server.");
      exit(1);
      }
   if (!svc_register(server, CALCPROG, CALCVERS,
                     calcprog_1, IPPROTO_TCP))
      {
      fprintf(stderr, "Error in register.");
      exit(1);
      }

   svc_run();
   fprintf(stderr, "Error in server.\n");
   exit(1);
}

/* Function to compute the desired output. */
 void *calcprog_1(service_request, server)
struct svc_req *service_request;
SVCXPRT *server;
{
```

```
double x;
double temp;
/* Determine the arguments in xdr format. */
if (!svc_getargs(server, xdr_double, &x) )
    {
    svcerr_decode(server);
    return;
temp = 2.0 * x + 3.0;

/* Illustrate that the computation is correct. */
printf("IN SERVER, value of temp = %lf\n", temp);

/* Send results back in xdr format.      */
if (!svc_sendreply(server, xdr_double, &temp))
    {
    fprintf(stderr,"Error in reply.\n");
    exit(1);
    }
return ;
}
```

Example 9.12: Lowest Level of RPC—Client Program

```
/* Client program for low-level RPC. */

#include <stdio.h>
#include <rpc/rpc.h>
#include "my_new.h"

static struct timeval TIME = {5, 0};

double f(x)
double x;
{
   return(2.0 * x + 3.0);
}

main(argc, argv)
int argc;
char * argv[];
{
```

```
    CLIENT *client;
    enum clnt_stat cl_status;
    double *x_ptr =(double *) malloc(sizeof(double));
    double x = 7.0, res;`

    if (argc < 2)
       {
       fprintf(stderr, "Error in arguments\n");
       exit(1);
       }
    *x_ptr = x;
    printf("The local procedure evaluated at 7.0");
    printf("is %5.11f\n", f(x));

    printf("CLIENT START \n");
    client = clnt_create(argv[1], CALCPROG, CALCVERS,
                           "tcp");
    if (client == NULL)
       {
       fprintf(stderr,"Error in client create\n");
       exit(1);
       }
    printf("CLIENT CREATED\n");

    res = 0.0;
    cl_status = clnt_call(client, F, xdr_double,
              x_ptr, xdr_double, &res, TIME);
    if (cl_status != RPC_SUCCESS)
      {
      clnt_perror(client, "RPC ERROR");
      exit(1);
      }
    printf("The remote procedure evaluated at 7.0");
    printf("is %5.11f\n", res);
}
```

It is appropriate to compare the intermediate and lowest levels of RPC. The lowest level was much more complex; however, it provided a level of control not available in the intermediate level. For example, we were able to specify the use of the protocol to be used for communication and the amount of time that we were willing to wait for a response. This cannot be done easily at the intermediate level.

Complex data types can be encoded and decoded more easily with the lowest level of RPC and user-defined conversion routines.

The lowest layer of RPC involves the use functions that are often only one step up in complexity from the use of sockets. The typical RPC library contains functions that perform some of the lower-level socket routines. These routines involve the use of the "application family" AF_INET instead of AF_UNIX. For the remaining details, consult the network programming manual for your system and one of the references for network programming or data communications.

9.4   RPC LANGUAGE AND THE rpcgen UTILITY

There are many details in the writing of programs that use RPC, especially at the lowest levels. Several of these details are repetitive. The easiest way to write low-level RPC programs is to use a utility called rpcgen that creates stubbed-in client and server programs.

The rpcgen utility takes as input a source code file written in a special language called RPC language, and produces as output a set of four output files in the C language. If the file in RPC language that is the input to the rpcgen utility is named "input.x," then the output files produced by the command rpcgen input.x are

- A header file named input.h.
- A set of XDR routines in a file named input_xdr.c.
- A set of stubbed-in C routines for the server in a file named input_svc.c.
- A set of stubbed-in C routines for the client program in a file named input_clnt.c.

The C preprocessor, cpp, is run on the input file prior to the use of rpcgen. Therefore, the C preprocessor statements are valid as long as they do not use these five constants:

```
RPC_HDR
RPC_XDR
RPC_SVC
RPC_CLNT
RPC_TBL
```

It is much easier to use the rpcgen utility than it is to learn the details of the various lower-level RPC library functions. At present, however, the RPC language is much more limited in its syntax and semantics than is C. In particular, the RPC language does not support nested structures or any of the scoping rules.

There are several examples of RPC-language programs in the standard Solaris 1.1 distribution. The `rpcgen` input file named `rnusers.x` can be used for the generation of code for the function `rnusers()`. This file can be found in the directory `rpcsvc` along with several other examples. It is not customary to include examples of RPC language files in the standard UNIX distribution.

In the `rpcgen` utility's current state of development, it is much easier to restrict programs that use `rpcgen` to a single source code file than to spread them over several source code files, as is common with C programs. (Only the RPC portion of a program must be restricted to a single file, not the entire program.)

Many programs that use RPC will have been developed originally as programs written in the C language that run on a single computer. The motivation for using the RPC mechanism is the usual one of achieving greater execution speed. We now describe the transformation of such a program from its original form to a network-based form.

9.4.1   Using the `rpcgen` Utility

Several steps are necessary to translate a program running on a single computer to one that uses other computers on the network for execution of remote procedures.

1. Determine the procedures that can have their computational load split among several computers on the network. (For the sake of this discussion, we will assume that our program consists of one such function and that the remainder of the program is best executed on a single computer.)
2. Place the procedure capable of being split over a network in a separate file. (This is not strictly necessary, but it makes the use of `rpcgen` on the program easier to understand.)
3. Determine which portion of the program will be the server and which will be the client. These two program portions should be placed in separate files with meaningful filenames.
4. If possible, determine the names of the computers on which the remote procedures will be run.
5. Write a small program in RPC language that executes the desired procedure remotely. Place this program in a file named `file.x`, where the string `file` has a meaningful name in terms of the procedure and has no conflict with any of the names of the other source code files making up the system.
6. Use the `rpcgen` utility to create the four files named `file.h`,

`file_xdr.c`, `file_svc.c`, and `file_clnt.c`. The source code file `file_xdr.c` contains everything necessary for the use of the XDR external data representation routines for data transfer. The other C files created include stubs for the functions.

7. Compile the files, using appropriate makefiles. Be sure that you have created one executable file that is a server and another executable file that is a client.

8. Copy the server and client executable files to the computers on which you wish them to execute. (This may not be necessary if either the client or the server is to run on the development computer.) Copying may involve getting appropriate permissions from system managers.

9. Execute the files on the appropriate computers, with the server running as a background process since servers are never supposed to terminate during normal execution.

Example 9.13 illustrates the use of `rpcgen`. The idea of the RPC program is to evaluate a function in the server program and report the results back to the client program. The function is a simple one used to compute the standard probability distribution. The code for this function, `f_1()`, is given in the file we have named `f_svc.c`. This name was chosen to reflect that the function is part of the code for the server.

Example 9.13: Function to Be Computed by a Server

```
/* File created to compute a function f */

#include "calc.h"
#include <math.h>

double * f_1(x)
double x;
{
double temp;
double *ptr;

printf("SERVER START \n");
temp = 1.0 /sqrt(2.0 * M_PI);
*ptr = temp * exp(-1.0 * x * x /2.0);
printf("SERVER BEFORE RETURN \n");
return ptr;
}
```

The input to the rpcgen utility is named calc.x. This file, which I created, is shown in example 9.14.

Example 9.14: An Input File for rpcgen

```
struct param
   {
   double x;
   };

program CALCPROG
   {
   version CALCVERS
      { double F(param) = 1;
      } = 1;
   } = 0x20001000; /* RPC program number */
```

The rpcgen utility then produces the header file, calc.h, the client stub, calc_clnt.c, the data organization file, calc_xdr.c, and the server stub, calc_svc.c. These files are produced in examples 9.15 through 9.18, with default format produced by rpcgen.

Example 9.15: Header File calc.h Created by rpcgen

```
/*
* Please do not edit this file.
* It was generated using rpcgen.
*/

#include <rpc/types.h>


struct param {
        double x;
};
typedef struct param param;
bool_t xdr_param();

#define CALCPROG ((u_long)0x20001000)
#define CALCVERS ((u_long)1)
#define F ((u_long)1)
    extern double *f_1();
```

Example 9.16: File `calc_clnt.c` Created by `rpcgen`

```
/*
 * Please do not edit this file.
 * It was generated using rpcgen.
 */

#include <rpc/rpc.h>
#include "calc.h"

/* Default timeout can be changed using clnt_control() */
static struct timeval TIMEOUT = { 25, 0 };

double *
f_1(argp, clnt)
        param *argp;
        CLIENT *clnt;
{

        static double res;

        bzero((char *)&res, sizeof(res));
        if (clnt_call(clnt, F, xdr_param, argp, xdr_double,
&res, TIMEOUT) != RPC_SUCCESS) {
                return (NULL);
        }
        return (&res);
}
```

Example 9.17: External Data Representation `calc_xdr.c` Created by `rpcgen`

```
/*
 * Please do not edit this file.
 * It was generated using rpcgen.
 */

#include <rpc/rpc.h>
#include "calc.h"

bool_t
xdr_param(xdrs, objp)
        XDR *xdrs;
```

```
        param *objp;
{
        if (!xdr_double(xdrs, &objp->x)) {
                return (FALSE);
        }
        return (TRUE);
}
```

Example 9.18: Server Stub `calc_svc.c` Created by `rpcgen`

```
* Please do not edit this file.
* It was generated using rpcgen.
*/

#include <stdio.h>
#include <rpc/rpc.h>
#include "calc.h"

static void calcprog_1();

main()
{
        register SVCXPRT *transp;

        (void) pmap_unset(CALCPROG, CALCVERS);

        transp = svcudp_create(RPC_ANYSOCK);
        if (transp == NULL) {
                fprintf(stderr, "cannot create udp
service.");
                exit(1);
        }
        if (!svc_register(transp, CALCPROG, CALCVERS,
calcprog_1, IPPROTO_UDP)) {
                fprintf(stderr, "unable to register
(CALCPROG, CALCVERS, udp).");
                exit(1);
        }

        transp = svctcp_create(RPC_ANYSOCK, 0, 0);
```

```
        if (transp == NULL) {
                fprintf(stderr, "cannot create tcp
service.");
                exit(1);
        }
        if (!svc_register(transp, CALCPROG, CALCVERS,
calcprog_1, IPPROTO_TCP)) {
                fprintf(stderr, "unable to register
(CALCPROG, CALCVERS, tcp).");
                exit(1);
        }

        svc_run();
        fprintf(stderr, "svc_run returned");
        exit(1);
        /* NOTREACHED */
}

static void
calcprog_1(rqstp, transp)
        struct svc_req *rqstp;
        register SVCXPRT *transp;
{
        union {
                param f_1_arg;
        } argument;
        char *result;
        bool_t (*xdr_argument)(), (*xdr_result)();
        char *(*local)();

        switch (rqstp->rq_proc) {
        case NULLPROC:
                (void) svc_sendreply(transp, xdr_void,
(char *)NULL);
                return;

        case F:
                xdr_argument = xdr_param;
                xdr_result = xdr_double;
                local = (char *(*)()) f_1;
                break;
```

```
        default:
                svcerr_noproc(transp);
                return;
        }
        bzero((char *)&argument, sizeof(argument));
        if (!svc_getargs(transp, xdr_argument,
            &argument)) {
                svcerr_decode(transp);
                return;
        }
        result = (*local)(&argument, rqstp);
        if (result != NULL && !svc_sendreply(transp,
xdr_result, result)) {
                svcerr_systemerr(transp);
        }
        if (!svc_freeargs(transp, xdr_argument,
            &argument))
{
                fprintf(stderr, "unable to free
                        arguments");
                exit(1);
        }
        return;
}
```

It remains to write a main driver program that will call the function f_1(). We omit the details, since our intention in this section has been to provide a brief overview of rpcgen. However, some of the functions appearing in the generated code require comment. The calls to send and receive data as well as the error logging function are similar to ones we have already seen. The function bzero() is used to initialize a set of bytes to 0.

We have made no mention of security with remote procedure calls other than that provided by password protection to files. A network file system would require a higher level of security and would use the secure facilities that are frequently grouped under the heading secure_rpc in an RPC manual. Consult your systems programming manual for more information.

9.5   PROCESS TRACING

The term *process tracing* refers to a situation in which one process runs entirely under the control of the another. The controlling process uses the kernel to keep track of all major changes in the process it controls.

Two prominent examples of process tracing in the UNIX operating system are debuggers and profilers, which behave in similar fashion. A debugger is used to find errors in software. The software being debugged is run as a process under the control of the debugger process. Breakpoints are set by the user either automatically or at specially chosen points, and the process being debugged runs until it hits these breakpoints. The process is then temporarily suspended so that the user can examine the contents of various registers and designed memory locations. After the user checks the values of these registers and memory locations, the suspended process can resume and will continue execution until it either makes a fatal error or arrives at the next breakpoint. This process control of software by the debuggers can continue as long as desired.

Profiling is similar to debugging, in the sense that one process runs under the control of another. However, the breakpoints are preset by the kernel for use by the *profiler*, frequently at each entrance and exit to a function and at each call to, and return from, a system call. Some profilers simply query the active portion of the code at predetermined intervals. By default, the system clock is queried at each breakpoint, and the results are kept in a file named mon.out that can be read by means of the UNIX prof or gprof utilities. The simplest way to profile a program is to use the -p option on the standard UNIX C, Pascal, or FORTRAN compilers. (This option may be available on other compilers also.)

For example, the C program toy.c can be compiled by the utility command cc -p toy.c. This creates the file mon.out, which is translated by the command prof (or gprof) into an easily read listing of all the functions and system calls used by toy.c. This list is sorted, which makes it easy to determine where the program spent most of its execution time.

Profilers are useful to speed up code that runs slower than it was designed to; they show where most of the problems are so that inefficient portions can be improved. After making the changes and testing the system, the new system is recompiled without the profiler being used so that the code will run faster. See the references by Bentley for an excellent discussion of the use of profilers in code improvement.

One last comment on process tracing. It requires a process to control the address space of another process, and thus it is difficult to avoid garbage if the controlled process has a fork() or exec(). Some modern debuggers such as adb in the standard Solaris distribution are now able to solve this problem and can trace processes with forks.

SUMMARY

Signals are used for interprocess communication when the main concern is notifying a process that an event has occurred. Some typical events are the interruption of the CPU because a disk data transfer is complete, the positioning of the mouse inside a window, or the pressing of a key.

Another use of signals is to inform a process that an error, such as a memory segment violation or a floating point error, has occurred. The effect of many such errors can be reduced by signal handler functions that allow a smooth reaction to the error. The signal handling function can be given as an argument to the `signal()` system call.

Sockets are used to connect processes on the same or different computers. The `socket()`, `bind()`, `listen()`, and `connect()` system calls control sockets. Programs that use sockets might not be portable.

An effective way of increasing computing power is remote procedure call (RPC). Many RPC programs can be implemented at several layers of complexity. The highest level of use is transparent to a user.

Two important calls at the intermediate level of RPC are `callrpc()` and `registerrpc()` (called `rpc_call()` and `rpc_reg()` in some versions of UNIX). All data transmitted must use the external data representation (XDR) format. Conditional compilation can aid in RPC portability.

The lowest level of RPC is more complicated and should be used only if additional control or security is needed, or if the desired transport protocols are not available at the intermediate level. The XDR format must also be used at this level for many forms of structured data.

Often, the simplest use of the lowest level of RPC is by the `rpcgen` utility, which allows a smooth connection between the main program and a remote procedure, and avoids the need for much lower-level programming. The `rpcgen` utility requires the rewriting of a portion of the program in a special language called RPC language. As before, all data transmitted must use the external data representation (XDR) format.

Process tracing is a complex ipc method that is used in profilers and debuggers.

REFERENCES

Bentley, J. *Programming Pearls*. Reading, Mass.: Addison-Wesley, 1986.

———. *More Programming Pearls*. Reading, Mass.: Addison-Wesley.

Burke, S. "Parallel Processing on Your UNIX Network, Part I." *SunEXPERT Magazine*, May 1993, 65–68.

———. "Parallel Processing on Your UNIX Network, Part II." *SunEXPERT Magazine*, June 1993, 62–65.

Rago, S. A. *UNIX System V Network Programming*. Reading, Mass.: Addison-Wesley, 1993.

Rochkind, M. *Advanced UNIX Programming*. Englewood Cliffs, N. J.: Prentice-Hall, 1985.

Stevens, W. R. *UNIX Network Programming*. Englewood Cliffs, N. J.: Prentice-Hall, 1991.

———. *Advanced Programming in the UNIX Environment*. Reading, Mass.: Addison-Wesley, 1992.

EXERCISES

1. Consider any short program (50–100 lines of code) you have written recently. Determine which signals can occur if there are errors in program execution. Be sure to consider the possibilities of running out of space for allocation of arrays; problems with file access such as wrong permissions, the file not existing, or being in the wrong directory; and hardware subsystem failures.

2. Design and implement an experiment to test the efficiency of the `socket()` system call:

   a. with two processes on the same computer.

   b. with two processes on different computers.

   Is the time noted in part b dependent on the distance between the computers?

3. Design and implement an experiment to determine if the old system calls `read()` and `write()` are more efficient than the new system calls `send()` and `receive()`.

4. Use remote procedure call to remotely monitor some activity such as CPU usage on another computer. Do this using the highest, intermediate, and lowest layers of RPC as indicated in the text. Compare the results in terms of performance.

5. Use the `rpcgen` utility to do exercise 4. Compare the performance of the resulting program with that of the other three.

6. Compare the set of utilities accessible via the remote shell (`rsh`) facility with the set of functions available in the `lrpcsvc` library.

7. For any of the RPC programs of this chapter, determine which signals can be sent and to which processes they are sent: server, client, or kernel.

IPC Comparison

In this chapter, we compare the various methods of interprocess communication. We present results of a timing experiment for several architectures and versions of UNIX.

10.1 INTRODUCTION: THE EXPERIMENT

Our continuing experiment on ipc efficiency uses the code given in Chapters 7, 8, and 9. The experiment was performed on an AT&T 3B2/310 running AT&T System V version 2.0 UNIX; a Sun 3/60 running SunOS 3.5; and a Sun SPARC 2 running SunOS 4.1.3 (Solaris 1.1). The systems were in single-user mode while the experiment was run. No changes were made to the process scheduling algorithm during the experiment. The nice() values of the processes were not changed, and thus priorities were set by the system.

The default system parameters were used in this experiment. On the AT&T 3B2/310, the maximum size of a shared memory segment is 8,192 bytes and the maximum number of semaphores, shared memory segments, or FIFOs is 10. On the Sun 3/60, the shared memory segment size is also 8,192 bytes and the maximum number of semaphores and shared memory segments is 60 and 100, respectively. On the more modern Sun SPARC 2, the maximum number of semaphores is 60 and the maximum number of shared memory segments is 100; however, the maximum size of a shared memory segment has been increased to 1,024 kilobytes. You may modify your system by either reconfiguring the kernel or fine-tuning performance by changing some constants.

The code for this experiment consisted of 19 C source code files, totaling 956 lines of code, which were combined into 14 executable files. The 14 executable files were grouped into 8 parent processes, some of which acted as sender processes, sending information to child processes that they created in order to receive communication from their parent. The organization is as follows.

For the file ipc test, the main process was `file_ipc`, which forked and executed the executable files `readfile` and `writefile`. The message ipc test was implemented with the executable file `message`, which used the processes `messerver` and `mesrec`. FIFOs required two processes, `fifoparent` and its child, `fiforec`. Pipes were tested with two processes named `pipetest`, the parent, and `childp`. All the other experiments used single executable files.

The largest executable file was 29,959 bytes, and the smallest was 6,149, at least on one system. Several of the C source code files were used in more than one executable file. For example, those containing functions to manipulate semaphores were used in the semaphore, shared file pointer, and shared memory experiments.

We have often followed the terminology of Rochkind in this book and have used two functions named `send()` and `receive()`. These two functions should not be confused with the relatively new system calls `send()` and `receive()` that are intended for use with sockets and RPC.

Each program read in the number of communications and the number of bytes communicated as command-line arguments. The command-line arguments were then changed to integer format.

The time command was used as part of a Bourne shell script, which ran the executable files three times for different values of the parameters. To distinguish the time of creation of the actual processes via the `fork()` and `exec()` mechanism, a separate time was computed for the running of the test programs with no parameters. This time represented the overhead of process creation and initialization; it was subtracted from the running times that are reported in the tables.

For example, the actual timing command for an executable file named `message` 50,000 times with a message size of 1,000 bytes was

```
time message 50000 1000 2>> output_file
```

This command redirected the output of the `time` command, which was written to file descriptor 2 (`stderr`), to the file called `output_file`. The time command was performed five times, and the average value was taken. The difference between this time and the time for a command such as

```
time message 0 0 2>> output_file
```

which represents the overhead for process creation and initialization using `fork()` and `exec()`, was reported. We had expected large variations in the times because of the potential for premature termination when using signals, but noticed none. This outcome is not guaranteed in future runs of the experiment. However, the relative times of the experiment using signals will not be decreased in any instance in which the signals are handled correctly.

The actual and relative execution times for the ipc methods running on the AT&T 3B2 computer are given in Table 10.1. Similar times for the Sun 3/60 computer are given in Table 10.2 and for the Sun SPARC 2 in Table 10.3. In each case, the interprocess communication was performed 50,000 times. Since both signals and semaphores are used to inform a process of a condition or to allow one process to execute its critical section while others wait, the number of bytes communicated is not relevant for either of these ipc methods. For all the other methods, the times for sending small messages of size 10 or 100 bytes are reported. To test the relationship between ipc speed and message size, "messages," or blocks of data, of 1,000 bytes were also considered. We used semaphores for synchronization of shared memory access.

Note that the relative times were computed on the basis of the time of the shared memory ipc for messages of the same size as the base. For example, the relative times given for messages were the quotients of the times for the ipc, with that message size divided by the corresponding times for shared memory (with no semaphores) using the same message sizes. The relative times for signals and semaphores were obtained by dividing the absolute times for these operations by the corresponding times for shared memory with 10-byte messages being communicated.

10.2   RESULTS FOR SVR3

UNIX ipc can be implemented via the file system (files, shared file pointers, pipes, FIFOs), signals, process tracing, and the System V ipc mechanisms (messages, semaphores, and shared memory). These methods naturally fall into four groups based on execution times observed in this experiment. (Recall that process tracing was not done.) Each group has features that affect the use of the ipc methods in certain applications.

The fastest group included both shared memory, without semaphores to prevent concurrent access, and messages. As expected, shared memory was the fastest method. However, this was the case only if no ipc method was being used for control of access to the shared memory locations. In our

Table 10.1.   Runtimes (in seconds) for 50,000 communications on an AT&T 3B2 computer under System V UNIX version 3.2

Number of Messages	Time (secs)	Relative Time
Shared memory: (no semaphores)		
10	174.2	1.0
100	183.1	1.0
1000	220.6	1.0
Messages:		
10	186.0	1.07
100	185.6	1.01
1000	1850.0	8.38
Semaphores:		
1000	265.9	1.59
Pipes:		
10	65.0	1.58
100	273.0	1.49
1000	273.0	1.24
FIFOs:		
10	320.0	1.84
100	325.0	1.86
1000	616.5	2.79
Signals:		
1000	401.1	2.30
Shared memory without semaphores:		
10	470.0	2.69
Shared memory with semaphores:		
100	478.3	2.61
1000	4999.2	22.66
Files:		
10	802.3	4.60
100	934.2	5.10
1000	2295.0	10.40
Shared file pointers:		
10	835.0	4.79
100	986.4	5.39
1000	1475.0	6.69

experiment, the time for shared memory access, with semaphores to prevent concurrent access to critical areas, was approximately 2.5 times greater than the time with no such protection for programs in which the amount of memory read was small (10 or 100 bytes). When the program required the writing of 1,000 bytes each time, it ran much slower.

In fact, the 1,000 bytes of memory caused the slowest running time. This was probably because there were more semaphore calls, since the writing of 1,000 bytes might have forced more switches of context between the two user processes, and thus the operating system would have to have made more system calls to reset the state of semaphores during context switches. Since few concurrent applications would allow the lack of memory protection that occurs without the use of some synchronizing system, we concluded that messages were the fastest general-purpose ipc method. If some type of synchronization of shared memory access is needed, then messages are probably better for synchronization than are semaphores.

The next fastest group included semaphores, pipes, and named pipes. Semaphores were the fastest of the three by a small amount. However, pipes performed nearly as fast, and they conveyed much more information (10 or 100 bytes), than the single bit of information provided by a binary semaphore or the single integer provided by a general semaphore, as is available in System V. There was only a small difference in time between pipes and FIFOs, at least for small messages. This difference was probably caused by the fact that atomicity is guaranteed when using FIFOs, and thus some system activity was slightly slowed. The major factor was the number of ipc events; increasing the size of a message to 1,000 bytes increased the time differential between pipes and FIFOs by less than 50 percent.

The third group included signals and shared memory with semaphores. As before, signals provided a restricted amount of information, while shared memory with semaphores provided potentially large amounts. The use of standard signals to indicate unusual events, such as keyboard interrupts, changes to a window on a screen, or termination of a process, was relatively fast. However, signals convey limited information in general.

The increase in time created by shared memory access controlled by semaphores would probably be acceptable for most applications.

The final group included files and shared file pointers. Files are slower than the previously discussed ipc methods by a factor of nearly two. However, this method may be necessary for certain applications that involve large data files. In general, shared file pointers are the slowest ipc method, although this may not always be true for larger files. Shared file pointers require a considerable amount of checking and updating, and for this reason, we suggest that they be avoided unless absolutely necessary. The version of UNIX System V used in the experiment did not support demand paging, so the times given do not really depend on disk activity but reflect actual time needed.

The results of the experiment would be different in different environments. Real-time requirements could cause significant difficulties, and obvious problems would occur if either the data files or the executable files required disk access. Average seek times would have to be added to the times described here. In addition, the relative times to change from user mode to kernel mode would probably be different on different systems.

10.3   RESULTS FOR SUNOS 3.5

We did not expect repetition of this experiment on a demand-paged system, such as Berkeley 4.3 or AT&T System V version 3.0, to produce significant changes in the results, assuming that the ipc facilities were available. The pipe, shared file pointer, semaphore, signal, message passing, and file ipc code ran successfully on a Sun 3/60 running SunOS version 3.5, but all other code needed changes to compile or to avoid execution failures, even though this operating system had ipc features. Generally, even if ipc features are available, changes in system data structures require changes in system calls and thus in ipc programs.

As we mentioned earlier, the UNIX kernel on the Sun 3/60 had to be reconfigured so that semaphores, messages, and shared memory would work. The shared memory programs (with and without semaphores) were awkward because of the large number of possible problems, such as the unavailability of segments and the overwriting of memory adjacent to the shared segments. Explicit checking of such segments was the major reason for the slow performance of shared memory when large data sizes were transferred.

In addition, the time for a `memcopy()` to complete the transfer of 1,000 items was probably larger than the time slice allotted for the process, and thus a context switch took place, slowing down the performance considerably. The checks needed for FIFOs were testing for limits on the size of a queue and the number of messages waiting to be sent to a queue, among others. We were unable to send any significant amount of data using FIFOs without including these checks, so we omitted these results from the table since the additional programming to ensure successful data communication was prohibitive. Thus, we have presented absolute times for data sizes of 10, 100, and 500 bytes, but not for 1,000 bytes, in our FIFO experiment.

The results of the experiment on a Sun 3/60 running SunOS 3.5 are shown in Table 10.2.

As expected, most of the programs using messages ran much faster on

Table 10.2.   Runtimes (in seconds) for 50,000 communications on a Sun 3/60 with SunOS 3.5

Number of Messages	Time (secs)	Relative Time
Shared memory:		
10	23.0	1.0 (no semaphores)
100	23.0	1.0
1000	34.1	1.0
Messages:		
10	30.0	1.30
100	30.1	1.31
1000	32.7	0.96
Semaphores:		
1000	129.2	5.62
Pipes:		
10	98.8	4.30
100	100.0	4.35
1000	99.9	2.93
FIFOs:		
10	45.5	1.98
100	45.7	1.98
500	45.7	1.34
1000	did not work	
Signals:		
1000	92.5	4.02
Shared memory with semaphores:		
10	100.2	4.36
100	1000.2	43.49
1000	5000.2	146.63
Files:		
10	330.0	14.34
100	380.0	16.52
1000	708.0	20.76
Shared file pointers:		
10	400.0	17.39
100	750.0	32.61
1000	2280.0	67.06

the Sun 3/60 than on the AT&T 3B2. The relative times for small messages were similar on the two systems and were so fast that we suggest messages be used whenever possible.

The relative performance of the other ipc methods was much slower on the Sun. The poor performance of the file methods was due primarily to the larger files created on the Sun than on the AT&T. Much of the increase in relative times on the Sun was probably due to the excess time for semaphores. Shared memory and messages were approximately six times faster on the Sun 3/60 than on the AT&T 3B2; however, semaphores were only two times faster. We again note that neither the Sun nor the AT&T versions of UNIX were fine-tuned to improve ipc performance, although fine-tuning might have dramatically improved some of the results. It is likely that the Sun ipc methods required much more frequent switches from user to kernel mode.

On the Sun 3/60, one file program created a file of over 40 MB. On the AT&T, the reading of files was so frequent that the largest file created was approximately 2 MB. The 40-MB intermediate file was close to the maximum possible file size of 50 MB (50,000 writes of 1,000 bytes each), which would occur only if all writes of data to the file preceded all reads.

10.4   RESULTS FOR SOLARIS 1.1

The next platform we used for our ipc experiment was a Sun SPARC 2 running Solaris version 1.1 (SunOS 4.1.3). Based on our experience with the failure of the FIFO code on the Sun 3/60 (SunOS 3.5) and the large size of intermediate files in the file ipc experiment, we anticipated some difficulties. However, with one exception, the code worked without any changes.

The ipc code using shared file pointers performed much faster than expected for message sizes (amount of data communicated) of 1,000, 2,000, or 3,000 bytes. The times for 1,000 communications of these sizes were 3.7 seconds, 4.4 seconds, and 6.1 seconds, respectively. Using a "message" size of 4,000 bytes, however, caused the program to take an exceptionally long time; it was aborted after 12 minutes in each test run. Since this is the least desirable method in general, unexpectedly slow performance in certain situations is not likely to be a major problem.

The SPARC 2 performed so much faster on the ipc experiments than the other two machines that comparisons between the different computers are meaningless.

The synchronization of reading and writing to files using a shared file pointer was much better on the SPARC running Solaris 1.1 (SunOS 4.1.3). While it was still possible to crash a file system, a crash occurred only with

Table 10.3. Runtimes (in seconds) for 50,000 communications on a Sun SPARC 2 computer running Solaris 1.1

Number of Messages	Time (secs)	Relative Time
Shared memory: (no semaphores)		
10	8.3	1.0
100	8.8	1.0
1000	8.9	1.0
Messages:		
10	11.7	1.41
100	11.9	1.35
1000	12.4	1.39
Semaphores:		
1000	29.1	3.51
Pipes:		
10	24.4	2.94
100	24.6	2.80
1000	25.0	2.81
FIFOs:		
10	12.9	1.55
100	13.1	1.49
1000	13.5	1.52
Signals:		
1000	37.4	4.51
Shared memory with semaphores:		
10	28.7	3.46
100	30.2	3.43
1000	52.1	5.85
FIFOs:		
10	149.2	17.98
100	161.9	18.40
1000	232.0	26.07
Shared file pointers:		
10	133.5	16.08
100	160.1	18.19
1000	351.0	39.44

very large numbers of communications between processes, indicating a fine-tuning of the buffer cache and better disk scheduling algorithms to speed up write performance.

In general, the ipc performance on the Sun SPARC 2 was impressive. All the ipc code worked readily, indicating the convergence of some of the different variants of UNIX toward a common standard. We will discuss this point again in Chapter 12, when we deal with standardization.

10.5   PROTECTION AND PORTABILITY ISSUES

The user of ipc should be aware of the relative levels of protection for a system using these methods. For example, ipc can fail if a file system is full. A more subtle problem can occur with memory protection. Any ipc program using shared memory that doesn't clearly set aside the proper amount of space for data is likely to have problems. Many of these problems are due to the C language's fundamental inability to determine if the definition

```
char * addr;
```

refers to a pointer to a single character or to an entire string.

Some UNIX installations are writing their own proprietary ipc methods for special purposes. However, special ipc mechanisms are not always portable to other UNIX installations; indeed, the ipc utilities package is an option with the current distribution of System V. The portability issue is probably best addressed by waiting for industrial acceptance of POSIX or some other standard.

Current trends in the computer industry suggest that many long-lived programs will eventually migrate to concurrent systems; these systems may be tightly coupled parallel or loosely coupled network-based systems. Different architectures have a direct influence on software architecture, at least for certain classes of software. Thus, it is reasonable to consider potential growth paths for hardware architecture when designing certain types of programs.

The choice is usually between tightly coupled parallel computers with shared memory, such as those produced by Alliant, or systems with distributed memory, which can be tightly coupled parallel computers (e.g., as hypercubes) or more loosely coupled systems (e.g., as networks).

If the expected migration path is to shared memory systems, then shared memory will be the ipc method of choice. On the other hand, if we expect to migrate to a distributed system, then messages (or remote procedure call, which we studied in Chapter 9) will be more appropriate.

A major factor in the speed at which processes communicate is process priority. It would be interesting to repeat the ipc experiments in this book using a CPU scheduling algorithm designed not to be fair but to continually give high priority to certain processes.

SUMMARY

The relative performance of the various ipc methods is easy to compare on identical platforms using the same version of the operating system. In general, shared memory is the fastest, but its raw performance is slowed down by the need for process synchronization using such methods as semaphores, signals, and messages.

REFERENCES

Bentley, J. *Programming Pearls*. Reading, Mass.: Addison-Wesley, 1986.
———. *More Programming Pearls*. Reading, Mass.: Addison-Wesley.
Rochkind, M. *Advanced UNIX Programming*. Englewood Cliffs, N. J.: Prentice-Hall, 1985.
Stevens, W. R. *Advanced Programming in the UNIX Environment*. Reading, Mass.: Addison-Wesley, 1992.

EXERCISES

1. Design and implement an experiment to test the efficiency of the `socket()` system call:
   a. with two processes on the same computer.
   b. with two processes on different computers.
   Is the time noted in part b dependent on the distance between the computers?

2. Design an experiment to test ipc efficiency if there are three processes running. What relationships (parent, child, sibling, etc.) must hold if all ipc methods are to be tested?

3. Implement the ipc tests you designed in exercise 2.

4. What happens if the ipc tests are performed with different amounts of data? Use a random number generator to generate the number of bytes in each communication.

5. What happens if we perform ipc with the same amount of data as the page size of the system?

6. What happens if we try to combine background processing with the UNIX shell command | in

```
ls *.p & | wc
```

or

```
ls *.p | wc &
```

Which ipc methods are used?

7. What problem should arise from a command like the following:

```
vi file &
```

Which ipc methods are used?

8. Consider a situation in which data exists in a database and is to be read by many processes but written to by one process at a time. Design an experiment to measure the efficiency of various ipc methods for querying the database by many processes at once. You should probably assume that the database is organized as a relational database.

9. List two advantages of each of the ipc methods discussed in this chapter. Also give a typical application of each method.

10. List two disadvantages of each of the ipc methods discussed in this chapter.

11. Design and implement an experiment to determine if the old system calls read() and write() are more efficient than the new system calls send() and receive().

11

Fault-Tolerant UNIX Software

UNIX has a considerable amount of support for the notion of *fault-tolerance*. The term *"fault-tolerance"* refers to the ability of a program to recover from unexpected errors. A software error is often called a *fault* or an *exception*. We will use the terms interchangeably.

11.1 INTRODUCTION TO FAULT-TOLERANCE

The philosophy of fault-tolerant software or hardware is that unexpected events do occur and systems must respond to them gracefully, without system crashes. Fault-tolerance is essential in life-critical medical software and in such systems as the air traffic control system that cannot afford to fail or to be unavailable for any time. In systems that must perform their computations within prescribed time limits, sufficient time might not be available for all the runtime checking that might prevent faults, and thus we often have to rely on fault detection and handling.

Fault-tolerance can occur at two levels: hardware and software. Hardware fault-tolerance is often achieved with redundant equipment. One example is the use of a backup system as a "hot spare." The hot spare is given the same computational load as other systems, but the results of its computations are ignored until one of those systems has a major problem such as a disk head crash or power loss. After the hardware fault occurs and is detected, the hot spare comes on line and performs in place of the system that had the failure. Computation resumes at this point. We will not discuss hardware fault-tolerance further in this book.

The basis of improving software fault-tolerance is the concept that the software faults of a system can often be corrected, or at least tolerated, if special code is used to ensure the system's continued performance. Techniques can be applied by a programmer or software designer to improve the survivability of existing code. They can also be used to provide a framework for incorporating existing, well-tested code into a larger system that supports a greater amount of fault-tolerance than does the original.

Software fault-tolerance can be achieved either by redundancy or by maintaining the correct "state" of a system, and returning control to a previously determined point in the program in the event of a software fault.

In this chapter, we briefly discuss some methods for increasing the fault-tolerance of programs running on the UNIX operating system. Most of these methods have been described in the available literature and can be accessed easily.

There is some controversy over the use of certain software fault-tolerance techniques. Some individuals feel that the software should address all possible cases and that no surprises should occur at runtime. Others feel that this is impractical because of the runtime overhead of fault-avoidance techniques, and that it is better to have software that is robust and efficient in nearly all cases, with a time penalty appropriate for repair of a software fault if the fault is rare enough.

Consider the simple example of a program that divides two floating point quantities. Obviously, we don't want division by zero, so one approach is to check every divisor to see if it is zero. In this approach, there is an additional overhead for every division because of the need to check. This method of "defensive programming" will avoid the possibility of the "division by 0" fault occurring. The overhead of a check of the divisor having the value 0 is negligible for a single division. However, if the division is repeated millions of times in a program whose time response is critical, a better approach might be to recognize that division by zero is an exceptional situation and thus should be treated by reacting to its occurrence rather than by defending against it. Another approach is to treat the division by zero as a runtime fault that can be efficiently detected and handled at runtime.

One way to improve fault-tolerance for this example is to allow the division to proceed but to generate a UNIX signal if there is a numerical error. The error is then treated by a signal handler, which switches control to an appropriate routine. This method of fault-tolerance requires some programming effort, but it allows the system to avoid the overhead of checking the divisor in each instance of a division. Moreover, it would likely produce faster execution of programs.

In the next section we describe three approaches to software fault-tolerance. The remainder of the chapter consists of examples illustrating how these approaches can be implemented using features of the UNIX operating system. The methods are more general than the examples presented here indicate, and you should be aware that there is a considerable amount of research in software fault-tolerance in non-UNIX systems.

11.2   SOME METHODS OF SOFTWARE FAULT-TOLERANCE

The first strategy we consider is the incorporation of fault-tolerance into the program by modifications of UNIX system calls and common C utility functions. This strategy emphasizes the detection of faults and their classification by the programmer. It was motivated by the terseness of several messages returned by failed UNIX system calls and the lack of information generally provided by C runtime systems about the nature of errors.

This strategy allows the programmer to determine the state of a system if a fault occurs, and allows appropriate actions. It is essentially a detection mechanism that allows the programmer to determine appropriate actions if a fault occurs.

The most important part of this strategy is the use of the shell with the C preprocessor that creates new include files for use with C programs. Our use of this strategy is not portable to non-UNIX systems, although the strategy itself might be.

The second fault-tolerant strategy is the rollback technique of Randell (see the references). In this technique, the program is considered correct until it reaches an error state due to a fault (either hardware or software). After the fault occurs and is detected, program execution is halted temporarily so that corrective action can be taken. Corrective action means resetting the program counter; changing the values of appropriate registers; clearing function calls, parameters, and return values from the system stack; and so forth. Rollback is an expensive operation in terms of execution time; the time needed for it is difficult to predict.

Our implementation of this strategy involves the use of signals and the UNIX system calls `setjmp()` and `longjmp()`, which operate on the system stack and allow us to restore the state of a program if a fault occurs.

This implementation works only on UNIX systems, since we must use specific system calls to manipulate the system stack.

The final fault-tolerant programming technique we consider is N-version programming, a method that has long been used for creating hardware fault-tolerance based on redundancy. The person most closely associated with this technique is Avizienis (see the references).

In an N-version programming system, several versions of a program's critical sections are active. These versions are coded by using different algorithms and, preferably, different programmers, so that the occurrence of a fault in one version will be independent of a fault in another version (which is difficult to achieve with the same algorithms or programmers). The results of these versions are compared frequently by a separate entity called a voter process, and a determination is made, by majority vote, of what the correct state of the program is. This method has a high but predictable overhead.

N-version programming clearly works best when the different versions and the voter process are concurrently running tasks or processes, preferably on different CPUs. However, interleaving on the same CPU is feasible. Our implementation makes use of the UNIX ipc method of messages.

11.3   A METHOD OF FAULT-TOLERANCE FOR GENERAL C PROGRAMS

The detection strategy we present for C programs is based on the use of the C preprocessor. It does not depend on UNIX system calls. It uses a UNIX Bourne shell script to automatically replace I/O system calls with fault-tolerant ones. This involves copying the user's files to temporary files. The strategy is illustrated in Figure 11.1.

The shell script file EXHcc, whose name stands for Exception Handling cc, replaces the command cc to compile the user's files. For example, the user has to type in the following in response to the command line prompt:

```
EXHcc -o main main.c print.c
main
```

This will compile the files and add the file exhand.o to the compilation. The file exhand.c contains the fault-tolerant routines needed to treat several standard I/O errors.

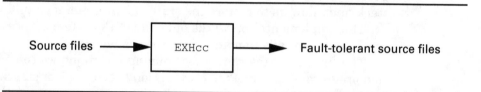

Figure 11.1.   A fault-tolerance strategy

The Bourne shell script EXHcc is presented in example 11.1 with line numbers to aid in readability. The line numbers are not part of the file.

Example 11.1: The Shell Script EXHcc

```
#FILE: EXHcc
1.   CC = cc
2.
3.   while [$# != 0]
4.   do
5.        case $1 in
6.        *.c)
7.                ccpp $1 > /tmp/$$$1
8.                CC = "$CC /tmp/$$$1"
9.                shift 1;;
10.         *)
11.                CC = "$CC $1"
12.                shift 1;;
13.        --)
14.                break;
15.        esac
16.   done
17.
18.   CC = "$CC exhand.o"
19.   eval $CC
```

Notice that on line 7 the positional parameter $1 denotes the C source code file to be compiled. The file is copied to the /tmp directory. The $$ prefix on the positional parameter $1 is equal to the process-id of the user's login shell. Since each process on the UNIX system is given a unique process-id, using $$ in the name of a file minimizes the possibility of another process using the same file. For example, a file with a name like

```
"/tmp/4567main.c
```

will be created in the directory /tmp when line 7 is executed from the script.

Line 8 shows the cc command being used to compile the file from /tmp. This compilation command is then stored in the shell variable CC. When there are multiple files to be compiled, line 9 will shift the positional parameter to the left by 1. On line 18, the variable CC will be assigned the statement on line 9. Line 19 uses the eval shell command in front of $CC. The net effect of the eval command is that the shell scans the command line twice before executing it.

With the -c option of the cc command, the user obtains the object file related to the source code file being compiled. For example, the user types in

```
cc -c exhand.c
```

which creates the file exhand.o. The exception handling routines reside within the file exhand.c. One such routine is shown in the following portion of the file exhand.c.

Example 11.2: The File exhand.c

```
/* FILE: exhand.c */
1.   _fclose(stream)
2.   FILE *fp;
3.   {
4.   int ret;
5.   ret = fclose(stream);
6.   if (ret == EOF)
7.      printf("Exception Handling Message\n");
8.   return(ret);
9.   }
```

Notice that the capturing of status information from the return of the input/output function by a fault-tolerant one requires writing fault-tolerant replacements for each such function. However, by doing so we get more complete information about the failure of such a function and can take some action if appropriate. This principle applies only to standard functions for which the user has written alternate versions that are to be substituted automatically.

Checking the return values can aid fault-tolerance because it allows the programmer to take corrective action, provided the return values are used properly. It is useful when the file containing more fault-tolerant system calls and functions is large enough to incorporate all those that are appropriate for an application. The size required can be very large in practice. These new exception handling include files should probably be organized in the same manner as the common C libraries are.

11.4   THE RECOVERY BLOCK METHOD IN UNIX

In this section, we describe the use of the UNIX signal() system call to provide software fault-tolerance in a simple case, division by zero. The technique is heavily operating-system dependent and is based on Randell's rollback method. It allows both the detection and the treatment of software faults. Numerical exceptions are detected with the UNIX signal mechanism. Treatment of faults is addressed by C system calls and subroutines.

The fundamental problems in any rollback technique are how to determine the appropriate place to roll program execution back to; and how to restore the state of the system at that place of execution after it has been determined.

There is an additional difficulty if the fault is detected while in the middle of a function, since the proper state of the system means a manipulation of the system stack so that parameters and return values can be ignored if they are no longer relevant. The UNIX system calls `setjmp()` and `longjmp()`, which manipulate the system stack, are a vital part of the handling mechanism of the rollback method once a software fault has been detected. Figure 11.2 describes the situation.

There are two handling options for floating point exceptions in C. These are based on C and ANSI/IEEE Standard 754-1985 (a standard for floating point arithmetic).

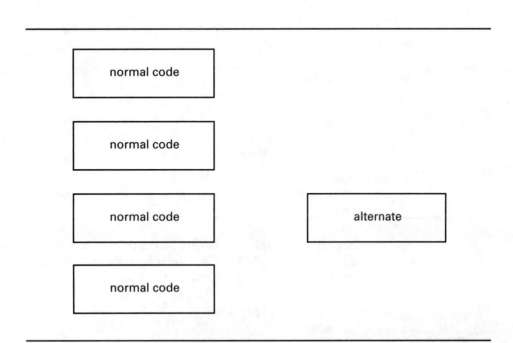

Figure 11.2.   The rollback method

11.4.1   Handling Floating Point Exceptions with `setjmp()` and `longjmp()`

The UNIX C compiler offers system-level detection and handling capabilities for some numeric exceptions. If the system has not been so configured to trap a given floating point exception, program execution will continue as normal, although the mathematical results may be erroneous. If it has been so configured, the trap will be done by the runtime system. In the event of a floating point exception, its corresponding exception signal will be raised and set to true. If no handler is provided, execution will halt and an error message will be printed.

Here, example 11.3 illustrates the use of signals to show a problem in arithmetic—division by 0. Notice the use of `setjmp()` and `longjmp()` to manipulate the system stack.

Example 11.3: A Floating Point Exception Handler

```
#include <stdio.h>
#include <signal.h>
#include <setjmp.h>

/*  "begin"  is  the  variable  containing  the
environment. */

jmp_buf begin;

main(argc, argv)
int argc;
char *argv[];
{
    int fpecatch();
    /*  "setjmp"  saves the  stack  environment  in
    "begin" */
    setjmp(begin);
    /* Should a floating point exception occur,  the
    signal  SIGFPE will  be  sent  and the  function
    fpecatch will be executed. */

    signal(SIGFPE, fpecatch);
    evaluate();
}
```

```
execerror(s, t)  /* recover from run-time error */
char *s, *t;
{
    warning(s, t);
    /* Use either longjmp() or abort(), not both. */
    /* The longjmp() function restores a stack
    environment previously saved in begin by
    setjmp() and program execution is restarted from
    the beginning.  */

    longjmp(begin, 0);

    /* abort execution of program */
    abort();
}

fpecatch()    /* catch floating point exceptions */
{
    execerror("floating point exception",
              (char *) 0);
}

warning(s, t)  /* print warning message */
char *s, *t;
{
    fprintf(stderr, " %s", s);
    if (t)
        fprintf(stderr, " %s", t);
}

evaluate()
{
    double x, y;
    scanf("%e%e", &x, &y);       /* error if y = 0 */
    x = x/y;
    printf(" The result of x/y is : %e ", x);
}
```

If the value of y is 0, program execution will halt, the error message will be printed, the preerror environment will be restored, and the user will be allowed to re-enter the data.

11.4.2   **Handling Floating Point Exceptions in IEEEFP Arithmetic**

An additional floating point exception handling feature is based on the IEEE standards and is available on AT&T UNIX System V. To implement a useful handle, the system calls `signal()`, `longjmp()`, `setjmp()`, and `abort()` and the function `fpgetround()` can be used. The code used in example 11.3 will be modified.

To catch a given floating point exception, previous exception traps are cleared and the trap (mask) bit is then set to catch the exception desired. Should the exception occur, it will be trapped and the variable `sticky_bit` will be assigned the value of the caught exception. The modified `evaluate()` function uses system functions that illustrate this.

```
evaluate()
{
    double x, y;
    int mask;

    fpsetsticky(FP_CLEAR);
        :
    fpsetmask(mask);
        :
    scanf("%e%e", &x,&y);
        :
}
```

To ascertain which exception has been raised, we perform the bitwise AND of `stick_bit` with the desired exception. If the result is the same as `stick_bit`, that exception has been raised, exclusive of any other exceptions. This can be seen in the modified `fpecatch()` function.

```
/* general signal-based error catcher for IEEE
floating point arithmetic */
fpecatch()
{
   int stick_bits;
   int retrn, mask;
   stick_bits = fpgetsticky();
   :
   retrn = ( mask & stick_bits );
   switch(retrn)
      {
```

```
        case (FP_X_DZ):
            execerror("Divide by zero exception",
                    (char *) 0);
            break;
        case (FP_X_OFL):
            execerror("Overflow exception",
                    (char *) 0);
            break;
        case (FP_X_UFL):
            execerror("Underflow exception",
                    (char *) 0);
            break;
        case (FP_X_IMP):
            execerror("Imprecision exception",
                    (char *) 0);
            break;
        default:
            execerror("Multiple exceptions",
                    (char *) 0);
            break;
    }   /* end switch */
}     /* end fpecatch */
```

Here, the floating point exception has been caught and a test is performed to isolate the precise exception detected.

The IEEEFP exception handler enables the user to determine which exception(s) have occurred, while the standard floating point exception handler for C places this responsibility in the hands of the user or the debugger. We now describe the handling of numerical exceptions using the IEEE standards. A simple case is presented in example 11.4.

Example 11.4: Exceptions and the IEEEFP Standards

```
/* Catch and handle divide by zero floating point
exceptions using IEEEFP Standards */
#include <stdio.h>
#include <signal.h>
#include <setjmp.h>
#include <ieeefp.h>

jmp_buf begin;
```

```
main(argc, argv)
int argc;
char *argv[];
{
   int fpecatch();
   setjmp(begin);
   signal(SIGFPE, fpecatch);
   evaluate();
}

execerror(s, t) /* Recover from run-time error. */
char *s, *t;
{
   warning(s, t);
   longjmp(begin, 0);
}


fpecatch()    /* catch floating point exceptions */
{
   int stick_bits;
   int retrn;

   /* interpret sticky bits */
   stick_bits = fpgetsticky();
   printf("stick_bits is 0x%x", stick_bits);
   retrn = (stick_bits & FP_X_DZ);
   if (retrn == FP_X_DZ)
      {
      puts(NUMERIC EXCEPTION - divide by zero");
      execerror("", (char *) 0);
      }
   else
      execerror("floating point exception",
                (char *) 0);
}
evaluate()
{
   float a, b;
   int round, mask, sticky;
```

```
    /* clear sticky bit at start of each loop */
    sticky = fpgetsticky(FP_CLEAR);
    fpsetround(FP_RP);
    mask = fpgetmask(FP_X_DZ);
    scanf("%f%f",&a,&b);
    a = a/b;
}
```

11.4.3   Rollback: Summary

To summarize the major features of the rollback method of fault-tolerance, we list the tasks performed in the examples:

- We identified the likely place in the source code that the software fault occurred. The type of fault was determined.
- We determined the type of signal that would be generated if this type of software fault occurred. This was done in the context of the type of arithmetic standards that would be used.
- We included code to catch the signal indicating that the software fault had occurred. This required the use of an appropriate UNIX signal for the software fault. We used the system call setjmp() to determine an appropriate place to return control to if the software fault occurred, and we had to roll back program execution to a presumably safe state.
- We used the longjmp() system call if the fault occurred so that we could clear the stack and return control to the safe place designated by the previous call to setjmp().
- Execution of the program now continues from the place where the setjmp() system call was found in the code. There is no erroneous information on the stack.

These operations are common to any programs that use the rollback technique to improve software fault-tolerance. Other operating systems and languages that use the rollback technique must have equivalent facilities. Use the sequence of steps indicated here as a template for a C language program that uses this method of software fault-tolerance on the UNIX operating system.

11.5   N-VERSION PROGRAMMING IN UNIX

N-version programming involves several distinct and independent processes, each of which has several common points called *breakpoints*. At each of these breakpoints, the results of the processes (or at least of their critical portions) are communicated to a particular process called the *voter* that wakes up and makes a decision. Figure 11.3 shows the situation.

11.5.1   The Voter

The voter's purpose is to determine the correct state of the machine and then to reset the processes to that state. The method is often as simple as using a majority of responses from the individual processes. The number of breakpoints appropriate for any particular application is still an open research question. Moreover, the effects of certain design choices for breakpoints and voters on fault-tolerance are not well understood at this time, although some rules of thumb are beginning to emerge.

Decisions concerning voter structure include

- How to compare results: Do numerical results have to be identical, or simply within a given tolerance? How character strings are to be compared.
- Selection of an appropriate methodology for performing the minimal number of comparison tests between versions.

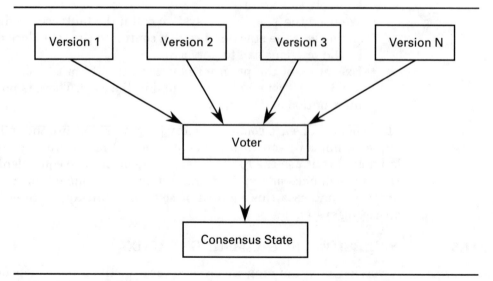

Figure 11.3.   N-version programming

- How to reject an algorithm version producing results deemed to be incorrect.
- How to proceed in the case of catastrophic version failure.
- What to do when the number of correct versions is below some minimal number (usually two).

An N-version programming system can be extremely complex, even if all the versions already exist. The versions of a program must be modified so that they communicate the results of intermediate computations to the voter process. The voter process must compare these results so that a majority decision about the correct state of the system can be obtained. It must allow for the possibility that some of the processes executing the various versions are much slower than the others in performing their computations. The voter itself must be fault-tolerant so that the system will not crash if one of the versions crashes.

11.5.2 Organization of N-Version Programming

For simplicity, we will present only a template for the organization of an N-version programming system. We will not discuss the fault-tolerance of the voter in the text proper, but will describe it in the exercises at the end of the chapter.

The organization of an N-version programming system with a voter process and one, two, or three separate processes could have the number of concurrent versions read in as command-line arguments. Such a system, in which the term "version" refers to a previously created system that performs a version of an essential computation, might look like example 11.5.

Example 11.5: Driver for a Complex N-Version Programming System

```
/* main driver for an N-version system. */
/* communication via message queues      */
#include <stdio.h>
#include <fcntl.h>

main(argc,argv)
int argc;
char *argv[];
{
    int i,j, pid, pid1, pid2, pid3, status;
```

```c
    int num_processes;

    /* Command line argument is interpreted as an integer */
    if (argc <= 2)
        {
        puts("Error- not enough arguments");
        exit(1);
        }
    else
        /* we have enough arguments - argv[1] is the number
        of processes and argv[2] is the name of the input
        file */
        {
        num_processes = atoi(argv[1]);
        switch (num_processes)
            {
            case 1:  /* one process, no voter and no forks */
                if(execl("version","version", argv[2], 0)
                    == -1)
                    {
                    fputs("Error in exec",stderr);
                    exit(1);
                    }
                /********* end of case 1 *********/


            case 2: /* two processes and voter - two forks */
                pid = fork() ;
                switch(pid)
                    {
                    case -1:
                      fputs("Error- fork failed", stderr);
                      exit(1);
                    case 0 : /* first and second processes */
                      pid1 = fork();
                      switch (pid1)
                      {
                      case -1:
                          fputs("Error: fork failed",stderr);
                          break;
                      case 0: /* first process */
```

```
            if(execl("version1","version1",argv[2],0)
                            == -1)
              {
              fputs("Error in exec",stderr);
              exit(1);
              }
         default: /* second process */
            if(execl("version","version",argv[2],0)
                            == -1)
              {
              fputs("Error in exec",stderr);
              exit(1);
              }
         }       /* end of switch pid1 */
      default :       /* voter */
      if(execl("voter","voter",argv[2],0) == -1)
            {
            puts("Error in execing voter");
            exit(1);
            }
      }       /* end of switch pid */
/**************** end of case 2 ****************/

case 3:          /* three processes and voter */
   pid = fork() ;
   switch(pid)
     case -1:
        puts("Error- fork failed");
        exit(1);
     case 0 :         /* first process */
        switch( pid1 = fork())
          {case -1:
              puts("Error- fork failed");
              exit(1);
           case 0:
            if(execl("version1","version1",argv[2],0)
                          == -1)
                {
                puts("Error in exec");
                exit(1);
```

```
                    }
             default:          /* second process */
               if(execl("version","version",argv[2],0)
                            == -1)
                   {
                   puts("Error in exec");
                   exit(1);
                   }
           }          /* end of switch pid1 */
         default:        /* third process and voter */
           switch (pid2 = fork())
           {
            case -1:
               fputs("Error- fork failed",stderr);
               exit(1);
            case 0:          /* third process */
              if(execl("version1","version1",argv[2],0)
                              == -1)
                 {
                 fputs("Error in exec",stderr);
                 exit(1);
                 }
             default:          /* voter process */
               if(execl("voter","voter",argv[2],0)
                            == -1)
                   {
                   puts("Error in exec voter");
                   exit(1);
                   }
              }           /* end of switch pid2 */
       }          /* end of switch pid */
      /*************** end of case 3 ***********/

    default: /* in parent - the voter process is here */
        if (execlp("voter","voter",0) == -1)
          {
          fputs("Error in voter", stderr);
          exit(1);
          }
} /* end of switch num_processes */
```

```
}  /* end else */
}      /* end of main */
```

The voter process must make decisions about the correct state of the system on the basis of the messages it has received from each of the versions.

We have not discussed the form of either the voter process or the individual versions. It is easier to illustrate the design by an example.

Consider a program that evaluates a two-dimensional array consisting of complicated mathematical expressions by performing a sequence of arithmetic operations on a large set of operands. Assume that there are several different methods for computing the array elements. The final result of the computation might be the determinant of the array. All the problems with floating point arithmetic that we described in section 11.4 are also applicable here. However, we may not wish to use the techniques described in that section because of the complexity of incorporating the system calls `setjmp()` and `longjmp()` correctly.

We can use N-version programming by determining that there are several methods for performing the desired computation. One method is to use formulas (which are assumed to be known) for computing the array elements and taking the evaluation of each newly computed array element as an event whose computation should be communicated to a voter. Assuming (as we are) that there are several different methods of computing the different array elements, it is easy to form the initial versions. We would make version 1 the program where method 1 is used for computing the elements of the array, version 2 the program where method 2 is used for computing the elements of the array, and so forth.

Once we have these versions, we incorporate them into an N-version programming system by sending a message to the voter process. The contents of this message are the indices of the array and the value of the array element. As many messages are sent from each version as there are array elements. One major advantage of message queues in an N-version programming system is that the voter process can determine which of the alternate versions is sent a particular message by embedding the number of the version in the message itself.

The voter process would have many messages sent to it: The total number of messages is the number of array elements multiplied by the number of versions. The voter process would have to determine the criteria for determining if two values were "close enough," since we would be using floating point arithmetic. This could be a difficult decision in practice. You will be asked to use this method in the exercises.

In general, a version has the form

```
/* algorithm version number  K */
i = 0;
while (!done)
    {
    compute (result[i]);
    send_message(result[i]) of type K to voter);
    i ++;
    }
```

The voter has the form

```
/*algorithm for voter process */
while (more_input)
    {
    receive_message(result[i]) for type K;
    store contents in the array temp[i][K];
    if (all messages from versions are received)
        compare( temp[i][1], ... temp[i][K]);
    produce the correct state of the system by
                determining consensus
    }
```

SUMMARY

Three methods of improving software fault-tolerance in the UNIX environment are replacement of system calls and I/O functions by those that automatically produce error messages and error values (which are used by the program); rollback techniques using the set jmp() and long jmp() system calls; and N-version programming, which uses multiple versions of an algorithm and determines the correct state of a system by a majority vote.

Each method has clear advantages and disadvantages. Using shell scripts and the C preprocessor is simple to use but is limited in the sense that it only works if we do a lot of preliminary work writing interfaces to system calls and commonly used functions. It also provides information only in the event of a failure of one of these system calls or functions, with no finer level of knowledge possible.

The rollback technique has the advantage of a fine level of control, in that we can be precise about where to send program control after a fault. However, the use of nonlocal gotos by means of set jmp() and long jmp() can make the flow of control in programs very difficult to understand.

N-version programming is the most flexible method. The flow of control of a modified program is easy to follow, and the errors in execution can be determined at specific places in the program. N-version programming requires considerable programming effort and a complicated decision on when two values are equal.

REFERENCES

Avizienis, A. "N-Version Approach to Fault-Tolerant Software." *IEEE Transactions on Software Engineering* SE-11 (1985): 1491–1501.

Coleman, D.M., and R. J. Leach. "Performance Issues in C Language Fault-Tolerant Software." *Computer Languages* 14 (1989): 1–9.

Randell, B. "System Structure for Software Fault-Tolerance." *IEEE Transactions on Software Engineering* SE-1 (1975): 220–232.

EXERCISES

1. Consider a program to perform a set of arithmetic operations on an expression in postfix form using an evaluation stack. The elements of the stack may be assumed to be integers. Write a fault-tolerant version of this program using the first method, namely, using C shell scripts and the preprocessor.

2. Repeat exercise 1 using the rollback method.

3. Repeat exercise 1 using the N-version programming method.

4. Repeat exercise 1 for a program that uses floating point numbers.

5. Repeat exercise 2 for a program that uses floating point numbers.

6. Repeat exercise 3 for a program that uses floating point numbers.

7. Which of the three fault-tolerance techniques discussed in this chapter is most appropriate for a system that controls an aircraft by detecting the air velocity at 100 different points using sensors, and sends the results of these sensor inputs to a single function that uses a mathematical algorithm that has been tested thousands of times in many different program environments? Describe a place in the software where fault-tolerance techniques are especially important and give reasons for your choice of method.

8. Describe the amount of extra design and coding effort needed to incorporate any one of the fault-tolerant approaches into an existing system.

9. Find a problem for which you are aware of two different programs that

serve as solutions. Combine them into an N-version programming system with N = 2. Develop a voter using message queues.

10. In Chapter 9, we studied remote procedure call. Describe how you would incorporate some of the fault-tolerance techniques of this chapter into programs that use `callrpc()` and `registerrpc()`.

11. Find a compiler for RPC language for which you have access to source code. Modify the `rpcgen` utility to include the fault-tolerant techniques you suggested in exercise 10.

12

Standardization and the Future of UNIX

In this chapter, we consider standardization efforts for UNIX. We also discuss research that addresses some of UNIX's perceived deficiencies.

12.1 STANDARDIZATION

There is always a battle between users and developers of a popular computer system. Users, especially commercial users, want a completely standard implementation, syntax, and functionality. Thus, they often push for early adoption of standards because it makes the planning of future projects easier and the transition path for new systems smoother. On the other hand, developers and researchers frequently don't want to standardize too early, since doing so limits their ability to enhance existing systems and create new ones.

The problem is especially acute for smaller companies, or even for large companies wishing to gain market share for a product in a new area, since they cannot compete with companies that have both a large share of the market and an effective means of keeping their technology up to date. Phrased simply, the pressures are to standardize early in the life of some technology, which results in the slowing or reducing of technological advances, or to standardize late, which results in wasteful development and research efforts. This is a constant battle, and the process of moving toward standards is an interesting one.

Different standards organizations use different methods. We describe a generic method for standardization here. Specific details will differ from standards organization to standards organization and from standard to standard.

Usually what happens is this. A technology is developed, and commercial products become available. Customers provide feedback about the products, and the producing company makes changes in response to customer needs. Other companies produce products that have some similarities, and their customers give them feedback, and these products also evolve. After several years of commercial operation, consensus begins to emerge that the systems being produced ought to have some common structures and interfaces.

At this point, an appropriate standards organization is consulted, and a survey is conducted to determine if there is any interest in standardization and if the technology is mature enough for the emergence of standards. The best-known standards organizations are the American National Standards Institute (ANSI), the Institute of Electronic and Electrical Engineers (IEEE), and the International Standards Organization (ISO). There are other standards organizations at national and other levels. The Department of Defense, for example, is the major force behind standardization of the new version of the computer language Ada, which will be released in the mid-1990s.

Once the need for the establishment of a standard is demonstrated, the standards organization announces its intentions and forms a committee consisting of users and developers from industry, academia, and government. The committee meets and produces draft reports that are disseminated to the members of the committee and to others who have expressed an interest. The intermediate reports are usually considered to be confidential until their release for comments from the community. After comments are received, the reports are finalized and sent out for a final vote. After a positive vote from the appropriate sponsoring group, the standard becomes operational.

It is important to note that the effectiveness of a computer software standard depends on marketplace compliance. Except for rare exceptions such as the computer language Ada, which is a trademark of the Department of Defense and whose description and usage are a matter of law, computer software standards are enforced by the marketplace. It is becoming common for the standards organization to develop a test suite to test systems for compliance with the standard. Unfortunately, there are no test suites currently intended for UNIX or related operating systems.

As an example of the effect of the marketplace, consider the specification of a common set of kernel-based and application-based standard interfaces that was submitted in September 1993 for possible inclusion in the XPG (*X Portability Guide*). The proposed standards were developed by several major vendors of UNIX operating systems such as Sun, Hewlett-Packard, and IBM. Hewlett-Packard's documentation often describes the degree of compliance with certain standards such as SVID, XPG, or POSIX. An interesting feature of this standardization effort is that many vendors of application programs were heavily involved. Thus, input was received from vendors of CASE tools, CAD-CAM systems, database systems, spreadsheet systems, and others.

Standards are a moving target, and they can overlap considerably, as is the case with the most common UNIX standards. Any program, whether kernel-based or application-based, that must be portable requires its designers and developers to have the relevant standards at their fingertips.

12.2   REAL-TIME PERFORMANCE

UNIX has several deficiencies in the area of real-time performance. Most, but not all, of these deficiencies are a function of the common UNIX algorithms for scheduling processes and queuing requests for disk access.

Recall that real-time systems have certain characteristics. The most important is the performance of critical actions within specified time limits. Thus, the performance of the system must be deterministic; that is, the time performance must be completely predictable. No algorithm that makes random decisions about timing response can ever be acceptable if the system has rigid time requirements. Even if the overall performance of such an algorithm is excellent, the unpredictability of time response may mean that some process will wait a long time, which is unsatisfactory for real-time systems.

Real-time requirements are generally incompatible with the efficient implementation of a multitasking, multiuser operating system, which is designed to improve throughput of processes and minimize perceived response time. A user of such a system expects that his or her job will make progress towards completion and that there will be no lapse in processing on any job. Dynamic computation of priorities is typical of such systems, since processes that are heavy CPU users are never starved for CPU access. Moreover, I/O bound processes that use the CPU infrequently get fast access to the CPU, so they are not penalized for having little past CPU usage and are not blocked for long.

A real-time system will behave differently. The timing performance of its processes can be predicted if the performance of the algorithms used in the source code, the type of code generated by the compiler, and the speed of the computer are known. This means that the process must be schedulable in such a way that its access to the CPU is completely predictable. Possible scheduling algorithms are round-robin, FIFO, and fixed-priority, all of which are preemptive—that is, a low-priority process can be immediately interrupted to give immediate access to a higher-priority process.

The interruption of a process in a real-time system and the associated process rescheduling in response to an external event are clearly different from what happens in UNIX. The UNIX signal implementation is different from that of a real-time system in the sense that a UNIX signal need not be immediately acted upon. Common UNIX process scheduling is different as well, since the priority of a process is adjusted according to the history of the process's use of the CPU and the number of runnable processes active in the system. Response to an external event of such a scheduling algorithm cannot possibly be predictable, although the optional scheduler in System V Release 4 provides some help in terms of run-time predictability.

Note that the use of the `nice()` system call does not satisfy the requirements of a real-time system. It cannot improve performance for the process that uses it unless it is called by the superuser. Changing the `nice` value of a process cannot make more than a temporary change in the priority of the calling process, since the priority is computed dynamically at regular intervals.

The use of the buffer cache to improve disk throughput is also incompatible with the demands of real-time performance. The priority of disk access for both reads and writes must be deterministic in a real-time system. In UNIX, the reading and writing of data to and from a disk is delayed until many requests can be queued up and the sent to a disk scheduler process based on an algorithm whose purpose is to minimize both disk head movement and seek time.

Most UNIX systems use some form of virtual memory with paging. The selection of the page to move out of memory in the event of a page fault is typically made by a general-purpose algorithm such as FIFO or LRU. A real-time system cannot afford the luxury of such decisions. Instead, the processes for which real-time performance is essential must be able to keep some specifically designated subset of their pages in memory, independently of the general page replacement algorithm.

The Mach operating system has evolved from a single-kernel operating system that provided the functionality of UNIX systems to a microkernel-based operating system that makes considerable use of the idea of lightweight processes. A microkernel allows a somewhat better fit with the client-server model of computation, especially over heterogeneous computer networks, than does a monolithic UNIX kernel. It contains a small but essential subset of the typical UNIX kernel's functionality. Operating system services not provided in the microkernel are run as kernel programs.

The idea of a microkernel is similar to that of computers designed to use RISC (reduced instruction set computer) chips as their CPUs. The philosophy is that overall performance will be enhanced if the most essential tasks are carried out as rapidly as possible and that tasks that are slowed down because of a smaller kernel (or multiple-step actions on a RISC machine) occur relatively infrequently.

Mach and its microkernel architecture provide good overall system performance in many situations. Golub et al. (see the references) describe a Mach environment in which UNIX is run as an *application program* rather than as the underlying operating system.

Bershad (see the references) states that for microkernel-based operating systems such as Mach, ipc performance is a less accurate predictor of overall system performance and throughput than is the degree to which the (hardware) cache memory is used efficiently. He is supported by several experiments and observations about the effect of good "localization schemes" that ensure good usage of the hardware memory cache. It is not at all clear that his arguments apply to UNIX systems with a large, monolithic kernel that contains full functionality.

The design choices in most implementations of UNIX emphasize throughput and general performance at the expense of the rapid, deterministic response necessary for real-time systems. They are the reason for the popularity of UNIX as a general-purpose operating system. Unfortunately, these design choices are not suited to real-time systems, although runtime predictability is improved in some ways. Real-time performance will be an important factor in new versions of UNIX.

12.3   POSIX

POSIX is an acronym for the Portable Operating System Interface for Computer Environments. It is an outcome of the work of the IEEE Standards Committee 1003, whose purpose was to specify some of the features of the operating system interface. This work should result in what is known as an *open system*—that is, a system that can be ported with minimal change across a wide variety of systems, can be easily integrated with other software that is also open, and can facilitate a consistent style of interaction with users. Many UNIX systems include some degree of POSIX compliance.

Several specifications make up the IEEE standard. A complete discussion of POSIX would require a large book just by itself, given that the standard contains more than 1,000 pages. We will be content with a limited overview here.

POSIX standards can be grouped into three broad categories.

- Platform External Interface Standards govern how a software system interacts with its external environment, especially its user interface.

- Application Program Interface Standards govern how the software system interacts with the underlying computer system, especially the operating system. These will be useful only if there are bindings to important computer languages. Bindings are either planned or existent for C, Ada, and FORTRAN.
- System Integration Interface Standards govern how various parts of an information processing system interface with one another.

POSIX includes a description of services that may always be expected from a command interpreter or shell. For example, a POSIX-compliant shell may have certain allowable exit codes that are used to account for possible errors in shell commands. These may not be consistent with actual exit codes in an existing UNIX system, even if they are consistent with a relatively new standard such as SVID (System V Interface Definition).

IEEE Standard 1003.1 specifies the interface between application programs and the operating system. IEEE Standard 1003.2 specifies the source-code-level interface to the command interpreter and a set of standard utility programs. IEEE Standard 1003.3 specifies the general requirements for test suites to ensure compliance of a POSIX system with the standard. IEEE Standard 1003.4 specifies the requirements for real-time systems adhering to the POSIX interface.

There are several differences between the IEEE standard 1003.4 for real-time performance and the most common implementations of UNIX (AT&T and BSD-based). We will describe some of the most important differences here.

The new POSIX standards require more accurate clock access and also often require that processes place a time stamp on events. Time stamping involves some conceptually simple changes, but its implementation is too complicated to present here. Just assume that the necessary changes to system clocks have been made.

The most obvious difference between UNIX and POSIX is in the area of process scheduling. POSIX's allowable scheduling algorithms include preemptable versions of round-robin and FIFO so that critical processes will get the CPU immediately. The newer versions of the AT&T System V kernel allow FIFO scheduling, but the scheduling of CPU use for a process is not preemptive. The real-time description in POSIX provides new system calls for process scheduling. These new system calls include `getscheduler()` and `setscheduler()` for determining which CPU scheduling algorithm will be used, and `yield()`, which allows a process to give up the CPU if it or its programmer knows that the CPU is not needed.

There is also an improvement in software performance because of attention being paid to interrupt latency and context switching time. The term *interrupt latency* refers to the longest possible interval for an interrupt to be received, acknowledged, and scheduled for service by an interrupt handling process (which might be the kernel or some other process that uses some kernel services via system calls). The term *context switching time* is more familiar and refers to the time needed to switch either to or from the task that is scheduled to handle the interrupt. The time for a context switch is clearly smaller if the interrupt handling process is a lightweight process, since only a small context must be saved. The availability of accurate benchmarks for computing these quantities is important to the designer of real-time systems.

Lightweight processes are now supported to some degree in many UNIX implementations. The treatment of input and output has also changed. Two new system calls, `aread()` and `awrite()`, perform the appropriate operations asychronously; that is, the process issuing the I/O request is not blocked from the CPU and can perform other computations. In ordinary UNIX, the `read()` and `write()` system calls perform synchronous input and output, and thus the process is blocked until the I/O operation is complete.

The fundamental data structure used for asynchronous input and output is the asynchronous I/O control block, or `aiocb`. This structure is known to the processes that use it by the address of the block. This information can be used in multiple I/O requests by a single process or a group of processes.

Real-time performance of synchronous I/O is also improved by processes avoiding the buffer cache and writing directly to disk. This is accomplished by means of new flags for file descriptors: `O_FSYNC` and `D_SYNC` (and of course new versions of the `open()` system call). Setting the first flag ensures that all future operations will place appropriate time stamps on disk events. The second flag says that the events will have time stamps placed on the disk when they are performed.

POSIX also allows the creation of a real-time file system with initial fast setup of files, and it allows the user to specify how the file will be placed on the disk so as to minimize disk movements necessary to read it. Files can be set up as contiguous sets of bytes and as files whose size is known before they are created. Thus, the files are not scattered all over the disk and the overhead of system calls to update i-nodes as the file grows in size is eliminated.

Some of the problems in real-time performance of paging systems have been eliminated in POSIX. The new system call `memlk()` forces a region to be locked into physical memory and will not permit a paging algorithm to page it out. The region can be as large as the entire virtual address space of the process or a small subset such as the data or stack address space. Other critical parts of processes such as frequently used regions can be locked into physical memory.

Other important changes to enhance real-time performance involve improved ipc methods. The improvements have come in binary semaphores, shared memory, and message passing. The primary change to semaphores is the availability of a nonblocked `wait()` created by the new system calls `semifwait()` and `semifpost()`. The P and V operations are handled by `semwait()` and `sempost()`. There are no major changes to general semaphores. The changes to shared memory and messages are relatively minor and should cause few problems in the porting of code written for older versions of UNIX to POSIX-based systems.

Working drafts of the POSIX standard are available electronically from several places, including the computer whose Internet address is `research.att.com` by means of anonymous `ftp`. See your system manager to find out if there is sufficient room for the drafts of this standard (or, indeed, if they have already been downloaded to your system).

12.4   SECURITY

There has been a great deal of publicity recently about the vulnerability of certain systems. Especially well publicized was a recent attempt to invade many computers on the Internet, which is the major computer network in the United States and which has worldwide connections. All the systems that were invaded ran operating systems based on the BSD version of UNIX or on something similar. We will briefly describe two of the methods of attack and what UNIX features allowed them.

The main objective of all of the methods of attack was to enter the computer's operating system not as an ordinary user but as root. There are two ways to do this: Find the password associated with root or bypass the password protection scheme entirely.

Finding the root password on many systems turned out to be much easier than one might think at first glance. Information about passwords and logins is kept in a file named `/etc/passwd`, which contains the user's name, login id, group, password, and some other information. At the time of the most publicized attack, this file was publicly readable; that is, anyone could read its contents. The password was always stored in encrypted form, so that some computational work had to be done to make an attempt at the root password, encrypt it, and compare it with the entry in the password file. Since the encryption algorithm was well known, this part was easy in principle.

The UNIX encryption algorithm worked in one direction only. That is, a user logging in through normal channels would enter his or her password, and the algorithm would produce a result that would be compared with the encrypted password in the password file. The user's version of the password was never stored in the system. If the encrypted password did not match, the user would be prompted again for the login id and the password. This process would continue until either the password was entered correctly or some timeout signal was reached, after which the connection would be closed, or the user would give up.

With anonymous `ftp`, a user can get read access to many remote machines and thus see an encrypted password for the root or superuser without logging on as root. Bypassing the login procedure entirely allowed the invader to try huge numbers of password combinations to find a match. After obtaining the match, the invader performed the login sequence with the found password, giving root permissions.

There are several reasons that this technique worked. The most important for many systems was that the password file was public. This has changed on the most recent versions of UNIX, so that a user cannot use his or her own system to compute passwords.

Another reason is that many passwords chosen by users were simple English words, using only alphabetical characters. Others were simple variations of the user's login name. Some system administrators were careless and used very short passwords that could be easily found in a dictionary.

Another method of attack used what is called a *back door*. This is a place in the operating system that can be entered without the usual login procedure. The term also refers to applications software that has "secret" entry points. A back door is placed in the code so that a designer can access the code quickly. It is useful while the system is under development and should be removed before delivery and installation of the software.

The back door that caused much of the problem was embedded in the BSD `sendmail` utility. It allowed a hacker to send a message of a certain size that contained special characters in a particular order that caused a buffer to overflow. The overflow of this buffer allowed the sender of the message to obtain root permissions on each machine in which the back door was still operating.

For more information on this attack on the network of UNIX computers, see Stoll's article or Denning's book, both listed in the references. For additional information, consult any text on computer security.

It is clear that UNIX is deficient in computer security. Some, but not all, of its deficiencies are caused by human failure to keep passwords secure; these deficiencies are addressed to some degree by the newer UNIX versions, which keep the password files private. Other causes are more complex. In general, UNIX system security is fairly good as large operating systems go. However, no system is completely safe.

12.5   THE ROLE OF ANSI C AND C++ IN FUTURE VERSIONS OF UNIX

You may have noticed that much of the code in this book is written in the Kernighan and Ritchie version of C rather than in the newer ANSI standard version. The problem is that the two versions are not completely compatible and that their differences can be quite subtle. Source code often compiles using standard compilers based on each of the two language standards, but the behavior of the executable code can be different. In addition, the standard SunOS software distribution (up through SunOS 4.1.3) includes compilers only for the older version of C.

The incompatability of the two C versions gives rise to problems in several areas, including arithmetic operations, assignments to pointers, and allocation of memory space. In general, the problems complicate the conversion of the UNIX operating system, which is currently written in Kernighan and Ritchie C, to a new version written in ANSI Standard C. This means that the weak type checking in the version of C currently used in the coding of UNIX will continue to dominate the strongly typed versions that would result from newer language implementations.

In general, only new UNIX utility programs are being written in ANSI Standard C. For reasons of compatibility with existing versions of UNIX, none of the basic system calls or major lower-level utilities are being written in this version.

The situation is somewhat different with regard to the rewriting of UNIX using C++ as an object-oriented programming language that supports object-oriented design. This is an appealing prospect because C++ supports abstract data types and allows objects to inherit structure and attributes from higher-level classes of objects.

C++ is generally considered a superset of C in the sense that C++ programs that do not use the object-oriented features of C++ are essentially C programs.

To understand the potential of C++ in simplifying an operating system, consider the notion of queue operations. Queues are used in many forms in operating systems: Process ready queues, disk request queues, terminal output queues, and print spooler queues are some of the most common. Each queue has a different structure, so the operating system designer has to write algorithms for manipulating queues individually. Large portions of the code have to be duplicated because these instances of queues are different in terms of the structure of queue elements. If the operating system were written in C++, the common code would need to be written only once and the individual queues would be coded as different instances of objects derived from the same object. In technical language, the properties of one class are inherited from the parent class, with their structure being basically the same as that of the original class, with some changes specific to the new class.

It has been estimated that the use of C++ would decrease the size of the operating system's most important feature, the kernel, by 20 to 25 percent. While the actual decrease cannot be determined until the system is implemented, changing to C++ would seem a worthwhile endeavor both from the perspective of decreasing the size of the kernel and from the perspective of making the operating system's design easier to understand and maintain.

There are two stumbling blocks in the way of a change to C++. The first is that C++ is a moving target in the sense that the language is evolving and its language definitions have not yet been locked in. In general, C++ is a superset of C, but there are many examples of programs written either in ANSI Standard C or in Kernighan and Ritchie C that either will not compile or produce incorrect output when the source code is run through a C++ compiler. This problem will probably be resolved in future generations of C++.

The other stumbling block is the unpredictability of runtime performance of code written in C++ or, indeed, in any object-oriented language. In particular, an instantiation of some object as a particular example of a class or a subclass may involve highly unpredictable runtime performance. The reason for this is that often each instance of an object of a new class or subclass requires a copy of the general code for the new class or subclass. This means that the system is performing no new computation when it is asked to but instead is spending its time creating new instances of new data types as abstract objects. Such behavior appears at this time to be incompatible with the requirements for real-time system performance.

This polymorphism of object-oriented languages and overloading of operators also creates many problems for the software tester. Leach and Hashemi (see the references) discuss some problems in porting software from C to C++.

It is likely that C++ will be used in the design and implementation of UNIX only after such language issues are resolved. The use of object-oriented methods of code will require significant changes in the design of UNIX. It will be interesting to see what happens.

REFERENCES

Bershad, B. "The Increasing Irrelevance of ipc Performance for Microkernel-Based Operating Systems." Carnegie Mellon University Technical Report, March 10, 1992.

Denning, P. *Computers Under Attack: Intruders, Worms and Viruses*. Reading, Mass.: Addison-Wesley, 1990.

Ellis, M. A., and B. Stroustrup. *The Annotated C++ Reference Manual*. Reading, Mass.: Addison-Wesley, 1990.

Golub, D., R. Dean, A. Forin, and R. Rashid. "UNIX as an Application Program." *Proceedings of the Summer 1990 USENIX Conference*, June 1990, 87–95.

Leach, R., and R. Hashemi. "Issues in Porting Software from C to C++." *Software: Practice and Experience* 23 (July 1992): 599–602.

Stoll, C. "Stalking the Wily Hacker." *Communications of the ACM* 31 (1988): 484–497.

Stroustrup, B. *The C++ Programming Language*. Reading, Mass.: Addison-Wesley, 1986.

About the Software

There is an optional disk available for this book. The disk includes source code for each of the examples in the book and many additional examples as well. Each program on the disk has been tested on a Sun SPARCStation 2 running Solaris 1.1 (which is also known as SunOS 4.1.3) using standard C compilers.

The software is provided on a 3.5 inch, high-density disk and is available in several formats. The standard one available from the publisher is in IBM PC format. Other formats are available, including UNIX tar (tape archive) and Macintosh formats.

1. INSTALLATION

There are two installation paths, depending on the availability of a 3.5 inch disk drive on the workstation on which the software is to be installed. In each case, the programs on the disk are in ASCII format, and the directories can be read easily. There is a readme file on the disk and most directories also have such a file.

1.1 Installation on workstations without 3.5 inch disk drives

If there is no such disk drive on the workstation, then the software must be uploaded from an IBM PC or compatible computer using a modem and communications software. Simply create a directory where you want the code and make the transfer using the commands of your communications software.

1.2   **Installation on workstations with 3.5 inch disk drives**

If you do not have a communications package, and there is a disk drive on the workstation, you can use the alternative technique of mounting a "PC file system," so that disks formatted for the IBM PC family can be read. This involves the use of the `mount` system call. Since this system call requires superuser privileges, you must either have these privileges or have the system administrator perform the installation.

The steps are:

1. Create a directory for the contents of the disk.

```
cd your_dir
```

2. Log in as superuser.
3. `Create a "PC file system,"`
   This step uses the mount command:

```
mount /pcfs
```

4. Check the contents.

```
ls -l /pcfs
```

This may take a while. There should be directories for the following: chapters 1 through 9, chapter 11, misc, and monitors. There should also be a global readme file.

5. Change to the Bourne shell.

```
sh
```

6. Run the following Bourne shell script:

```
for i in /pcfs/*
do
  mkdir $i
done
```

This creates the subdirectories named `chap1.. chap11` in your directory. Do the same for the subdirectories `misc` and `monitors`.

7. Repeat for each subdirectory
   For each subdirectory, copy the files from the disk to your subdirectory, using the filter `dos2unix` so that the code is formatted properly on the UNIX system: Be sure to use the complete path name of the directory `your_dir` instead of the name `complete_dir`.

```
for i in [1-9]
do
  cd /pcfs/$i
  for j in *
  do
    dos2unix $j complete_dir /$j
  done
  cd ..
done
```

You will have to convert the contents of the other directories `chap11`, `misc`, and `monitors` manually. You should use the script

```
for j in *
do
  dos2unix $j complete_dir /$j
done
```

to install the files in a directory. Note that you will have to repeat this step whenever a directory has subdirectories.

8. Check for correct transfer

```
ls -Ral /pcfs
ls -Ral complete_dir
```

These two should agree.

9. Unmount the "PC file system."

```
umount /pcfs
```

10. Log off as superuser

```
exit
```

2.   **CONTENTS OF THE DISK**

The contents of the disk include the example programs in the book. There are additional programs provided in the misc and monitor directories.

All programs are grouped into directories, with the names of the directories matching the contents of the different chapters of the book. Each directory contains a readme file explaining its contents. Makefiles are also included as appropriate.

Some of the programs in the later chapters are given in both ANSI and the older Kernighan & Ritchie versions of C. In this case, they are placed into separate directories.

3.   **SYSTEM REQUIREMENTS**

The programs included on the disk were tested on a Sun SPARCStation 2 running Solaris 1.1 Except for the programs of Chapter 8, which depend on installation of the System V ipc Package for semaphore, messages, and shared memory, most programs should be relatively portable. Minor changes may be necessary in some environments.

No serious demands are made on the operating system. The ipc code in chapters 7, 8, or 9 may exhaust system resources for large values of the arguments.

Index